W9-CPO-215

The
GOURMAN REPORT

A Rating of Graduate and Professional Programs in American and International Universities

SEVENTH EDITION
Revised

Dr. Jack Gourman

National Education Standards

Editorial inquiries concerning this book should be addressed to:
Editor
National Education Standards
One Wilshire Building
Suite 2900
624 South Grand Avenue
Los Angeles, California 90017

International Standard Serial Number (ISSN) 1049-717X

Library of Congress Catalog Card Number 95-072303

ISBN: 0-918192-17-X

Printed in the United States of America

This book is dedicated to the memory of
BLANKA GOURMAN
a kind and generous spirit.

PREFACE to the seventh edition

As with previous editions, THE GOURMAN REPORT: A RATING OF GRADUATE AND PROFESSIONAL PROGRAMS addresses the need for a qualitative evaluation of higher-level education in the United States, Canada, and International universities. We have tried to organize the data so educators, administrators, corporations, students and others can quickly and efficiently locate the material of interest to them. To this end, several new fields have been added. These new programs reflect the importance of the respective disciplines to our nation's economic and technical development. Excluded from the seventh edition are the Soviet universities because of internal affairs and political instability.

As always, the greatest and most important change is in the ratings themselves. I regret that, in all too many cases, readers will turn to the ranking for their own programs and discover a lower score than in the last book. Let me be blunt: higher education is in ill health today. Years of fiscal malnutrition have taken their toll. Public indifference, irresponsible statements and actions from elected officials and others in a position of authority, and growing cynicism on the part of faculty and administrators combine to compound the symptoms. And, while the "patient" is the institution, those most aggrieved are the students themselves. Perhaps naively, young men and women still look to higher education for the knowledge and understanding they will need in later life. At many of today's schools, their chances of finding what they seek are not good.

Even among established schools, many institutions again scored poorly based on one or more of the following shortcomings:

1. Objectives of the program are ill-defined and misunderstood.

2. The present program is not constituted to meet the needs and problems of students and faculty.

3. Institutional reports are not evaluated and beneficial changes are not recommended.

4. Administrators are reluctant to reveal the weakness of programs.

5. The public relations of the institution provides a false image to cover up deficiencies in programs.

6. Requisite improvements are not made in the quality of administrators, faculty instruction, curriculum, library resources and the physical plant.

7. Graduate training is offered by institutions with inferior undergraduate programs.

8. Students suffer from poor counseling.

9. Funds designation for the improvement of faculty, curriculum, library resources and physical areas are misused.

10. Teacher education programs and training are below average.[1]

11. Graduate schools of education below average.[2]

12. Criminal Justice/Criminology Correction programs are inadequate.[3]

13. Special interest pressure is exerted by administrators, to the detriment of the educators and teaching experience.

14. Student grants and scholarships are inadequate or nonexistent.

15. Faculty salaries are inadequate.

16. Funds for faculty research are inadequate.

17. Computer facility not sufficient to support current research activities for both faculty and students.

18. Insufficient funding for research equipment and infrastructure.

19. Number of teaching and research assistantships inadequate.

20. Major research laboratories inadequate.

---

[1] Credential Note:
A student with a baccalaureate degree or higher (and approved by THE GOURMAN REPORT) with a 3.5 grade point average in the major (excluding education majors) and an overall 3.3 grade point average are eligible for a teaching credential.
In addition, the candidate must submit two letters from faculty who can assess their professional potential.
Prospective candidates would apply directly to the state board of education for a teaching credential.
We strongly recommend credential programs be *discontinued* by the educational institution.

[2] The Graduate Schools of Education are not approved by THE GOURMAN REPORT and should be *discontinued* by the educational institution.

[3] Criminal Justice/Criminology and Correction programs are not approved by THE GOURMAN REPORT.

Jack Gourman
Los Angeles, California
August, 1996

Preface
Introduction
Table of Contents

The Disciplines – A Rating of Graduate and Professional Programs

Part I

GRADUATE PROGRAMS

Table of Contents

Table of Contents

Table of Contents

The GOURMAN REPORT
PART I

GRADUATE PROGRAMS

Aerospace Engineering
Agricultural Economics
Agricultural Engineering
Agricultural Sciences
Agronomy/Soil Sciences
Anthropology
Applied Mathematics
Applied Physics
Architecture
Art History
Astronomy
Biochemistry
Biomedical Engineering
Botany
Cell Biology
Ceramic Sciences and Engineering
Chemical Engineering
Chemistry
Child Development-Psychology
City/Regional Planning
Civil Engineering
Classics
Clinical Psychology
Cognitive-Psychology
Comparative Literature
Computer Science
Developmental Psychology
Drama/Theatre
Economics
Electrical Engineering
English
Entomology
Environmental Engineering
Experimental Psychology (General)
Forestry
French
Geography
Geosciences
German
History
Horticulture
Industrial Engineering
Industrial/Labor Relations

Industrial/Organizational Psychology
Inorganic Chemistry
Journalism
Landscape Architecture
Library Science
Linguistics
Materials Science
Mathematics
Mechanical Engineering
Microbiology
Molecular Genetics
Music
Near and Middle Eastern Studies
Neurosciences
Nuclear Engineering
Nutrition
Occupational Therapy
Oceanography
Organic Chemistry
Personality-Pyschology
Petroleum Engineering
Pharmacology
Plant Pathology
Philosophy
Physical Chemistry
Physical Therapy
Physics
Physiology
Political Science
Psychology
Public Administration
Radio/TV/Film
Russian
Sensation and Perception-Psychology
Slavic Languages
Social Psychology
Social Welfare/Social Work
Sociology
Spanish
Speech Pathology/Audiology
Statistics
Toxicology

A RATING OF GRADUATE PROGRAMS IN AEROSPACE ENGINEERING
Leading Institutions

Thirty institutions with scores in the 4.0-5.0 range, in rank order

INSTITUTION	Rank	Score
CAL TECH	1	4.93
M.I.T.	2	4.92
STANFORD	3	4.91
PRINCETON	4	4.90
MICHIGAN (Ann Arbor)	5	4.89
CORNELL (N.Y.)	6	4.88
PURDUE (Lafayette)	7	4.86
TEXAS (Austin)	8	4.84
GEORGIA TECH	9	4.82
CALIFORNIA, SAN DIEGO	10	4.81
UCLA	11	4.80
MINNESOTA (Minneapolis)	12	4.78
COLORADO (Boulder)	13	4.76
ILLINOIS (Urbana)	14	4.74
V.P.I. & STATE U.	15	4.73
NORTH CAROLINA STATE (Raleigh)	16	4.72
TEXAS A&M (College Station)	17	4.70
PENN STATE (University Park)	18	4.68
WASHINGTON (Seattle)	19	4.65
MARYLAND (College Park)	20	4.64
IOWA STATE (Ames)	21	4.62
RENSSELAER (N.Y.)	22	4.61
CINCINNATI	23	4.60
NOTRE DAME	24	4.59
OHIO STATE (Columbus)	25	4.57
KANSAS	26	4.53
FLORIDA (Gainesville)	27	4.50
SUNY (Buffalo)	28	4.48
TENNESSEE (Knoxville)	29	4.45
AUBURN	30	4.41

A RATING OF GRADUATE PROGRAMS IN AGRICULTURAL ECONOMICS
Leading Institutions

Thirty-four institutions with scores in the 4.0-5.0 range, in rank order

INSTITUTION	Rank	Score
CORNELL (N.Y.)	1	4.92
MICHIGAN STATE	2	4.91
ILLINOIS (Urbana)	3	4.90
MINNESOTA (Minneapolis)	4	4.87
CALIFORNIA, DAVIS	5	4.86
PURDUE (Lafayette)	6	4.84
WISCONSIN (Madison)	7	4.80
CALIFORNIA, BERKELEY	8	4.76
STANFORD	9	4.73
PENN STATE (University Park)	10	4.72
MISSOURI (Columbia)	11	4.71
FLORIDA (Gainesville)	12	4.66
TEXAS A&M (College Station)	13	4.63
IOWA STATE (Ames)	14	4.62
OHIO STATE (Columbus)	15	4.60
OREGON STATE	16	4.54
CONNECTICUT (Storrs)	17	4.53
MARYLAND (College Park)	18	4.51
KANSAS STATE	19	4.48
V.P.I. & STATE U.	20	4.45
WASHINGTON STATE	21	4.40
NEBRASKA (Lincoln)	22	4.38
KENTUCKY	23	4.33
MASSACHUSETTS (Amherst)	24	4.31
NORTH CAROLINA STATE (Raleigh)	25	4.29
AUBURN (Auburn)	26	4.26
LSU (Baton Rouge)	27	4.23
COLORADO STATE	28	4.19
GEORGIA (Athens)	29	4.17
OKLAHOMA STATE	30	4.15
MISSISSIPPI STATE	31	4.14
TENNESSEE (Knoxville)	32	4.12
TEXAS TECH	33	4.11
HAWAII (Manoa)	34	4.10

A RATING OF GRADUATE PROGRAMS IN AGRICULTURAL ENGINEERING
Leading Institutions

Thirty-two institutions with scores in the 4.0-5.0 range, in rank order

INSTITUTION	Rank	Score
CORNELL (N.Y.)	1	4.92
MICHIGAN STATE	2	4.91
IOWA STATE (Ames)	3	4.90
ILLINOIS (Urbana)	4	4.88
PURDUE (Lafayette)	5	4.87
MINNESOTA (Minneapolis)	6	4.84
OHIO STATE (Columbus)	7	4.82
TEXAS A&M (College Station)	8	4.81
PENN STATE (University Park)	9	4.79
WISCONSIN (Madison)	10	4.75
CALIFORNIA, DAVIS	11	4.73
MARYLAND (College Park)	12	4.70
MISSOURI (Columbia)	13	4.66
COLORADO STATE	14	4.64
NORTH CAROLINA STATE (Raleigh)	15	4.62
TENNESSEE (Knoxville)	16	4.59
WASHINGTON STATE	17	4.54
FLORIDA (Gainesville)	18	4.52
KANSAS STATE	19	4.50
CLEMSON	20	4.46
V.P.I. & STATE U.	21	4.43
NEBRASKA (Lincoln)	22	4.40
OKLAHOMA STATE	23	4.33
OREGON STATE	24	4.32
KENTUCKY	25	4.28
UTAH STATE	26	4.26
LSU (Baton Rouge)	27	4.22
AUBURN (Auburn)	28	4.20
TEXAS TECH	29	4.18
IDAHO (Moscow)	30	4.16
NORTH DAKOTA STATE	31	4.15
MAINE (Orono)	32	4.12

A RATING OF GRADUATE PROGRAMS IN AGRICULTURAL SCIENCES
Leading Institutions

Thirty-two institutions with scores in the 4.0-5.0 range, in rank order

INSTITUTION	Rank	Score
CORNELL (N.Y.)	1	4.91
TEXAS A&M (College Station)	2	4.89
ILLINOIS (Urbana)	3	4.87
PURDUE (Lafayette)	4	4.85
IOWA STATE (Ames)	5	4.81
MICHIGAN STATE	6	4.79
CALIFORNIA, DAVIS	7	4.75
WISCONSIN (Madison)	8	4.72
MINNESOTA (Minneapolis)	9	4.69
OHIO STATE (Columbus)	10	4.65
KANSAS STATE	11	4.62
MISSOURI (Columbia)	12	4.59
PENN STATE (University Park)	13	4.57
LSU (Baton Rouge)	14	4.55
NEBRASKA (Lincoln)	15	4.51
MARYLAND (College Park)	16	4.49
NORTH CAROLINA STATE (Raleigh)	17	4.47
OKLAHOMA STATE	18	4.43
GEORGIA (Athens)	19	4.40
OREGON STATE	20	4.37
TENNESSEE (Knoxville)	21	4.35
COLORADO STATE	22	4.33
MASSACHUSETTS (Amherst)	23	4.31
UTAH STATE	24	4.27
ARIZONA (Tucson)	25	4.22
TEXAS TECH	26	4.20
FLORIDA (Gainesville)	27	4.17
AUBURN (Auburn)	28	4.15
CLEMSON	29	4.14
CONNECTICUT (Storrs)	30	4.12
WASHINGTON STATE	31	4.09
MAINE (Orono)	32	4.07

A RATING OF GRADUATE PROGRAMS IN AGRONOMY/SOIL SCIENCES
Leading Institutions

Twenty-six institutions with scores in the 4.0-5.0 range, in rank order

INSTITUTION	Rank	Score
CORNELL (N.Y.)	1	4.86
TEXAS A&M (College Station)	2	4.84
WISCONSIN (Madison)	3	4.80
CALIFORNIA, DAVIS	4	4.79
MINNESOTA (Minneapolis)	5	4.78
ILLINOIS (Urbana)	6	4.75
OHIO STATE (Columbus)	7	4.72
PENN STATE (University Park)	8	4.69
PURDUE (Lafayette)	9	4.68
IOWA STATE (Ames)	10	4.66
KANSAS STATE	11	4.62
MICHIGAN STATE	12	4.58
GEORGIA (Athens)	13	4.55
FLORIDA (Gainesville)	14	4.51
NEBRASKA (Lincoln)	15	4.50
LSU (Baton Rouge)	16	4.46
V.P.I. & STATE U.	17	4.43
OREGON STATE	18	4.40
MARYLAND (College Park)	19	4.38
ARKANSAS (Fayetteville)	20	4.37
NORTH CAROLINA STATE (Raleigh)	21	4.33
OKLAHOMA STATE	22	4.31
CALIFORNIA, RIVERSIDE	23	4.26
MASSACHUSETTS, (Amherst)	24	4.24
UTAH STATE	25	4.21
ARIZONA (Tucson)	26	4.19

A RATING OF GRADUATE PROGRAMS IN ANTHROPOLOGY
Leading Institutions

Thirty-one institutions with scores in the 4.0-5.0 range, in rank order

INSTITUTION	Rank	Score
MICHIGAN (Ann Arbor)	1	4.92
CALIFORNIA, BERKELEY	2	4.91
CHICAGO	3	4.90
HARVARD	4	4.88
ARIZONA (Tucson)	5	4.86
PENNSYLVANIA	6	4.84
STANFORD	7	4.82
UCLA	8	4.81
YALE	9	4.80
CALIFORNIA, SAN DIEGO	10	4.79
TEXAS (Austin)	11	4.78
FLORIDA (Gainesville)	12	4.76
NYU	13	4.75
ILLINOIS (Urbana)	14	4.72
CALIFORNIA, DAVIS	15	4.71
COLUMBIA (N.Y.)	16	4.68
WASHINGTON (St. Louis)	17	4.66
DUKE	18	4.64
WISCONSIN (Madison)	19	4.63
CALIFORNIA, SANTA BARBARA	20	4.62
JOHNS HOPKINS	21	4.60
CUNY (Graduate School)	22	4.59
VIRGINIA (Charlottesville)	23	4.55
RUTGERS (New Brunswick)	24	4.53
PITTSBURGH (Pittsburgh)	25	4.50
ARIZONA STATE	26	4.48
PRINCETON	27	4.46
INDIANA (Bloomington)	28	4.44
WASHINGTON (Seattle)	29	4.40
NORTH CAROLINA (Chapel Hill)	30	4.37
CORNELL (N.Y.)	31	4.36

A RATING OF GRADUATE PROGRAMS IN APPLIED MATHEMATICS
Leading Institutions

Twenty-four institutions with scores in the 4.0-5.0 range, in rank order

INSTITUTION	Rank	Score
HARVARD	1	4.88
PRINCETON	2	4.84
CHICAGO	3	4.82
M.I.T.	4	4.80
YALE	5	4.76
WISCONSIN (Madison)	6	4.73
COLUMBIA (N.Y.)	7	4.69
CAL TECH	8	4.66
CORNELL (N.Y.)	9	4.64
BROWN	10	4.60
RICE	11	4.57
WASHINGTON (Seattle)	12	4.53
NORTHWESTERN (Evanston)	13	4.50
MARYLAND (College Park)	14	4.48
PURDUE (Lafayette)	15	4.41
JOHNS HOPKINS	16	4.33
INDIANA (Bloomington)	17	4.29
VIRGINIA (Charlottesville)	18	4.25
PENN STATE (University Park)	19	4.20
COLORADO (Boulder)	20	4.18
MICHIGAN STATE	21	4.16
IOWA (Iowa City)	22	4.14
FLORIDA (Gainesville)	23	4.10
KANSAS (Lawrence)	24	4.09

A RATING OF GRADUATE PROGRAMS IN APPLIED PHYSICS
Leading Institutions

Eleven institutions with scores in the 4.0-5.0 range, in rank order

INSTITUTION	Rank	Score
CAL TECH	1	4.87
HARVARD	2	4.84
PRINCETON	3	4.82
CORNELL (N.Y.)	4	4.79
STANFORD	5	4.76
MICHIGAN (Ann Arbor)	6	4.74
COLUMBIA (N.Y.)	7	4.70
YALE	8	4.66
RENSSELAER (N.Y.)	9	4.63
CARNEGIE-MELLON	10	4.60
COLORADO (Boulder)	11	4.57

A RATING OF GRADUATE PROGRAMS IN ARCHITECTURE
Leading Institutions

Twenty-nine institutions with scores in the 4.0-5.0 range, in rank order

INSTITUTION	Rank	Score
HARVARD	1	4.91
M.I.T.	2	4.90
PRINCETON	3	4.88
CALIFORNIA, BERKELEY	4	4.86
PENNSYLVANIA	5	4.83
CARNEGIE-MELLON	6	4.80
MICHIGAN (Ann Arbor)	7	4.75
GEORGIA TECH	8	4.73
RICE	9	4.70
COLUMBIA (N.Y.)	10	4.66
TEXAS (Austin)	11	4.60
YALE	12	4.59
TEXAS A&M (College Station)	13	4.54
UCLA	14	4.50
WASHINGTON (Seattle)	15	4.48
OHIO STATE (Columbus)	16	4.47
ILLINOIS (Urbana)	17	4.40
V.P.I. & STATE U.	18	4.39
OREGON (Eugene)	19	4.35
ARIZONA STATE	20	4.32
WASHINGTON (St. Louis)	21	4.26
HAWAII (Manoa)	22	4.25
FLORIDA (Gainesville)	23	4.20
RENSSELAER (N.Y.)	24	4.19
NEW MEXICO (Albuquerque)	25	4.18
HOUSTON (University Park)	26	4.15
VIRGINIA (Charlottesville)	27	4.13
MINNESOTA (Minneapolis)	28	4.12
OKLAHOMA (Norman)	29	4.08

A RATING OF GRADUATE PROGRAMS IN ART HISTORY
Leading Institutions

Thirty institutions with scores in the 4.0-5.0 range, in rank order

INSTITUTION	Rank	Score
N.Y.U.	1	4.90
HARVARD	2	4.88
YALE	3	4.85
COLUMBIA (N.Y.)	4	4.80
PRINCETON	5	4.78
CALIFORNIA, BERKELEY	6	4.73
STANFORD	7	4.68
MICHIGAN (Ann Arbor)	8	4.63
BRYN MAWR	9	4.55
JOHNS HOPKINS	10	4.48
PENNSYLVANIA	11	4.47
NORTHWESTERN (Evanston)	12	4.43
UCLA	13	4.41
CHICAGO	14	4.37
NORTH CAROLINA (Chapel Hill)	15	4.35
CORNELL (N.Y.)	16	4.31
PITTSBURGH (Pittsburgh)	17	4.29
INDIANA (Bloomington)	18	4.24
VIRGINIA (Charlottesville)	19	4.21
KANSAS (Lawrence)	20	4.18
BOSTON U.	21	4.15
BROWN	22	4.13
MARYLAND (College Park)	23	4.12
RUTGERS (New Brunswick)	24	4.11
MINNESOTA (Minneapolis)	25	4.10
TEXAS (Austin)	26	4.09
CALIFORNIA, SANTA BARBARA	27	4.07
ILLINOIS (Urbana)	28	4.06
WASHINGTON (Seattle)	29	4.05
OHIO STATE (Columbus)	30	4.03

A RATING OF GRADUATE PROGRAMS IN ASTRONOMY
Leading Institutions

Twenty-seven institutions with scores in the 4.0-5.0 range, in rank order

INSTITUTION	Rank	Score
CAL TECH	1	4.92
CALIFORNIA, BERKELEY	2	4.90
HARVARD	3	4.88
CHICAGO	4	4.87
CALIFORNIA, SANTA CRUZ	5	4.85
M.I.T.	6	4.82
ARIZONA (Tucson)	7	4.80
CORNELL (N.Y.)	8	4.75
TEXAS (Austin)	9	4.72
HAWAII (Manoa)	10	4.69
ILLINOIS (Urbana)	11	4.63
WISCONSIN (Madison)	12	4.62
UCLA	13	4.60
VIRGINIA (Charlottesville)	14	4.58
YALE	15	4.53
COLUMBIA (N.Y.)	16	4.50
MARYLAND (College Park)	17	4.48
PENN STATE (University Park)	18	4.46
OHIO STATE (Columbus)	19	4.37
MINNESOTA (Minneapolis)	20	4.35
MICHIGAN (Ann Arbor)	21	4.33
SUNY (Stony Brook)	22	4.29
BOSTON U.	23	4.25
INDIANA (Bloomington)	24	4.23
LSU (Baton Rouge)	25	4.21
IOWA STATE (Ames)	26	4.15
FLORIDA (Gainesville)	27	4.13

A RATING OF GRADUATE PROGRAMS IN BIOCHEMISTRY
Leading Institutions

Thirty institutions with scores in the 4.0-5.0 range, in rank order

INSTITUTION	Rank	Score
CALIFORNIA, SAN FRANCISCO	1	4.94
STANFORD	2	4.92
M.I.T.	3	4.91
CALIFORNIA, BERKELEY	4	4.90
HARVARD	5	4.89
CAL TECH	6	4.87
YALE	7	4.86
WISCONSIN (Madison)	8	4.85
CALIFORNIA, SAN DIEGO	9	4.84
JOHNS HOPKINS	10	4.82
COLUMBIA (N.Y.)	11	4.80
WASHINGTON (St. Louis)	12	4.78
COLORADO (Boulder)	13	4.77
DUKE	14	4.76
UCLA	15	4.75
PENNSYLVANIA	16	4.73
WASHINGTON (Seattle)	17	4.71
BAYLOR COLLEGE OF MEDICINE	18	4.68
BRANDEIS	19	4.66
U. OF TEXAS SOUTHWESTERN MEDICAL CENTER (Dallas)	20	4.65
ROCKEFELLER, U. (New York)	21	4.64
CORNELL (Ithaca)	22	4.62
MICHIGAN SCHOOL OF MEDICINE (Ann Arbor)	23	4.61
CHICAGO	24	4.60
MICHIGAN (Ann Arbor)	25	4.58
ALBERT EINSTEIN COLLEGE OF MEDICINE	26	4.56
OREGON (Eugene)	27	4.55
NORTH CAROLINA (Chapel Hill)	28	4.53
VANDERBILT	29	4.51
UTAH (Salt Lake City)	30	4.49

A RATING OF GRADUATE PROGRAMS IN BIOMEDICAL ENGINEERING
Leading Institutions

Twenty-six institutions with scores in the 4.0-5.0 range, in rank order

INSTITUTION	Rank	Score
M.I.T.	1	4.90
CALIFORNIA, SAN DIEGO	2	4.88
DUKE	3	4.87
PENNSYLVANIA	4	4.85
WASHINGTON (Seattle)	5	4.83
JOHNS HOPKINS	6	4.77
CALIFORNIA, SAN FRANCISCO	7	4.76
CALIFORNIA, BERKELEY	8	4.70
RICE	9	4.69
MICHIGAN (Ann Arbor)	10	4.65
STANFORD	11	4.63
UTAH (Salt Lake City)	12	4.59
CASE WESTERN RESERVE	13	4.56
ROCHESTER (N.Y.)	14	4.50
NORTHWESTERN (Evanston)	15	4.47
VANDERBILT	16	4.36
MINNESOTA (Minneapolis)	17	4.35
TEXAS (Austin)	18	4.33
NORTH CAROLINA (Chapel Hill)	19	4.27
PENN STATE (University Park)	20	4.25
VIRGINIA (Charlottesville)	21	4.21
DREXEL U.	22	4.18
CALIFORNIA, DAVIS	23	4.16
OHIO STATE (Columbus)	24	4.14
IOWA (Iowa City)	25	4.12
ALABAMA (Birmingham)	26	4.10

A RATING OF GRADUATE PROGRAMS IN BOTANY
Leading Institutions

Forty institutions with scores in the 4.0-5.0 range, in rank order

INSTITUTION	Rank	Score
CALIFORNIA, DAVIS	1	4.92
TEXAS (Austin)	2	4.90
CALIFORNIA, BERKELEY	3	4.88
WISCONSIN (Madison)	4	4.86
CORNELL (N.Y.)	5	4.85
MICHIGAN (Ann Arbor)	6	4.84
DUKE	7	4.83
YALE	8	4.80
ILLINOIS (Urbana)	9	4.76
CALIFORNIA, RIVERSIDE	10	4.74
MICHIGAN STATE	11	4.72
NORTH CAROLINA STATE (Raleigh)	12	4.69
UCLA	13	4.66
PENN STATE (University Park)	14	4.63
INDIANA (Bloomington)	15	4.62
MINNESOTA (Minneapolis)	16	4.61
NORTH CAROLINA (Chapel Hill)	17	4.59
GEORGIA (Athens)	18	4.57
WASHINGTON (St. Louis)	19	4.54
PURDUE (Lafayette)	20	4.51
OREGON STATE	21	4.49
WASHINGTON (Seattle)	22	4.46
OHIO STATE (Columbus)	23	4.44
KENTUCKY	24	4.40
IOWA STATE (Ames)	25	4.38
MASSACHUSETTS (Amherst)	26	4.37
FLORIDA (Gainesville)	27	4.35
CLAREMONT GRADUATE SCHOOL	28	4.32
NEBRASKA (Lincoln)	29	4.29
SUNY (C. Environ., Sci. & Forestry	30	4.27
OKLAHOMA (Norman)	31	4.25
CALIFORNIA, IRVINE	32	4.21
RUTGERS (New Brunswick)	33	4.19
WASHINGTON STATE	34	4.16
CHICAGO	35	4.14
COLORADO STATE	36	4.13
HAWAII (Manoa)	37	4.12
MARYLAND (College Park)	38	4.11
MISSOURI (Columbia)	39	4.10
IOWA (Iowa City)	40	4.09

A RATING OF GRADUATE PROGRAMS IN CELL BIOLOGY
Leading Institutions

Thirty-five institutions with scores in the 4.0-5.0 range, in rank order

INSTITUTION	Rank	Score
ROCKEFELLER U. (N.Y.)	1	4.93
CALIFORNIA, SAN FRANCISCO	2	4.92
M.I.T.	3	4.91
HARVARD	4	4.90
CALIFORNIA, SAN DIEGO	5	4.88
CAL TECH	6	4.86
STANFORD (Medical School)	7	4.85
YALE	8	4.83
PRINCETON	9	4.82
WASHINGTON (Seattle)	10	4.80
CALIFORNIA, BERKELEY	11	4.77
DUKE	12	4.76
WASHINGTON (St. Louis)	13	4.74
WISCONSIN (Madison)	14	4.72
UCLA	15	4.69
STANFORD (Humanities & Sciences)	16	4.68
COLUMBIA (N.Y.)	17	4.67
JOHNS HOPKINS	18	4.65
TEXAS U. OF (Southwestern Medical Center) (Dallas)	19	4.63
PENNSYLVANIA	20	4.61
BAYLOR COLLEGE OF MEDICINE	21	4.58
COLORADO SCHOOL OF MEDICINE (Denver)	22	4.57
NYU	23	4.54
ALBERT EINSTEIN COLLEGE OF MEDICINE	24	4.52
ILLINOIS (Urbana)	25	4.50
NORTH CAROLINA (Chapel Hill)	26	4.48
VANDERBILT	27	4.45
MICHIGAN (Ann Arbor)	28	4.42
NORTHWESTERN (Evanston)	29	4.39
CALIFORNIA, DAVIS	30	4.36
CORNELL (N.Y.)	31	4.33
INDIANA (Bloomington)	32	4.29
MINNESOTA SCHOOL OF MEDICINE (Minneapolis)	33	4.25
BRANDEIS	34	4.22
SUNY (Stony Brook)	35	4.20

A RATING OF GRADUATE PROGRAMS IN CERAMIC SCIENCES AND ENGINEERING
Leading Institutions

Nine institutions with scores in the 4.0-5.0 range, in rank order

INSTITUTION	Rank	Score
ALFRED (SUNY)	1	4.91
ILLINOIS (Urbana)	2	4.88
OHIO STATE (Columbus)	3	4.84
RUTGERS (New Brunswick)	4	4.82
PENN STATE (University Park)	5	4.79
GEORGIA TECH	6	4.73
WASHINGTON (Seattle)	7	4.66
MISSOURI (Rolla)	8	4.60
IOWA STATE (Ames)	9	4.53

A RATING OF GRADUATE PROGRAMS IN CHEMICAL ENGINEERING
Leading Institutions

Thirty-seven institutions with scores in the 4.0-5.0 range, in rank order

INSTITUTION	Rank	Score
MINNESOTA (Minneapolis)	1	4.93
M.I.T.	2	4.91
CAL TECH	3	4.90
CALIFORNIA, BERKELEY	4	4.89
STANFORD	5	4.88
DELAWARE (Newark)	6	4.87
WISCONSIN (Madison)	7	4.86
ILLINOIS (Urbana)	8	4.85
PRINCETON	9	4.83
TEXAS (Austin)	10	4.82
PENNSYLVANIA	11	4.79
CARNEGIE-MELLON	12	4.77
CORNELL (N.Y.)	13	4.76
NORTHWESTERN (Evanston)	14	4.75
PURDUE (Lafayette)	15	4.74
MICHIGAN (Ann Arbor)	16	4.72
NOTRE DAME	17	4.70
CALIFORNIA, SANTA BARBARA	18	4.69
WASHINGTON (Seattle)	19	4.68
HOUSTON	20	4.64
MASSACHUSETTS (Amherst)	21	4.62
RICE	22	4.60
CUNY (Graduate School)	23	4.56
PENN STATE (University Park)	24	4.54
COLORADO (Boulder)	25	4.53
NORTH CAROLINA STATE (Raleigh)	26	4.51
CALIFORNIA, DAVIS	27	4.49
SUNY (Buffalo)	28	4.46
LEHIGH	29	4.45
YALE	30	4.41
GEORGIA TECH	31	4.40
IOWA STATE (Ames)	32	4.38
FLORIDA (Gainesville)	33	4.36
RENSSELAER (N.Y.)	34	4.34
JOHNS HOPKINS	35	4.32
TEXAS A&M (College Station)	36	4.31
VIRGINIA (Charlottesville)	37	4.30

A RATING OF GRADUATE PROGRAMS IN CHEMISTRY
Leading Institutions

Forty institutions with scores in the 4.0-5.0 range, in rank order

INSTITUTION	Rank	Score
HARVARD	1	4.93
CALIFORNIA, BERKELEY	2	4.92
CAL TECH	3	4.90
M.I.T.	4	4.88
COLUMBIA (N.Y.)	5	4.87
STANFORD	6	4.85
ILLINOIS (Urbana)	7	4.83
UCLA	8	4.82
CHICAGO	9	4.80
CORNELL (N.Y.)	10	4.79
WISCONSIN (Madison)	11	4.78
NORTHWESTERN (Evanston)	12	4.76
PRINCETON	13	4.74
YALE	14	4.72
TEXAS (Austin)	15	4.70
NORTH CAROLINA (Chapel Hill)	16	4.66
OHIO STATE (Columbus)	17	4.65
TEXAS A&M (College Station)	18	4.64
CALIFORNIA, SAN DIEGO	19	4.62
INDIANA (Bloomington)	20	4.60
PENN STATE (University Park)	21	4.58
PURDUE (Lafayette)	22	4.55
MINNESOTA (Minneapolis)	23	4.54
CALIFORNIA, SAN FRANCISCO	24	4.50
PENNSYLVANIA	25	4.48
IOWA STATE (Ames)	26	4.46
JOHNS HOPKINS	27	4.44
RICE	28	4.42
FLORIDA (Gainesville)	29	4.41
WASHINGTON (Seattle)	30	4.38
UTAH (Salt Lake City)	31	4.36
PITTSBURGH (Pittsburgh)	32	4.35
EMORY	33	4.33
ROCHESTER (N.Y.)	34	4.27
CALIFORNIA, SANTA BARBARA	35	4.25
MICHIGAN (Ann Arbor)	36	4.21
CALIFORNIA, IRVINE	37	4.20
NOTRE DAME	38	4.18
MICHIGAN STATE	39	4.17
OREGON (Eugene)	40	4.16

A RATING OF GRADUATE PROGRAMS IN
CHILD DEVELOPMENT-PSYCHOLOGY
Leading Institutions

Fourteen institutions with scores in the 4.0-5.0 range, in rank order

INSTITUTION	Rank	Score
STANFORD	1	4.43
YALE	2	4.40
ILLINOIS (Urbana)	3	4.36
MINNESOTA (Minneapolis)	4	4.32
CALIFORNIA, BERKELEY	5	4.30
CARNEGIE-MELLON	6	4.27
CORNELL (N.Y.)	7	4.26
WISCONSIN (Madison)	8	4.25
TEXAS (Austin)	9	4.21
VIRGINIA (Charlottesville)	10	4.18
NORTH CAROLINA (Chapel Hill)	11	4.15
DUKE	12	4.13
IOWA (Iowa City)	13	4.12
FLORIDA (Gainesville)	14	4.10

A RATING OF GRADUATE PROGRAMS IN CITY/REGIONAL PLANNING
Leading Institutions

Seventeen institutions with scores in the 4.0-5.0 range, in rank order

INSTITUTION	Rank	Score
M.I.T.	1	4.83
GEORGIA TECH	2	4.81
USC (Los Angeles)	3	4.79
RUTGERS (New Brunswick)	4	4.76
NORTH CAROLINA (Chapel Hill)	5	4.75
CALIFORNIA, BERKELEY	6	4.74
V.P.I. & STATE U.	7	4.70
ILLINOIS (Urbana)	8	4.68
UCLA	9	4.65
PRINCETON	10	4.62
WISCONSIN (Madison)	11	4.60
MICHIGAN (Ann Arbor)	12	4.55
WASHINGTON (Seattle)	13	4.53
OHIO STATE (Columbus)	14	4.51
CORNELL (N.Y.)	15	4.47
TEXAS A&M (College Station)	16	4.44
HARVARD	17	4.42

A RATING OF GRADUATE PROGRAMS IN CIVIL ENGINEERING
Leading Institutions

Forty institutions with scores in the 4.0-5.0 range, in rank order

INSTITUTION	Rank	Score
CALIFORNIA, BERKELEY	1	4.92
M.I.T.	2	4.90
ILLINOIS (Urbana)	3	4.89
CAL TECH	4	4.88
STANFORD	5	4.87
TEXAS (Austin)	6	4.86
CORNELL (N.Y.)	7	4.85
NORTHWESTERN (Evanston)	8	4.84
PRINCETON	9	4.83
MICHIGAN (Ann Arbor)	10	4.82
PURDUE (Lafayette)	11	4.80
CARNEGIE-MELLON	12	4.79
MINNESOTA (Minneapolis)	13	4.77
WASHINGTON (Seattle)	14	4.74
NORTH CAROLINA (Chapel Hill)	15	4.73
CALIFORNIA, DAVIS	16	4.72
GEORGIA TECH	17	4.71
LEHIGH	18	4.69
TEXAS A&M (College Station)	19	4.68
UCLA	20	4.67
WISCONSIN (Madison)	21	4.65
RICE	22	4.63
COLORADO (Boulder)	23	4.62
COLORADO STATE	24	4.60
JOHNS HOPKINS	25	4.58
DUKE	26	4.56
COLUMBIA (N.Y.)	27	4.53
IOWA (Iowa City)	28	4.51
PENN STATE (University Park)	29	4.48
SUNY (Buffalo)	30	4.47
ARIZONA (Tucson)	31	4.46
CALIFORNIA, IRVINE	32	4.43
RENSSELAER (N.Y.)	33	4.40
NOTRE DAME	34	4.38
FLORIDA (Gainesville)	35	4.36
MARYLAND (College Park)	36	4.34
VIRGINIA (Charlottesville)	37	4.32
OHIO STATE (Columbus)	38	4.30
V.P.I. & STATE U.	39	4.28
NORTH CAROLINA STATE (Raleigh)	40	4.26

A RATING OF GRADUATE PROGRAMS IN CLASSICS
Leading Institutions

Thirty institutions with scores in the 4.0-5.0 range, in rank order

INSTITUTION	Rank	Score
HARVARD	1	4.90
CALIFORNIA, BERKELEY	2	4.88
PRINCETON	3	4.86
YALE	4	4.84
MICHIGAN (Ann Arbor)	5	4.81
BROWN	6	4.77
CHICAGO	7	4.76
TEXAS (Austin)	8	4.70
UCLA	9	4.67
COLUMBIA (N.Y.)	10	4.64
CORNELL (N.Y.)	11	4.63
PENNSYLVANIA	12	4.59
NORTH CAROLINA (Chapel Hill)	13	4.56
DUKE	14	4.51
BRYN MAWR	15	4.45
STANFORD	16	4.41
ILLINOIS (Urbana)	17	4.36
VIRGINIA (Charlottesville)	18	4.32
WISCONSIN (Madison)	19	4.28
OHIO STATE (Columbus)	20	4.25
WASHINGTON (Seattle)	21	4.20
OHIO STATE (Columbus)	22	4.18
CALIFORNIA, SANTA BARBARA	23	4.17
JOHNS HOPKINS	24	4.15
MINNESOTA (Minneapolis)	25	4.14
N.Y.U.	26	4.13
BOSTON U.	27	4.10
CINCINNATI	28	4.09
CATHOLIC U. (D.C.)	29	4.08
FORDHAM	30	4.06

A RATING OF GRADUATE PROGRAMS IN CLINICAL PSYCHOLOGY
Leading Institutions

Twenty-four institutions with scores in the 4.0-5.0 range, in rank order

INSTITUTION	Rank	Score
YALE	1	4.67
PENNSYLVANIA	2	4.65
MICHIGAN (Ann Arbor)	3	4.61
MINNESOTA (Minneapolis)	4	4.58
CALIFORNIA, BERKELEY	5	4.57
UCLA	6	4.53
INDIANA (Bloomington)	7	4.50
OREGON (Eugene)	8	4.49
COLORADO (Boulder)	9	4.48
WASHINGTON (Seattle)	10	4.45
TEXAS (Austin)	11	4.43
NORTH CAROLINA (Chapel Hill)	12	4.41
NORTHWESTERN (Evanston)	13	4.40
N.Y.U.	14	4.38
PENN STATE (University Park)	15	4.37
DUKE	16	4.36
RUTGERS (New Brunswick)	17	4.27
IOWA (Iowa City)	18	4.25
OHIO STATE (Columbus)	19	4.22
WASHINGTON (St. Louis)	20	4.20
PURDUE (Lafayette)	21	4.18
SUNY (Stony Brook)	22	4.15
USC (Los Angeles)	23	4.11
VANDERBILT	24	4.05

A RATING OF GRADUATE PROGRAMS IN COGNITIVE-PSYCHOLOGY
Leading Institutions

Thirty-one institutions with scores in the 4.0-5.0 range, in rank order

INSTITUTION	Rank	Score
STANFORD	1	4.58
MICHIGAN (Ann Arbor)	2	4.56
YALE	3	4.54
UCLA	4	4.53
MINNESOTA (Minneapolis)	5	4.52
PENNSYLVANIA	6	4.50
CALIFORNIA, BERKELEY	7	4.49
CARNEGIE-MELLON	8	4.46
CORNELL (N.Y.)	9	4.43
WISCONSIN (Madison)	10	4.40
COLUMBIA (N.Y.)	11	4.37
TEXAS (Austin)	12	4.36
INDIANA (Bloomington)	13	4.35
VIRGINIA (Charlottesville)	14	4.34
OHIO STATE (Columbus)	15	4.33
OREGON (Eugene)	16	4.32
COLORADO (Boulder)	17	4.31
NORTHWESTERN (Evanston)	18	4.30
NORTH CAROLINA (Chapel Hill)	19	4.28
MASSACHUSETTS (Amherst)	20	4.26
DUKE	21	4.25
RUTGERS (New Brunswick)	22	4.23
ROCHESTER (N.Y.)	23	4.20
JOHNS HOPKINS	24	4.18
PURDUE (Lafayette)	25	4.17
IOWA (Iowa City)	26	4.15
SUNY (Buffalo)	27	4.14
VANDERBILT	28	4.12
SUNY (Stony Brook)	29	4.10
FLORIDA (Gainesville)	30	4.08
USC (Los Angeles)	31	4.05

A RATING OF GRADUATE PROGRAMS IN COMPARATIVE LITERATURE
Leading Institutions

Thirty institutions with scores in the 4.0-5.0 range, in rank order

INSTITUTION	Rank	Score
YALE	1	4.82
DUKE	2	4.74
HARVARD	3	4.73
COLUMBIA (N.Y.)	4	4.68
PRINCETON	5	4.64
CORNELL (N.Y.)	6	4.59
JOHNS HOPKINS	7	4.58
CALIFORNIA, IRVINE	8	4.54
STANFORD	9	4.50
CALIFORNIA, BERKELEY	10	4.46
PENNSYLVANIA	11	4.41
N.Y.U.	12	4.36
CHICAGO	13	4.31
WASHINGTON (Seattle)	14	4.28
MICHIGAN (Ann Arbor)	15	4.25
UCLA	16	4.21
NORTHWESTERN (Evanston)	17	4.16
CALIFORNIA, SAN DIEGO	18	4.15
INDIANA (Bloomington)	19	4.13
BROWN	20	4.12
TEXAS (Austin)	21	4.10
RUTGERS (New Brunswick)	22	4.09
USC (Los Angeles)	23	4.08
EMORY	24	4.07
WASHINGTON (St. Louis)	25	4.06
PENN STATE (University Park)	26	4.05
MINNESOTA (Minneapolis)	27	4.04
IOWA (Iowa City)	28	4.03
ILLINOIS (Urbana)	29	4.02
CALIFORNIA, RIVERSIDE	30	4.01

A RATING OF GRADUATE PROGRAMS IN COMPUTER SCIENCE
Leading Institutions

Forty-one institutions with scores in the 4.0-5.0 range, in rank order

INSTITUTION	Rank	Score
M.I.T.	1	4.92
STANFORD	2	4.91
CARNEGIE-MELLON	3	4.90
CALIFORNIA, BERKELEY	4	4.88
CORNELL (N.Y.)	5	4.86
PRINCETON	6	4.85
TEXAS (Austin)	7	4.82
ILLINOIS (Urbana)	8	4.80
WASHINGTON (Seattle)	9	4.79
HARVARD	10	4.78
WISCONSIN (Madison)	11	4.73
CAL TECH	12	4.71
BROWN	13	4.69
UCLA	14	4.67
YALE	15	4.65
MARYLAND (College Park)	16	4.63
MASSACHUSETTS (Amherst)	17	4.59
N.Y.U.	18	4.56
RICE	19	4.53
MICHIGAN (Ann Arbor)	20	4.50
USC (Los Angeles)	21	4.46
COLUMBIA (N.Y.)	22	4.43
CHICAGO	23	4.40
PENNSYLVANIA	24	4.38
CALIFORNIA, SAN DIEGO	25	4.37
PURDUE (Lafayette)	26	4.32
RUTGERS (New Brunswick)	27	4.28
DUKE	28	4.25
ROCHESTER (N.Y.)	29	4.22
NORTH CAROLINA (Chapel Hill)	30	4.21
SUNY (Stony Brook)	31	4.20
ARIZONA (Tucson)	32	4.18
GEORGIA TECH	33	4.16
CALIFORNIA, IRVINE	34	4.14
VIRGINIA (Charlottesville)	35	4.13
JOHNS HOPKINS	36	4.12
INDIANA (Bloomington)	37	4.11
NORTHWESTERN (Evanston)	38	4.10
OHIO STATE (Columbus)	39	4.09
COLORADO (Boulder)	40	4.08
UTAH (Salt Lake City)	41	4.06

A RATING OF GRADUATE PROGRAMS IN DEVELOPMENTAL PSYCHOLOGY
Leading Institutions

Twenty-six institutions with scores in the 4.0-5.0 range, in rank order

INSTITUTION	Rank	Score
STANFORD	1	4.61
MICHIGAN (Ann Arbor)	2	4.60
YALE	3	4.57
ILLINOIS (Urbana)	4	4.53
UCLA	5	4.52
PENNSYLVANIA	6	4.48
MINNESOTA (Minneapolis)	7	4.46
CARNEGIE-MELLON	8	4.43
CALIFORNIA, BERKELEY	9	4.42
CORNELL (N.Y.)	10	4.41
TEXAS (Austin)	11	4.38
WASHINGTON (Seattle)	12	4.36
INDIANA (Bloomington)	13	4.35
VIRGINIA (Charlottesville)	14	4.32
OHIO STATE (Columbus)	15	4.30
NORTH CAROLINA (Chapel Hill)	16	4.26
OREGON (Eugene)	17	4.25
CALIFORNIA, IRVINE	18	4.23
RUTGERS (New Brunswick)	19	4.22
PURDUE (Lafayette)	20	4.21
PENN STATE (University Park)	21	4.19
ROCHESTER (N.Y.)	22	4.16
DUKE	23	4.14
IOWA (Iowa City)	24	4.13
MASSACHUSETTS (Amherst)	25	4.11
USC (Los Angeles)	26	4.10

A RATING OF GRADUATE PROGRAMS IN DRAMA/THEATRE
Leading Institutions

Thirty-two institutions with scores in the 4.0-5.0 range, in rank order

INSTITUTION	Rank	Score
YALE	1	4.90
UCLA	2	4.89
NORTHWESTERN (Evanston)	3	4.88
STANFORD	4	4.87
IOWA (Iowa City)	5	4.84
MINNESOTA (Minneapolis)	6	4.79
INDIANA (Bloomington)	7	4.76
N.Y.U.	8	4.74
USC (Los Angeles)	9	4.73
CALIFORNIA, BERKELEY	10	4.71
CARNEGIE-MELLON	11	4.70
WISCONSIN (Madison)	12	4.69
WASHINGTON (Seattle)	13	4.68
FLORIDA STATE	14	4.65
CORNELL (N.Y.)	15	4.62
ILLINOIS (Urbana)	16	4.60
OHIO STATE (Columbus)	17	4.58
CALIFORNIA, SANTA BARBARA	18	4.55
TEXAS (Austin)	19	4.53
NORTH CAROLINA (Chapel Hill)	20	4.50
MICHIGAN (Ann Arbor)	21	4.48
COLUMBIA (N.Y.)	22	4.46
CASE WESTERN RESERVE	23	4.42
WAYNE STATE (Detroit)	24	4.38
OREGON (Eugene)	25	4.35
MARYLAND (College Park)	26	4.30
TULANE	27	4.27
CATHOLIC U. (D.C.)	28	4.25
MICHIGAN STATE	29	4.21
TUFTS	30	4.18
KANSAS (Lawrence)	31	4.16
PITTSBURGH (Pittsburgh)	32	4.13

A RATING OF GRADUATE PROGRAMS IN ECONOMICS
Leading Institutions

Forty institutions with scores in the 4.0-5.0 range, in rank order

INSTITUTION	Rank	Score
CHICAGO	1	4.92
M.I.T.	2	4.91
HARVARD	3	4.90
PRINCETON	4	4.89
STANFORD	5	4.88
YALE	6	4.86
CALIFORNIA, BERKELEY	7	4.84
PENNSYLVANIA	8	4.82
NORTHWESTERN (Evanston)	9	4.80
MINNESOTA (Minneapolis)	10	4.79
UCLA	11	4.76
COLUMBIA (N.Y.)	12	4.73
MICHIGAN (Ann Arbor)	13	4.68
UCLA	14	4.66
ROCHESTER (N.Y.)	15	4.63
WISCONSIN (Madison)	16	4.60
CORNELL (N.Y.)	17	4.59
N.Y.U.	18	4.55
CALIFORNIA, SAN DIEGO	19	4.53
MARYLAND (College Park)	20	4.52
BOSTON U.	21	4.49
DUKE	22	4.44
BROWN	23	4.42
NORTH CAROLINA (Chapel Hill)	24	4.41
VIRGINIA (Charlottesville)	25	4.39
MICHIGAN STATE	26	4.36
WASHINGTON (Seattle)	27	4.33
ILLINOIS (Urbana)	28	4.31
WASHINGTON (St. Louis)	29	4.29
IOWA (Iowa City)	30	4.27
TEXAS (Austin)	31	4.22
JOHNS HOPKINS	32	4.21
TEXAS A&M (College Station)	33	4.20
PITTSBURGH (Pittsburgh)	34	4.19
OHIO STATE (Columbus)	35	4.17
ARIZONA (Tucson)	36	4.16
CALIFORNIA, DAVIS	37	4.14
SUNY (Stony Brook)	38	4.12
FLORIDA (Gainesville)	39	4.11
USC (Los Angeles)	40	4.09

A RATING OF GRADUATE PROGRAMS IN ELECTRICAL ENGINEERING
Leading Institutions

Thirty-five institutions with scores in the 4.0-5.0 range, in rank order

INSTITUTION	Rank	Score
STANFORD	1	4.92
M.I.T.	2	4.91
ILLINOIS (Urbana)	3	4.90
CALIFORNIA, BERKELEY	4	4.88
CAL TECH	5	4.87
CORNELL (N.Y.)	6	4.86
MICHIGAN (Ann Arbor)	7	4.85
PURDUE (Lafayette)	8	4.84
PRINCETON	9	4.83
USC (Los Angeles)	10	4.82
UCLA	11	4.81
CARNEGIE-MELLON	12	4.79
GEORGIA TECH	13	4.78
TEXAS (Austin)	14	4.77
COLUMBIA (N.Y.)	15	4.75
WISCONSIN (Madison)	16	4.72
MARYLAND (College Park)	17	4.70
MINNESOTA (Minneapolis)	18	4.68
CALIFORNIA, SANTA BARBARA	19	4.66
CALIFORNIA, SAN DIEGO	20	4.64
NORTH CAROLINA STATE (Raleigh)	21	4.62
OHIO STATE (Columbus)	22	4.61
RENSSELAER (N.Y.)	23	4.60
POLYTECHNIC UNIVERSITY (Brooklyn, N.Y.)	24	4.54
WASHINGTON (Seattle)	25	4.51
RICE	26	4.50
V.P.I. & STATE U.	27	4.48
PENN STATE (University Park)	28	4.47
MASSACHUSETTS (Amherst)	29	4.46
YALE	30	4.42
FLORIDA (Gainesville)	31	4.40
TEXAS A&M (College Station)	32	4.38
CALIFORNIA, DAVIS	33	4.34
JOHNS HOPKINS	34	4.32
BROWN	35	4.30

A RATING OF GRADUATE PROGRAMS IN ENGLISH
Leading Institutions

Thirty-seven institutions with scores in the 4.0-5.0 range, in rank order

INSTITUTION	Rank	Score
YALE	1	4.93
CALIFORNIA, BERKELEY	2	4.92
HARVARD	3	4.91
DUKE	4	4.90
VIRGINIA (Charlottesville)	5	4.89
CORNELL (N.Y.)	6	4.88
STANFORD	7	4.87
COLUMBIA (N.Y.)	8	4.86
PENNSYLVANIA	9	4.83
CHICAGO	10	4.82
JOHNS HOPKINS	11	4.81
PRINCETON	12	4.80
UCLA	13	4.77
CALIFORNIA, IRVINE	14	4.76
BROWN	15	4.74
MICHIGAN (Ann Arbor)	16	4.71
RUTGERS (New Brunswick)	17	4.70
INDIANA (Bloomington)	18	4.69
NYU	19	4.66
CUNY (Graduate School)	20	4.64
TEXAS (Austin)	21	4.63
WISCONSIN (Madison)	22	4.61
WASHINGTON (Seattle)	23	4.60
NORTH CAROLINA (Chapel Hill)	24	4.58
PITTSBURGH (Pittsburgh)	25	4.57
SUNY (Buffalo)	26	4.56
ILLINOIS (Urbana)	27	4.52
NORTHWESTERN (Evanston)	28	4.49
NOTRE DAME	29	4.48
VANDERBILT	30	4.46
USC (Los Angeles)	31	4.43
EMORY	32	4.41
OHIO STATE (Columbus)	33	4.40
CALIFORNIA, SANTA BARBARA	34	4.38
MINNESOTA (Minneapolis)	35	4.36
CALIFORNIA, SAN DIEGO	36	4.35
BOSTON U.	37	4.32

A RATING OF GRADUATE PROGRAMS IN ENTOMOLOGY
Leading Institutions

Thirty-one institutions with scores in the 4.0-5.0 range, in rank order

INSTITUTION	Rank	Score
CALIFORNIA, BERKELEY	1	4.92
CORNELL (N.Y.)	2	4.91
ILLINOIS (Urbana)	3	4.90
CALIFORNIA, DAVIS	4	4.89
MINNESOTA (Minneapolis)	5	4.88
MICHIGAN STATE	6	4.86
WISCONSIN (Madison)	7	4.83
PURDUE (Lafayette)	8	4.81
KANSAS (Lawrence)	9	4.80
OHIO STATE (Columbus)	10	4.79
IOWA STATE (Ames)	11	4.76
CALIFORNIA, RIVERSIDE	12	4.74
OREGON STATE	13	4.72
KANSAS STATE	14	4.70
NORTH CAROLINA STATE (Raleigh)	15	4.66
TEXAS A&M (College Station)	16	4.63
RUTGERS (New Brunswick)	17	4.61
LSU (Baton Rouge)	18	4.55
FLORIDA (Gainesville)	19	4.53
PENN STATE (University Park)	20	4.51
MASSACHUSETTS (Amherst)	21	4.46
MISSOURI (Columbia)	22	4.43
ARIZONA (Tucson)	23	4.41
WASHINGTON STATE	24	4.40
MARYLAND (College Park)	25	4.38
COLORADO STATE	26	4.37
AUBURN (Auburn)	27	4.32
NEBRASKA (Lincoln)	28	4.28
GEORGIA (Athens)	29	4.22
OKLAHOMA STATE	30	4.20
V.P.I. & STATE U.	31	4.18

A RATING OF GRADUATE PROGRAMS IN ENVIRONMENTAL ENGINEERING
Leading Institutions

Ten institutions with scores in the 4.0-5.0 range, in rank order

INSTITUTION	Rank	Score
CAL TECH	1	4.86
CINCINNATI	2	4.82
TEXAS (Austin)	3	4.81
GEORGIA TECH	4	4.77
V.P.I. & STATE U.	5	4.74
NORTH CAROLINA (Chapel Hill)	6	4.70
FLORIDA (Gainesville)	7	4.66
MASSACHUSETTS (Amherst)	8	4.64
COLORADO STATE	9	4.61
CLEMSON	10	4.56

A RATING OF GRADUATE PROGRAMS IN EXPERIMENTAL PSYCHOLOGY (GENERAL)
Leading Institutions

Sixteen institutions with scores in the 4.0-5.0 range, in rank order

INSTITUTION	Rank	Score
YALE	1	4.55
MINNESOTA (Minneapolis)	2	4.53
WASHINGTON (Seattle)	3	4.51
CORNELL (N.Y.)	4	4.49
COLUMBIA (N.Y.)	5	4.48
PENNSYLVANIA	6	4.46
OHIO STATE (Columbus)	7	4.43
COLORADO (Boulder)	8	4.42
NORTH CAROLINA (Chapel Hill)	9	4.39
PENN STATE (University Park)	10	4.37
N.Y.U.	11	4.34
DUKE	12	4.33
JOHNS HOPKINS	13	4.30
BROWN	14	4.28
IOWA (Iowa City)	15	4.25
SUNY (Stony Brook)	16	4.20

A RATING OF GRADUATE PROGRAMS IN FORESTRY
Leading Institutions

Thirty-one institutions with scores in the 4.0-5.0 range, in rank order

INSTITUTION	Rank	Score
WASHINGTON (Seattle)	1	4.91
OREGON STATE	2	4.90
GEORGIA (Athens)	3	4.88
SUNY (College of Environmental Science and Forestry, Syracuse)	4	4.87
MAINE (Orono)	5	4.86
MINNESOTA (Minneapolis)	6	4.85
UTAH STATE	7	4.83
CALIFORNIA, BERKELEY	8	4.82
NORTH CAROLINA STATE (Raleigh)	9	4.81
YALE	10	4.80
DUKE	11	4.79
IDAHO (Moscow)	12	4.75
MONTANA (Missoula)	13	4.72
MICHIGAN (Ann Arbor)	14	4.70
PURDUE (Lafayette)	15	4.68
WISCONSIN (Madison)	16	4.65
AUBURN (Auburn)	17	4.64
CLEMSON	18	4.62
MISSISSIPPI STATE	19	4.58
PENN STATE (University Park)	20	4.55
MISSOURI (Columbia)	21	4.52
COLORADO STATE	22	4.49
MICHIGAN STATE	23	4.48
V.P.I. & STATE U.	24	4.44
TEXAS A&M (College Station)	25	4.41
WEST VIRGINIA (Morgantown)	26	4.40
STEPHEN F. AUSTIN STATE U.	27	4.37
MASSACHUSETTS (Amherst)	28	4.33
LSU (Baton Rouge)	29	4.26
IOWA STATE (Ames)	30	4.25
FLORIDA (Gainesville)	31	4.24

A RATING OF GRADUATE PROGRAMS IN FRENCH
Leading Institutions

Thirty-two institutions with scores in the 4.0-5.0 range, in rank order

INSTITUTION	Rank	Score
YALE	1	4.93
PRINCETON	2	4.92
COLUMBIA (N.Y.)	3	4.91
DUKE	4	4.90
PENNSYLVANIA	5	4.86
STANFORD	6	4.85
CALIFORNIA, BERKELEY	7	4.83
CORNELL (N.Y.)	8	4.82
MICHIGAN (Ann Arbor)	9	4.81
WISCONSIN (Madison)	10	4.80
N.Y.U.	11	4.75
HARVARD	12	4.73
VIRGINIA (Charlottesville)	13	4.71
EMORY	14	4.68
CHICAGO	15	4.66
JOHNS HOPKINS	16	4.64
CUNY (Graduate School)	17	4.62
CALIFORNIA, IRVINE	18	4.59
UCLA	19	4.56
BROWN	20	4.55
RUTGERS (New Brunswick)	21	4.52
TEXAS (Austin)	22	4.51
WASHINGTON (St. Louis)	23	4.48
INDIANA (Bloomington)	24	4.46
LSU (Baton Rouge)	25	4.44
MINNESOTA (Minneapolis)	26	4.40
IOWA (Iowa City)	27	4.39
NORTHWESTERN (Evanston)	28	4.32
OHIO STATE (Columbus)	29	4.26
RICE	30	4.25
CALIFORNIA, DAVIS	31	4.20
ILLINOIS (Urbana)	32	4.18

A RATING OF GRADUATE PROGRAMS IN GEOGRAPHY
Leading Institutions

Thirty institutions with scores in the 4.0-5.0 range, in rank order

INSTITUTION	Rank	Score
MINNESOTA (Minneapolis)	1	4.92
PENN STATE (University Park)	2	4.91
CALIFORNIA, BERKELEY	3	4.89
WISCONSIN (Madison)	4	4.87
CALIFORNIA, SANTA BARBARA	5	4.85
OHIO STATE (Columbus)	6	4.83
UCLA	7	4.81
CLARK (Massachusetts)	8	4.74
WASHINGTON (Seattle)	9	4.68
ILLINOIS (Urbana)	10	4.63
SYRACUSE	11	4.56
IOWA (Iowa City)	12	4.51
SUNY (Buffalo)	13	4.46
LSU (Baton Rouge)	14	4.38
TEXAS (Austin)	15	4.31
COLORADO (Boulder)	16	4.26
JOHNS HOPKINS	17	4.21
ARIZONA STATE	18	4.18
ARIZONA (Tucson)	19	4.16
KENTUCKY	20	4.12
RUTGERS (New Brunswick)	21	4.10
GEORGIA (Athens)	22	4.09
NORTH CAROLINA (Chapel Hill)	23	4.08
FLORIDA (Gainesville)	24	4.07
INDIANA (Bloomington)	25	4.06
MARYLAND (College Park)	26	4.05
OREGON (Eugene)	27	4.04
HAWAII (Manoa)	28	4.03
KANSAS (Lawrence)	29	4.02
WISCONSIN (Milwaukee)	30	4.01

A RATING OF GRADUATE PROGRAMS IN GEOSCIENCES
Leading Institutions

Thirty-nine institutions with scores in the 4.0-5.0 range, in rank order

INSTITUTION	Rank	Score
CAL TECH	1	4.91
M.I.T.	2	4.90
CALIFORNIA, BERKELEY	3	4.89
STANFORD	4	4.88
COLUMBIA (N.Y.)	5	4.87
HARVARD	6	4.86
CHICAGO	7	4.85
CALIFORNIA, SAN DIEGO	8	4.83
UCLA	9	4.80
CORNELL (N.Y.)	10	4.78
PRINCETON	11	4.76
PENN STATE (University Park)	12	4.74
TEXAS (Austin)	13	4.73
ARIZONA (Tucson)	14	4.71
BROWN	15	4.69
MICHIGAN (Ann Arbor)	16	4.68
JOHNS HOPKINS	17	4.65
CALIFORNIA, SANTA BARBARA	18	4.64
NORTHWESTERN (Evanston)	19	4.60
WASHINGTON (Seattle)	20	4.54
WISCONSIN (Madison)	21	4.52
CALIFORNIA, SANTA CRUZ	22	4.47
RICE	23	4.46
ILLINOIS (Urbana)	24	4.42
USC (Los Angeles)	25	4.39
MINNESOTA (Minneapolis)	26	4.38
V.P.I. & STATE U.	27	4.36
ARIZONA STATE (Tempe)	28	4.35
WASHINGTON (St. Louis)	29	4.34
CALIFORNIA, DAVIS	30	4.31
SUNY (Stony Brook)	31	4.29
HAWAII (Manoa)	32	4.25
TEXAS A&M (College Station)	33	4.20
OREGON (Eugene)	34	4.18
COLORADO (Boulder)	35	4.16
DARTMOUTH COLLEGE	36	4.14
COLORADO SCHOOL OF MINES	37	4.12
PURDUE (Lafayette)	38	4.10
RENSSELAER (N.Y.)	39	4.09

A RATING OF GRADUATE PROGRAMS IN GERMAN
Leading Institutions

Thirty-one institutions with scores in the 4.0-5.0 range, in rank order

INSTITUTION	Rank	Score
CALIFORNIA, BERKELEY	1	4.91
PRINCETON	2	4.90
HARVARD	3	4.88
YALE	4	4.86
WASHINGTON (St. Louis)	5	4.85
STANFORD	6	4.81
CORNELL (N.Y.)	7	4.80
INDIANA (Bloomington)	8	4.75
VIRGINIA (Charlottesville)	9	4.72
JOHNS HOPKINS	10	4.68
WISCONSIN (Madison)	11	4.67
WASHINGTON (Seattle)	12	4.65
TEXAS (Austin)	13	4.62
PENNSYLVANIA	14	4.60
CALIFORNIA, IRVINE	15	4.58
OHIO STATE (Columbus)	16	4.53
NORTH CAROLINA (Chapel Hill)	17	4.50
MINNESOTA (Minneapolis)	18	4.46
ILLINOIS (Urbana)	19	4.42
MICHIGAN (Ann Arbor)	20	4.40
UCLA	21	4.36
N.Y.U.	22	4.35
CALIFORNIA, DAVIS	23	4.30
MASSACHUSETTS (Amherst)	24	4.22
PENN STATE (University Park)	25	4.21
CALIFORNIA, SANTA BARBARA	26	4.20
GEORGETOWN (D.C.)	27	4.18
PITTSBURGH (Pittsburgh)	28	4.16
SUNY (Buffalo)	29	4.14
RUTGERS (New Brunswick)	30	4.12
SUNY (Albany)	31	4.11

A RATING OF GRADUATE PROGRAMS IN HISTORY
Leading Institutions

Thirty-seven institutions with scores in the 4.0-5.0 range, in rank order

INSTITUTION	Rank	Score
YALE	1	4.93
CALIFORNIA, BERKELEY	2	4.92
PRINCETON	3	4.91
HARVARD	4	4.90
MICHIGAN (Ann Arbor)	5	4.89
STANFORD	6	4.88
COLUMBIA (N.Y.)	7	4.87
CHICAGO	8	4.86
JOHNS HOPKINS	9	4.85
WISCONSIN (Madison)	10	4.84
UCLA	11	4.83
INDIANA (Bloomington)	12	4.82
CORNELL (N.Y.)	13	4.80
BROWN	14	4.79
PENNSYLVANIA	15	4.78
NORTH CAROLINA (Chapel Hill)	16	4.76
NORTHWESTERN (Evanston)	17	4.74
ROCHESTER (N.Y.)	18	4.72
DUKE	19	4.69
VIRGINIA (Charlottesville)	20	4.66
BRANDEIS	21	4.63
CUNY (Graduate School)	22	4.61
TEXAS (Austin)	23	4.58
N.Y.U.	24	4.55
MINNESOTA (Minneapolis)	25	4.53
IOWA (Iowa City)	26	4.50
CALIFORNIA, SANTA BARBARA	27	4.48
RUTGERS (New Brunswick)	28	4.44
ILLINOIS (Urbana)	29	4.42
CALIFORNIA, SAN DIEGO	30	4.40
WASHINGTON (Seattle)	31	4.38
VANDERBILT	32	4.35
CALIFORNIA, DAVIS	33	4.32
NOTRE DAME	34	4.30
MARYLAND (College Park)	35	4.28
EMORY	36	4.27
RICE	37	4.26

A RATING OF GRADUATE PROGRAMS IN HORTICULTURE
Leading Institutions

Twenty-seven institutions with scores in the 4.0-5.0 range, in rank order

INSTITUTION	Rank	Score
CORNELL (N.Y.)	1	4.91
TEXAS A&M (College Station)	2	4.89
IOWA STATE (Ames)	3	4.87
PURDUE (Lafayette)	4	4.84
ILLINOIS (Urbana)	5	4.82
MICHIGAN STATE	6	4.80
WISCONSIN (Madison)	7	4.78
MINNESOTA (Minneapolis)	8	4.76
OHIO STATE (Columbus)	9	4.74
KANSAS STATE	10	4.72
MISSOURI (Columbia)	11	4.71
PENN STATE (University Park)	12	4.70
COLORADO STATE	13	4.68
LSU (Baton Rouge)	14	4.66
MARYLAND (College Park)	15	4.64
GEORGIA (Athens)	16	4.60
NORTH CAROLINA STATE (Raleigh)	17	4.58
OREGON STATE	18	4.56
TENNESSEE (Knoxville)	19	4.55
NEBRASKA (Lincoln)	20	4.50
FLORIDA (Gainesville)	21	4.48
AUBURN (Auburn)	22	4.46
WASHINGTON STATE	23	4.43
HAWAII (Manoa)	24	4.40
V.P.I. & STATE U.	25	4.33
RUTGERS (New Brunswick)	26	4.30
WASHINGTON (Seattle)	27	4.26

A RATING OF GRADUATE PROGRAMS IN INDUSTRIAL ENGINEERING
Leading Institutions

Thirty institutions with scores in the 4.0-5.0 range, in rank order

INSTITUTION	Rank	Score
GEORGIA TECH	1	4.91
CALIFORNIA, BERKELEY	2	4.90
PURDUE (Lafayette)	3	4.88
MICHIGAN (Ann Arbor)	4	4.87
TEXAS A&M (College Station)	5	4.86
NORTHWESTERN (Evanston)	6	4.84
STANFORD	7	4.82
PENN STATE (University Park)	8	4.80
WISCONSIN (Madison)	9	4.76
V.P.I. & STATE U.	10	4.73
NORTH CAROLINA STATE (Raleigh)	11	4.72
OHIO STATE (Columbus)	12	4.69
ILLINOIS (Urbana)	13	4.65
RENSSELAER (N.Y.)	14	4.62
LEHIGH	15	4.58
OKLAHOMA STATE	16	4.54
ARIZONA STATE	17	4.51
SUNY (Buffalo)	18	4.50
FLORIDA (Gainesville)	19	4.47
AUBURN (Auburn)	20	4.46
USC (Los Angeles)	21	4.45
IOWA STATE (Ames)	22	4.44
PITTSBURGH (Pittsburgh)	23	4.42
IOWA (Iowa City)	24	4.39
OKLAHOMA (Norman)	25	4.38
ARKANSAS (Fayettville)	26	4.37
MASSACHUSETTS (Amherst)	27	4.36
NEBRASKA (Lincoln)	28	4.35
KANSAS STATE	29	4.33
CLEMSON	30	4.32

A RATING OF GRADUATE PROGRAMS IN INDUSTRIAL/LABOR RELATIONS
Leading Institutions

Eight institutions with scores in the 4.0-5.0 range, in rank order

INSTITUTION	Rank	Score
CORNELL (N.Y.)	1	4.82
CASE WESTERN RESERVE	2	4.78
ILLINOIS (Urbana)	3	4.74
RUTGERS (New Brunswick)	4	4.71
WISCONSIN (Madison)	5	4.66
MINNESOTA (Minneapolis)	6	4.63
OHIO STATE (Columbus)	7	4.60
MICHIGAN STATE	8	4.52

A RATING OF GRADUATE PROGRAMS IN INDUSTRIAL/ORGANIZATIONAL PSYCHOLOGY
Leading Institutions

Seventeen institutions with scores in the 4.0-5.0 range, in rank order

INSTITUTION	Rank	Score
MICHIGAN (Ann Arbor)	1	4.61
MINNESOTA (Minneapolis)	2	4.60
OHIO STATE (Columbus)	3	4.58
PURDUE (Lafayette)	4	4.55
N.Y.U.	5	4.52
PENN STATE (University Park)	6	4.50
CUNY (Graduate School)	7	4.46
MICHIGAN STATE	8	4.43
NORTH CAROLINA STATE (Raleigh)	9	4.41
HOUSTON (Houston)	10	4.38
SUNY (Buffalo)	11	4.35
GEORGIA TECH	12	4.32
ILLINOIS INSTITUTE OF TECHNOLOGY	13	4.29
CINCINNATI	14	4.26
GEORGE WASHINGTON	15	4.22
TEXAS A&M (College station)	16	4.19
WAYNE STATE (Detroit)	17	4.16

A RATING OF GRADUATE PROGRAMS IN INORGANIC CHEMISTRY
Leading Institutions

Sixteen institutions with scores in the 4.0-5.0 range, in rank order

INSTITUTION	Rank	Score
MINNESOTA (Minneapolis)	1	4.90
M.I.T.	2	4.87
OHIO STATE (Columbus)	3	4.84
PURDUE (Lafayette)	4	4.81
HARVARD	5	4.79
COLUMBIA (N.Y.)	6	4.76
MICHIGAN (Ann Arbor)	7	4.73
RUTGERS (New Brunswick)	8	4.70
TEXAS A&M (College Station)	9	4.66
MARYLAND (College Park)	10	4.62
FLORIDA (Gainesville)	11	4.59
PITTSBURGH (Pittsburgh)	12	4.54
MISSOURI (Columbia)	13	4.52
YALE	14	4.49
NOTRE DAME	15	4.46
RENSSELAER (N.Y.)	16	4.42

A RATING OF GRADUATE PROGRAMS IN JOURNALISM
Leading Institutions

Twenty-two institutions with scores in the 4.0-5.0 range, in rank order

INSTITUTION	Rank	Score
COLUMBIA (N.Y.)	1	4.92
NORTHWESTERN (Evanston)	2	4.91
MISSOURI (Columbia)	3	4.89
MINNESOTA (Minneapolis)	4	4.87
ILLINOIS (Urbana)	5	4.85
WISCONSIN (Madison)	6	4.83
MICHIGAN (Ann Arbor)	7	4.81
STANFORD	8	4.80
TEXAS (Austin)	9	4.77
INDIANA (Bloomington)	10	4.74
IOWA (Iowa City)	11	4.72
USC (Los Angeles)	12	4.68
N.Y.U.	13	4.65
BOSTON U.	14	4.60
MARYLAND (College Park)	15	4.58
WAYNE STATE (Detroit)	16	4.53
SYRACUSE	17	4.49
MICHIGAN STATE	18	4.46
NORTH CAROLINA (Chapel Hill)	19	4.43
PENN STATE (University Park)	20	4.42
OHIO STATE (Columbus)	21	4.39
OHIO U. (Athens)	22	4.33

A RATING OF GRADUATE PROGRAMS IN LANDSCAPE ARCHITECTURE
Leading Institutions

Seventeen institutions with scores in the 4.0-5.0 range, in rank order

INSTITUTION	Rank	Score
HARVARD	1	4.89
CALIFORNIA, BERKELEY	2	4.84
MICHIGAN (Ann Arbor)	3	4.81
PENNSYLVANIA	4	4.78
SUNY (College of Environmental Science & Forestry)	5	4.75
ILLINOIS (Urbana)	6	4.70
CORNELL (N.Y.)	7	4.69
KANSAS STATE	8	4.62
MASSACHUSETTS (Amherst)	9	4.57
GEORGIA (Athens)	10	4.53
WASHINGTON (Seattle)	11	4.50
NORTH CAROLINA STATE (Raleigh)	12	4.43
OHIO STATE (Columbus)	13	4.42
COLORADO (Denver)	14	4.38
LSU (Baton Rouge)	15	4.34
MINNESOTA (Minneapolis)	16	4.30
VIRGINIA (Charlottesville)	17	4.29

A RATING OF GRADUATE PROGRAMS IN LIBRARY SCIENCE

Twenty institutions with scores in the 4.0-5.0 range, in rank order

INSTITUTION	Rank	Score
MICHIGAN (Ann Arbor)	1	4.91
ILLINOIS (Urbana)	2	4.90
INDIANA (Bloomington)	3	4.86
WISCONSIN (Madison)	4	4.84
UCLA	5	4.82
RUTGERS (New Brunswick)	6	4.80
PITTSBURGH (Pittsburgh)	7	4.77
NORTH CAROLINA (Chapel Hill)	8	4.74
SIMMONS (Massachusetts)	9	4.71
TEXAS (Austin)	10	4.66
WASHINGTON (Seattle)	11	4.62
MARYLAND (College Park)	12	4.58
FLORIDA STATE	13	4.55
SYRACUSE	14	4.51
DREXEL	15	4.47
PRATT INSTITUTE	16	4.43
SUNY (Albany)	17	4.41
WAYNE STATE (Detroit)	18	4.38
CATHOLIC U. (D.C.)	19	4.36
LSU (Baton Rouge)	20	4.35

A RATING OF GRADUATE PROGRAMS IN LINGUISTICS
Leading Institutions

Thirty-two institutions with scores in the 4.0-5.0 range, in rank order

INSTITUTION	Rank	Score
M.I.T.	1	4.90
STANFORD	2	4.89
UCLA	3	4.86
CHICAGO	4	4.84
CALIFORNIA, BERKELEY	5	4.83
MASSACHUSETTS (Amherst)	6	4.79
CALIFORNIA, SAN DIEGO	7	4.78
PENNSYLVANIA	8	4.75
OHIO STATE (Columbus)	9	4.74
CORNELL (N.Y.)	10	4.72
CALIFORNIA, SANTA CRUZ	11	4.67
TEXAS (Austin)	12	4.65
USC (Los Angeles)	13	4.62
ARIZONA (Tucson)	14	4.61
CALIFORNIA, SAN DIEGO	15	4.58
CONNECTICUT (Storrs)	16	4.55
CUNY (Graduate School)	17	4.50
WASHINGTON (Seattle)	18	4.47
ILLINOIS (Urbana)	19	4.46
BROWN	20	4.42
GEORGETOWN (D.C.)	21	4.37
HARVARD	22	4.32
SUNY (Buffalo)	23	4.29
PITTSBURGH (Pittsburgh)	24	4.26
WISCONSIN (Madison)	25	4.23
HAWAII (Manoa)	26	4.20
SUNY (Stony Brook)	27	4.19
OREGON (Eugene)	28	4.18
INDIANA (Bloomington)	29	4.17
BOSTON U.	30	4.12
YALE	31	4.10
MICHIGAN (Ann Arbor)	32	4.09

A RATING OF GRADUATE PROGRAMS IN MATERIALS SCIENCE
Leading Institutions

Thirty-six institutions with scores in the 4.0-5.0 range, in rank order

INSTITUTION	Rank	Score
M.I.T.	1	4.93
NORTHWESTERN (Evanston)	2	4.92
CORNELL (N.Y.)	3	4.91
STANFORD	4	4.90
CALIFORNIA, BERKELEY	5	4.89
ILLINOIS (Urbana)	6	4.88
MASSACHUSETTS (Amherst)	7	4.86
CARNEGIE-MELLON	8	4.85
CAL TECH	9	4.83
PENN STATE (University Park)	10	4.82
CALIFORNIA, SANTA BARBARA	11	4.79
PENNSYLVANIA	12	4.78
RENSSELAER (N.Y.)	13	4.76
WISCONSIN (Madison)	14	4.73
FLORIDA (Gainesville)	15	4.72
MICHIGAN (Ann Arbor)	16	4.71
MINNESOTA (Minneapolis)	17	4.70
CASE WESTERN RESERVE	18	4.65
TEXAS (Austin)	19	4.63
OHIO STATE (Columbus)	20	4.60
VIRGINIA (Charlottesville)	21	4.58
LEHIGH	22	4.55
NORTH CAROLINA STATE (Raleigh)	23	4.53
RUTGERS (New Brunswick)	24	4.50
UCLA	25	4.46
ARIZONA STATE	26	4.44
COLUMBIA (N.Y.)	27	4.42
ARIZONA (Tucson)	28	4.39
BROWN	29	4.36
PURDUE (Lafayette)	30	4.30
JOHNS HOPKINS	31	4.26
VANDERBILT	32	4.22
UTAH (Salt Lake City)	33	4.21
ROCHESTER (N.Y.)	34	4.20
AKRON, U. OF	35	4.16
DREXEL U.	36	4.12

A RATING OF GRADUATE PROGRAMS IN MATHEMATICS
Leading Institutions

Forty-seven institutions with scores in the 4.0-5.0 range, in rank order

INSTITUTION	Rank	Score
PRINCETON	1	4.94
CALIFORNIA, BERKELEY	2	4.93
HARVARD	3	4.92
M.I.T.	4	4.91
CHICAGO	5	4.90
STANFORD	6	4.89
N.Y.U.	7	4.88
YALE	8	4.87
WISCONSIN (Madison)	9	4.86
COLUMBIA (N.Y.)	10	4.85
MICHIGAN (Ann Arbor)	11	4.84
BROWN	12	4.83
CORNELL (N.Y.)	13	4.82
UCLA	14	4.81
ILLINOIS (Urbana)	15	4.80
CAL TECH	16	4.79
MINNESOTA (Minneapolis)	17	4.78
CALIFORNIA, SAN DIEGO	18	4.77
PENNSYLVANIA	19	4.72
TEXAS (Austin)	20	4.69
PURDUE (Lafayette)	21	4.68
RUTGERS (New Brunswick)	22	4.66
WASHINGTON (Seattle)	23	4.64
SUNY (Stony Brook)	24	4.63
MARYLAND (College Park)	25	4.59
NORTHWESTERN (Evanston)	26	4.58
RICE	27	4.52
JOHNS HOPKINS	28	4.47
CUNY (Graduate School)	29	4.45
OHIO STATE (Columbus)	30	4.43
PENN STATE (University Park)	31	4.40
BRANDEIS	32	4.39
VIRGINIA (Charlottesville)	33	4.34
NOTRE DAME	34	4.31
DUKE	35	4.28
NORTH CAROLINA (Chapel Hill)	36	4.24
UTAH (Salt Lake City)	37	4.23
ILLINOIS (Chicago)	38	4.20
GEORGIA TECH	39	4.18
RENSSELAER (N.Y.)	40	4.16
WASHINGTON (St. Louis)	41	4.13
CARNEGIE-MELLON	42	4.11
INDIANA (Bloomington)	43	4.09
USC (Los Angeles)	44	4.07
MICHIGAN STATE	45	4.06
OREGON (Eugene)	46	4.03
DARTMOUTH COLLEGE	47	4.01

A RATING OF GRADUATE PROGRAMS IN MECHANICAL ENGINEERING
Leading Institutions

Thirty-six institutions with scores in the 4.0-5.0 range, in rank order

INSTITUTION	Rank	Score
M.I.T.	1	4.93
STANFORD	2	4.92
CALIFORNIA, BERKELEY	3	4.91
CAL TECH	4	4.90
MICHIGAN (Ann Arbor)	5	4.89
PRINCETON	6	4.88
CORNELL (N.Y.)	7	4.86
MINNESOTA (Minneapolis)	8	4.84
ILLINOIS (Urbana)	9	4.83
PURDUE (Lafayette)	10	4.82
CALIFORNIA, SAN DIEGO	11	4.80
BROWN	12	4.77
NORTHWESTERN (Evanston)	13	4.75
RENSSELAER (N.Y.)	14	4.73
TEXAS (Austin)	15	4.72
UCLA	16	4.70
GEORGIA TECH	17	4.66
PENN STATE (University Park)	18	4.62
CARNEGIE-MELLON	19	4.60
CASE WESTERN RESERVE	20	4.58
WISCONSIN (Madison)	21	4.55
PENNSYLVANIA	22	4.52
LEHIGH	23	4.49
NORTH CAROLINA STATE (Raleigh)	24	4.47
OHIO STATE (Columbus)	25	4.46
CALIFORNIA, DAVIS	26	4.43
RICE	27	4.41
TEXAS A&M (College Station)	28	4.40
COLUMBIA (N.Y.)	29	4.38
V.P.I. & STATE U.	30	4.37
RUTGERS (new Brunswick)	31	4.35
MARYLAND (College Park)	32	4.34
WASHINGTON (Seattle)	33	4.33
NOTRE DAME	34	4.32
ARIZONA (Tucson)	35	4.30
CALIFORNIA, IRVINE	36	4.29

A RATING OF GRADUATE PROGRAMS IN MICROBIOLOGY
Leading Institutions

Forty institutions with scores in the 4.0-5.0 range, in rank order

INSTITUTION	Rank	Score
M.I.T.	1	4.93
ROCKEFELLER (N.Y.)	2	4.92
CALIFORNIA, SAN DIEGO	3	4.91
JOHNS HOPKINS	4	4.90
DUKE	5	4.89
WASHINGTON (Seattle)	6	4.88
UCLA	7	4.87
CHICAGO	8	4.86
ILLINOIS (Urbana)	9	4.85
PENNSYLVANIA	10	4.84
HARVARD	11	4.83
CALIFORNIA, DAVIS	12	4.82
WISCONSIN (Madison)	13	4.81
MICHIGAN (Ann Arbor)	14	4.80
STANFORD	15	4.79
COLUMBIA (N.Y.)	16	4.77
CALIFORNIA, SAN FRANCISCO	17	4.76
YALE	18	4.75
N.Y.U.	19	4.73
CALIFORNIA, BERKELEY	20	4.72
ALABAMA (Birmingham)	21	4.70
MINNESOTA (Minneapolis)	22	4.69
RUTGERS (New Brunswick)	23	4.68
PURDUE (Lafayette)	24	4.67
CORNELL (Medical Center) (N.Y.)	25	4.66
CORNELL (Ithaca, N.Y.)	26	4.64
MICHIGAN STATE	27	4.62
NORTH CAROLINA (Chapel Hill)	28	4.60
ALBERT EINSTEIN (College of Medicine) (N.Y.)	29	4.58
TEXAS (Austin)	30	4.57
CALIFORNIA, IRVINE	31	4.54
VANDERBILT	32	4.52
ROCHESTER (N.Y.)	33	4.50
FLORIDA (Gainesville)	34	4.49
VIRGINIA (Charlottesville)	35	4.46
OREGON (Eugene)	36	4.45
TUFTS	37	4.42
V.P.I. & STATE U.	38	4.40
INDIANA (Bloomington)	39	4.38
IOWA (Iowa City)	40	4.34

A RATING OF GRADUATE PROGRAMS IN MOLECULAR GENETICS
Leading Institutions

Thirty-six institutions with scores in the 4.0-5.0 range, in rank order

INSTITUTION	Rank	Score
CALIFORNIA, SAN FRANCISCO	1	4.92
HARVARD	2	4.91
M.I.T.	3	4.90
STANFORD	4	4.88
CALIFORNIA, SAN DIEGO	5	4.86
CAL TECH	6	4.83
YALE	7	4.80
JOHNS HOPKINS	8	4.79
WISCONSIN (Madison)	9	4.76
CHICAGO	10	4.73
CALIFORNIA, BERKELEY	11	4.70
COLUMBIA (N.Y.)	12	4.68
DUKE	13	4.66
BAYLOR COLLEGE OF MEDICINE	14	4.65
WASHINGTON (St. Louis)	15	4.64
PENNSYLVANIA	16	4.60
TEXAS U. OF (Southwestern Medical Center, Dallas)	17	4.57
WASHINGTON (Seattle)	18	4.54
UTAH (Salt Lake City)	19	4.52
MICHIGAN (Ann Arbor)	20	4.48
CORNELL (N.Y.)	21	4.45
ALBERT EINSTEIN COLLEGE OF MEDICINE	22	4.41
ROCHESTER (N.Y.)	23	4.39
SUNY (Stony Brook)	24	4.38
NORTH CAROLINA (Chapel Hill)	25	4.37
TEXAS U. OF (Health Science Center, Houston)	26	4.35
RUTGERS (New Brunswick)	27	4.32
EMORY	28	4.30
INDIANA (Bloomington)	29	4.27
TEXAS (Austin)	30	4.24
ILLINOIS (Urbana)	31	4.23
VANDERBILT	32	4.20
BRANDEIS	33	4.18
NORTH CAROLINA STATE (Raleigh)	34	4.15
ARIZONA (Tucson)	35	4.13
PENN STATE (University Park)	36	4.10

A RATING OF GRADUATE PROGRAMS IN MUSIC
Leading Institutions

Thirty-six institutions with scores in the 4.0-5.0 range, in rank order

INSTITUTION	Rank	Score
HARVARD	1	4.91
CHICAGO	2	4.90
CALIFORNIA, BERKELEY	3	4.88
PRINCETON	4	4.86
YALE	5	4.85
CORNELL (N.Y.)	6	4.81
ILLINOIS (Urbana)	7	4.80
COLUMBIA (N.Y.)	8	4.79
MICHIGAN (Ann Arbor)	9	4.77
CUNY (Graduate School)	10	4.76
PENNSYLVANIA	11	4.74
N.Y.U.	12	4.73
STANFORD	13	4.72
ROCHESTER (N.Y.)	14	4.70
NORTH CAROLINA (Chapel Hill)	15	4.68
INDIANA (Bloomington)	16	4.66
UCLA	17	4.64
BRANDEIS	18	4.62
DUKE	19	4.60
TEXAS (Austin)	20	4.57
USC (Los Angeles)	21	4.56
RUTGERS (New Brunswick)	22	4.54
NORTHWESTERN (Evanston)	23	4.53
OHIO STATE (Columbus)	24	4.51
NORTH TEXAS (Denton)	25	4.50
SUNY (Stony Brook)	26	4.47
WASHINGTON (Seattle)	27	4.45
MARYLAND (College Park)	28	4.43
CALIFORNIA, SANTA BARBARA	29	4.42
FLORIDA STATE	30	4.40
IOWA (Iowa City)	31	4.36
MINNESOTA (Minneapolis)	32	4.33
WISCONSIN	33	4.32
WASHINGTON (St. Louis)	34	4.26
CALIFORNIA, SAN DIEGO	35	4.23
CINCINNATI, U. OF	36	4.22

A RATING OF GRADUATE PROGRAMS IN
NEAR AND MIDDLE EASTERN STUDIES
Leading Institutions

Thirteen institutions with scores in the 4.0-5.0 range, in rank order

INSTITUTION	Rank	Score
HARVARD	1	4.82
COLUMBIA (N.Y.)	2	4.78
JOHNS HOPKINS	3	4.76
PRINCETON	4	4.73
CALIFORNIA, BERKELEY	5	4.70
CHICAGO	6	4.66
CORNELL (N.Y.)	7	4.65
MICHIGAN (Ann Arbor)	8	4.62
PENNSYLVANIA	9	4.58
UCLA	10	4.53
N.Y.U.	11	4.49
BRANDEIS	12	4.45
GEORGETOWN (D.C.)	13	4.42

A RATING OF GRADUATE PROGRAMS IN NEUROSCIENCES
Leading Institutions

Thirty-five institutions with scores in the 4.0-5.0 range, in rank order

INSTITUTION	Rank	Score
YALE	1	4.93
HARVARD	2	4.92
CALIFORNIA, SAN FRANCISCO	3	4.91
CALIFORNIA, SAN DIEGO	4	4.90
COLUMBIA (N.Y.)	5	4.87
JOHNS HOPKINS	6	4.86
STANFORD	7	4.83
CALIFORNIA, BERKELEY	8	4.81
CAL TECH	9	4.78
PENNSYLVANIA	10	4.75
WASHINGTON (St. Louis)	11	4.73
ROCKEFELLER U.	12	4.71
DUKE	13	4.68
WASHINGTON (Seattle)	14	4.67
CASE WESTERN RESERVE	15	4.64
UCLA	16	4.62
M.I.T.	17	4.60
MICHIGAN (Ann Arbor)	18	4.57
CHICAGO	19	4.53
BAYLOR COLLEGE OF MEDICINE	20	4.51
CALIFORNIA, IRVINE	21	4.48
CORNELL (N.Y.)	22	4.45
NORTHWESTERN (Evanston)	23	4.40
WISCONSIN (Madison)	24	4.36
NORTH CAROLINA (Chapel Hill)	25	4.33
VANDERBILT	26	4.31
ALBERT EINSTEIN COLLEGE OF MEDICINE	27	4.29
IOWA (Iowa City)	28	4.24
SUNY (Stony Brook)	29	4.22
VIRGINIA (Charlottesville)	30	4.19
MAYO GRADUATE SCHOOL	31	4.16
BRANDEIS	32	4.14
EMORY	33	4.13
MINNESOTA (Minneapolis)	34	4.11
OREGON (Eugene)	35	4.10

A RATING OF GRADUATE PROGRAMS IN NUCLEAR ENGINEERING
Leading Institutions

Twenty-five institutions with scores in the 4.0-5.0 range, in rank order

INSTITUTION	Rank	Score
M.I.T.	1	4.91
MICHIGAN (Ann Arbor)	2	4.90
CORNELL (N.Y.)	3	4.88
CALIFORNIA, BERKELEY	4	4.86
GEORGIA TECH	5	4.85
ILLINOIS (Urbana)	6	4.82
RENSSELAER (N.Y.)	7	4.81
TEXAS A&M (College Station)	8	4.80
OHIO STATE (Columbus)	9	4.76
WISCONSIN (Madison)	10	4.72
PURDUE (Lafayette)	11	4.71
VIRGINIA (Charlottesville)	12	4.67
NORTH CAROLINA STATE (Raleigh)	13	4.65
PENN STATE (University Park)	14	4.63
FLORIDA (Gainesville)	15	4.60
NORTHWESTERN (Evanston)	16	4.57
CINCINNATI	17	4.50
ARIZONA (Tucson)	18	4.47
WASHINGTON (Seattle)	19	4.45
MISSOURI (Columbia)	20	4.41
KANSAS STATE	21	4.34
MARYLAND (College Park)	22	4.32
MISSOURI (Rolla)	23	4.28
COLUMBIA (N.Y.)	24	4.24
OKLAHOMA (Norman)	25	4.20

A RATING OF GRADUATE PROGRAMS IN NUTRITION
Leading Institutions

Thirty-eight institutions with scores in the 4.0-5.0 range, in rank order

INSTITUTION	Rank	Score
CORNELL (N.Y.)	1	4.92
COLUMBIA (N.Y.)	2	4.91
EMORY	3	4.89
TUFTS	4	4.88
JOHNS HOPKINS	5	4.87
CHICAGO	6	4.86
PURDUE (Lafayette)	7	4.83
IOWA STATE (Ames)	8	4.81
HARVARD	9	4.78
PENN STATE (University Park)	10	4.77
ALABAMA (Birmingham)	11	4.75
CALIFORNIA, DAVIS	12	4.73
ILLINOIS (Urbana)	13	4.72
OHIO STATE (Columbus)	14	4.69
MINNESOTA (Minneapolis)	15	4.68
MICHIGAN STATE	16	4.65
KANSAS STATE	17	4.63
WISCONSIN (Madison)	18	4.61
WASHINGTON (Seattle)	19	4.60
CALIFORNIA, BERKELEY	20	4.58
RUTGERS (New Brunswick)	21	4.57
MISSOURI (Columbia)	22	4.53
PITTSBURGH (Pittsburgh)	23	4.51
TEXAS (Austin)	24	4.48
ARIZONA (Tucson)	25	4.45
COLORADO STATE	26	4.42
NORTH CAROLINA (Chapel Hill)	27	4.39
TEXAS A&M (College Station)	28	4.35
AUBURN (Auburn)	29	4.34
MARYLAND (College Park)	30	4.30
CASE WESTERN RESERVE	31	4.28
FLORIDA (Gainesville)	32	4.24
FLORIDA STATE	33	4.21
USC (Los Angeles)	34	4.20
DREXEL	35	4.19
OREGON STATE	36	4.15
NORTH CAROLINA STATE (Raleigh)	37	4.12
CLEMSON	38	4.10

A RATING OF GRADUATE PROGRAMS IN OCCUPATIONAL THERAPY
Leading Institutions

Twenty institutions with scores in the 4.0-5.0 range, in rank order

INSTITUTION	Rank	Score
BOSTON U.	1	4.86
COLUMBIA	2	4.82
TUFTS	3	4.77
TEMPLE (Philadelphia)	4	4.73
NORTH CAROLINA (Chapel Hill)	5	4.68
OHIO STATE (Columbus)	6	4.64
N.Y.U.	7	4.60
COLORADO STATE	8	4.57
USC (Los Angeles)	9	4.54
FLORIDA (Gainesville)	10	4.50
WAYNE STATE (Detroit)	11	4.49
WASHINGTON (St. Louis)	12	4.47
ALABAMA (Birmingham)	13	4.43
KANSAS (Lawrence)	14	4.39
MEDICAL U. OF SOUTH CAROLINA	15	4.36
TEXAS WOMAN'S U.	16	4.34
PITTSBURGH (Pittsburgh)	17	4.32
WASHINGTON (Seattle)	18	4.29
ILLINOIS (Chicago)	19	4.26
SUNY (Buffalo)	20	4.22

A RATING OF GRADUATE PROGRAMS IN OCEANOGRAPHY
Leading Institutions

Twenty-four institutions with scores in the 4.0-5.0 range, in rank order

INSTITUTION	Rank	Score
CALIFORNIA, SAN DIEGO	1	4.91
M.I.T.	2	4.90
COLUMBIA (N.Y.)	3	4.88
WASHINGTON (Seattle)	4	4.85
OREGON STATE	5	4.82
HAWAII (Manoa)	6	4.81
SUNY (Stony Brook)	7	4.78
FLORIDA STATE	8	4.76
MARYLAND (College Park)	9	4.73
MIAMI (Florida)	10	4.70
TEXAS A&M (College Station)	11	4.68
RHODE ISLAND (Kingston)	12	4.66
SOUTH FLORIDA (Tampa)	13	4.62
WISCONSIN (Madison)	14	4.59
NORTH CAROLINA (Chapel Hill)	15	4.55
STANFORD	16	4.53
DUKE	17	4.51
SOUTH CAROLINA (Columbia)	18	4.48
ALASKA (Fairbanks)	19	4.46
NORTH CAROLINA STATE (Raleigh)	20	4.42
LSU (Baton Rouge)	21	4.38
NAVAL POST GRADUATE SCHOOL (Monterey)	22	4.35
FLORIDA INSTITUTE OF TECHNOLOGY	23	4.32
MASSACHUSETTS (Amherst)	24	4.29

A RATING OF GRADUATE PROGRAMS IN ORGANIC CHEMISTRY
Leading Institutions

Thirteen institutions with scores in the 4.0-5.0 range, in rank order

INSTITUTION	Rank	Score
HARVARD	1	4.85
PURDUE (Lafayette)	2	4.82
CORNELL (N.Y.)	3	4.79
M.I.T.	4	4.75
MICHIGAN (Ann Arbor)	5	4.73
MARYLAND (College Park)	6	4.70
COLUMBIA (N.Y.)	7	4.66
RUTGERS (New Brunswick)	8	4.63
PITTSBURGH (Pittsburgh)	9	4.58
MISSOURI (Columbia)	10	4.54
YALE	11	4.51
NOTRE DAME	12	4.48
RENSSELAER (N.Y.)	13	4.43

A RATING OF GRADUATE PROGRAMS IN PERSONALTY-PSYCHOLOGY
Leading Institutions

Eighteen institutions with scores in the 4.0-5.0 range, in rank order

INSTITUTION	Rank	Score
STANFORD	1	4.49
MICHIGAN (Ann Arbor)	2	4.46
YALE	3	4.42
MINNESOTA (Minneapolis)	4	4.39
CALIFORNIA, BERKELEY	5	4.38
WASHINGTON (Seattle)	6	4.37
CORNELL (N.Y.)	7	4.33
WISCONSIN (Madison)	8	4.30
COLUMBIA (N.Y.)	9	4.28
TEXAS (Austin)	10	4.26
OREGON (Eugene)	11	4.25
NORTHWESTERN (Evanston)	12	4.22
DUKE	13	4.19
JOHNS HOPKINS	14	4.18
N.Y.U.	15	4.17
PURDUE (Lafayette)	16	4.16
MASSACHUSETTS (Amherst)	17	4.15
SUNY (Stony Brook)	18	4.14

A RATING OF GRADUATE PROGRAMS IN PETROLEUM ENGINEERING
Leading Institutions

Fourteen institutions with scores in the 4.0-5.0 range, in rank order

INSTITUTION	Rank	Score
TEXAS (Austin)	1	4.89
STANFORD	2	4.85
USC (Los Angeles)	3	4.83
TULSA	4	4.80
TEXAS A&M (College Station)	5	4.77
OKLAHOMA (Norman)	6	4.74
LSU (Baton Rouge)	7	4.70
CALIFORNIA, BERKELEY	8	4.66
KANSAS (Lawrence)	9	4.63
PENN STATE (University Park)	10	4.59
COLORADO (Mines)	11	4.54
MISSOURI (Rolla)	12	4.45
HOUSTON (Houston)	13	4.40
NEW MEXICO (Mining & Technology)	14	4.37

A RATING OF GRADUATE PROGRAMS IN PHARMACOLOGY
Leading Institutions

Thirty institutions with scores in the 4.0-5.0 range, in rank order

INSTITUTION	Rank	Score
CALIFORNIA, SAN DIEGO	1	4.93
JOHNS HOPKINS	2	4.92
DUKE	3	4.91
YALE	4	4.90
VANDERBILT	5	4.89
WASHINGTON (Seattle)	6	4.86
PENNSYLVANIA	7	4.83
M.I.T.	8	4.82
NORTH CAROLINA (Chapel Hill)	9	4.80
TEXAS U. OF (Southwestern Medical Center, Dallas)	10	4.77
N.Y.U.	11	4.75
MICHIGAN (Ann Arbor)	12	4.72
WISCONSIN (Madison)	13	4.71
STANFORD	14	4.70
COLORADO (Boulder)	15	4.66
ROCHESTER (N.Y.)	16	4.63
EMORY	17	4.60
COLUMBIA (N.Y.)	18	4.58
IOWA (Iowa City)	19	4.55
KANSAS (Lawrence)	20	4.52
CHICAGO	21	4.50
MINNESOTA (Minneapolis)	22	4.48
SUNY (Stony Brook)	23	4.47
TEXAS (Austin)	24	4.44
VIRGINIA (Charlottesville)	25	4.40
ALBERT EINSTEIN COLLEGE OF MEDICINE	26	4.37
MAYO GRADUATE SCHOOL	27	4.35
CALIFORNIA, DAVIS	28	4.32
MICHIGAN STATE U.	29	4.29
GEORGETOWN (D.C.)	30	4.25

A RATING OF GRADUATE PROGRAMS IN PLANT PATHOLOGY
Leading Institutions

Thirty institutions with scores in the 4.0-5.0 range, in rank order

INSTITUTION	Rank	Score
CORNELL (N.Y.)	1	4.87
PURDUE (Lafayette)	2	4.85
IOWA STATE (Ames)	3	4.82
MICHIGAN STATE	4	4.80
OHIO STATE (Columbus)	5	4.76
CALIFORNIA, DAVIS	6	4.75
MINNESOTA (Minneapolis)	7	4.74
WISCONSIN (Madison)	8	4.71
CALIFORNIA, BERKELEY	9	4.69
TEXAS A&M (College Station)	10	4.65
PENN STATE (University Park)	11	4.64
KANSAS STATE	12	4.62
ILLINOIS (Urbana)	13	4.61
MISSOURI (Columbia)	14	4.58
GEORGIA (Athens)	15	4.55
COLORADO STATE	16	4.53
ARIZONA (Tucson)	17	4.50
FLORIDA (Gainesville)	18	4.47
CALIFORNIA, RIVERSIDE	19	4.46
HAWAII (Manoa)	20	4.43
NORTH CAROLINA STATE (Raleigh)	21	4.41
LSU (Baton Rouge)	22	4.39
AUBURN (Auburn)	23	4.37
RUTGERS (New Brunswick)	24	4.35
OREGON STATE	25	4.32
V.P.I. & STATE U.	26	4.28
KENTUCKY	27	4.24
MISSISSIPPI STATE	28	4.22
MASSACHUSETTS (Amherst)	29	4.21
WASHINGTON STATE	30	4.20

A RATING OF GRADUATE PROGRAMS IN PHILOSOPHY
Leading Institutions

Forty institutions with scores in the 4.0-5.0 range, in rank order

INSTITUTION	Rank	Score
PRINCETON	1	4.92
PITTSBURGH (Pittsburgh)	2	4.91
HARVARD	3	4.90
CALIFORNIA, BERKELEY	4	4.88
STANFORD	5	4.87
UCLA	6	4.86
CHICAGO	7	4.84
MICHIGAN (Ann Arbor)	8	4.82
CORNELL (N.Y.)	9	4.80
M.I.T.	10	4.78
NOTRE DAME	11	4.76
RUTGERS (New Brunswick)	12	4.73
BROWN	13	4.71
ARIZONA (Tucson)	14	4.68
NORTH CAROLINA (Chapel Hill)	15	4.67
ILLINOIS (Chicago)	16	4.63
CUNY (Graduate School)	17	4.60
MASSACHUSETTS (Amherst)	18	4.56
CALIFORNIA, SAN DIEGO	19	4.53
WISCONSIN (Madison)	20	4.50
CALIFORNIA, IRVINE	21	4.47
OHIO STATE (Columbus)	22	4.43
NORTHWESTERN (Evanston)	23	4.41
PENNSYLVANIA	24	4.39
TEXAS (Austin)	25	4.38
COLUMBIA (N.Y.)	26	4.35
SYRACUSE	27	4.34
BOSTON U.	28	4.31
JOHNS HOPKINS	29	4.29
INDIANA (Bloomington)	30	4.27
MINNESOTA (Minneapolis)	31	4.25
ROCHESTER (N.Y.)	32	4.24
ILLINOIS (Urbana)	33	4.21
RICE	34	4.18
VANDERBILT	35	4.16
USC (Los Angeles)	36	4.12
EMORY	37	4.11
VIRGINIA (Charlottesville)	38	4.10
DUKE	39	4.08
MARYLAND (College Park)	40	4.06

A RATING OF GRADUATE PROGRAMS IN PHYSICAL CHEMISTRY
Leading Institutions

Sixteen institutions with scores in the 4.0-5.0 range, in rank order

INSTITUTION	Rank	Score
MINNESOTA (Minneapolis)	1	4.88
OHIO STATE (Columbus)	2	4.84
HARVARD	3	4.83
COLUMBIA (N.Y.)	4	4.80
M.I.T.	5	4.77
PURDUE (Lafayette)	6	4.74
MICHIGAN (Ann Arbor)	7	4.72
TEXAS A&M (College Station)	8	4.69
RUTGERS (New Brunswick)	9	4.68
MARYLAND (College Park)	10	4.65
MISSOURI (Columbia)	11	4.61
PITTSBURGH (Pittsburgh)	12	4.59
YALE	13	4.58
FLORIDA (Gainesville)	14	4.54
NOTRE DAME	15	4.52
RENSSELAER (N.Y.)	16	4.49

A RATING OF GRADUATE PROGRAMS IN PHYSICAL THERAPY
Leading Institutions

Twenty-one institutions with scores in the 4.0-5.0 range, in rank order

INSTITUTION	Rank	Score
BOSTON U.	1	4.88
COLUMBIA (N.Y.)	2	4.85
WASHINGTON (St. Louis)	3	4.81
DUKE	4	4.76
USC (Los Angeles)	5	4.70
EMORY	6	4.63
IOWA (Iowa City)	7	4.58
PITTSBURGH (Pittsburgh)	8	4.52
LONG ISLAND U. (Brooklyn)	9	4.44
ALABAMA (Birmingham)	10	4.40
MIAMI (Florida)	11	4.39
MEDICAL COLLEGE OF PENNSYLVANIA/HAHNEMANN	12	4.38
KANSAS (Lawrence)	13	4.37
CALIFORNIA, SAN FRANCISCO	14	4.36
NORTH CAROLINA (Chapel Hill)	15	4.32
MEDICAL U. OF SOUTH CAROLINA	16	4.31
U. OF TEXAS MEDICAL BRANCH AT GALVESTON	17	4.29
TEXAS WOMAN'S U.	18	4.25
TEMPLE (Philadelphia)	19	4.23
SAINT LOUIS U.	20	4.22
BAYLOR U.	21	4.20

A RATING OF GRADUATE PROGRAMS IN PHYSICS
Leading Institutions

Forty-one institutions with scores in the 4.0-5.0 range, in rank order

INSTITUTION	Rank	Score
HARVARD	1	4.93
CAL TECH	2	4.92
CORNELL (N.Y.)	3	4.91
PRINCETON	4	4.90
M.I.T.	5	4.88
CALIFORNIA, BERKELEY	6	4.86
STANFORD	7	4.84
CHICAGO	8	4.83
ILLINOIS (Urbana)	9	4.82
COLUMBIA (N.Y.)	10	4.81
YALE	11	4.80
CALIFORNIA, SANTA BARBARA	12	4.77
PENNSYLVANIA	13	4.76
MICHIGAN (Ann Arbor)	14	4.75
UCLA	15	4.73
TEXAS (Austin)	16	4.71
WASHINGTON (Seattle)	17	4.70
CALIFORNIA, SAN DIEGO	18	4.68
MARYLAND (College Park)	19	4.66
ROCKEFELLER (N.Y.)	20	4.65
SUNY (Stony Brook)	21	4.63
WISCONSIN (Madison)	22	4.61
RUTGERS (New Brunswick)	23	4.58
MINNESOTA (Minneapolis)	24	4.55
ROCHESTER (N.Y.)	25	4.53
BROWN	26	4.51
JOHNS HOPKINS	27	4.50
OHIO STATE (Columbus)	28	4.48
CARNEGIE-MELLON	29	4.46
PURDUE (Lafayette)	30	4.45
MICHIGAN STATE	31	4.44
CALIFORNIA, IRVINE	32	4.42
COLORADO (Boulder)	33	4.39
INDIANA (Bloomington)	34	4.36
NORTHWESTERN (Evanston)	35	4.34
CUNY (Graduate School)	36	4.30
BOSTON U.	37	4.29
FLORIDA (Gainesville)	38	4.25
DUKE	39	4.23
PITTSBURGH (Pittsburgh)	40	4.21
RICE	41	4.19

A RATING OF GRADUATE PROGRAMS IN PHYSIOLOGY
Leading Institutions

Thirty institutions with scores in the 4.0-5.0 range, in rank order

INSTITUTION	Rank	Score
YALE	1	4.91
CALIFORNIA, SAN FRANCISCO	2	4.90
CALIFORNIA, SAN DIEGO	3	4.89
BAYLOR COLLEGE OF MEDICINE	4	4.87
PENNSYLVANIA	5	4.85
UCLA	6	4.81
STANFORD	7	4.78
WASHINGTON (Seattle)	8	4.74
VIRGINIA (Charlottesville)	9	4.71
COLUMBIA (N.Y.)	10	4.67
CHICAGO	11	4.63
CAL TECH	12	4.59
N.Y.U.	13	4.58
IOWA (Iowa City)	14	4.57
MICHIGAN (Ann Arbor)	15	4.56
VANDERBILT	16	4.53
ALBERT EINSTEIN (College of Medicine, N.Y.)	17	4.49
JOHNS HOPKINS	18	4.44
ILLINOIS (Urbana)	19	4.42
MAYO GRADUATE SCHOOL	20	4.39
ALABAMA (Birmingham)	21	4.37
EMORY	22	4.35
ARIZONA (Tucson)	23	4.30
WISCONSIN (Madison)	24	4.29
TEXAS HEALTH SCIENCE CENTER (Houston)	25	4.25
NORTHWESTERN (Evanston)	26	4.22
DUKE	27	4.18
CALIFORNIA, DAVIS	28	4.16
DARTMOUTH COLLEGE	29	4.12
CORNELL (N.Y.)	30	4.10

A RATING OF GRADUATE PROGRAMS IN POLITICAL SCIENCE
Leading Institutions

Thirty-four institutions with scores in the 4.0-5.0 range, in rank order

INSTITUTION	Rank	Score
YALE	1	4.92
MICHIGAN (Ann Arbor)	2	4.91
CALIFORNIA, BERKELEY	3	4.90
HARVARD	4	4.88
CHICAGO	5	4.86
PRINCETON	6	4.85
STANFORD	7	4.84
WISCONSIN (Madison)	8	4.82
UCLA	9	4.80
CORNELL (N.Y.)	10	4.78
M.I.T.	11	4.76
COLUMBIA (N.Y.)	12	4.74
ROCHESTER (N.Y.)	13	4.72
MINNESOTA (Minneapolis)	14	4.67
DUKE	15	4.66
NORTH CAROLINA (Chapel Hill)	16	4.65
TEXAS (Austin)	17	4.63
JOHNS HOPKINS	18	4.61
OHIO STATE (Columbus)	19	4.58
NOTRE DAME	20	4.56
INDIANA (Bloomington)	21	4.53
ILLINOIS (Urbana)	22	4.51
CALIFORNIA, SAN DIEGO	23	4.45
VIRGINIA (Charlottesville)	24	4.42
PENNSYLVANIA	25	4.37
NORTHWESTERN (Evanston)	26	4.34
PITTSBURGH (Pittsburgh)	27	4.31
WASHINGTON (Seattle)	28	4.26
MICHIGAN STATE	29	4.24
ILLINOIS (Urbana)	30	4.21
WASHINGTON (St. Louis)	31	4.16
EMORY	32	4.14
RUTGERS (New Brunswick)	33	4.12
GEORGETOWN (D.C.)	34	4.09

A RATING OF GRADUATE PROGRAMS IN PSYCHOLOGY
Leading Institutions

Forty institutions with scores in the 4.0-5.0 range, in rank order

INSTITUTION	Rank	Score
STANFORD	1	4.72
YALE	2	4.70
PENNSYLVANIA	3	4.69
MICHIGAN (Ann Arbor)	4	4.68
MINNESOTA (Minneapolis)	5	4.66
HARVARD	6	4.65
CALIFORNIA, BERKELEY	7	4.63
ILLINOIS (Urbana)	8	4.60
UCLA	9	4.58
CHICAGO	10	4.55
CALIFORNIA, SAN DIEGO	11	4.53
CARNEGIE-MELLON	12	4.52
INDIANA (Bloomington)	13	4.49
COLUMBIA (N.Y.)	14	4.47
PRINCETON	15	4.45
WISCONSIN (Madison)	16	4.43
OREGON (Eugene)	17	4.42
VIRGINIA (Charlottesville)	18	4.41
TEXAS (Austin)	19	4.40
WASHINGTON (Seattle)	20	4.39
CORNELL (N.Y.)	21	4.38
COLORADO (Boulder)	22	4.36
BROWN	23	4.35
NORTH CAROLINA (Chapel Hill)	24	4.33
NORTHWESTERN (Evanston)	25	4.30
JOHNS HOPKINS	26	4.29
OHIO STATE (Columbus)	27	4.28
PURDUE (Lafayette)	28	4.27
DUKE	29	4.26
ROCHESTER (N.Y.)	30	4.25
SUNY (Stony Brook)	31	4.23
RUTGERS (New Brunswick)	32	4.20
IOWA (Iowa City)	33	4.18
PENN STATE (University Park)	34	4.17
VANDERBILT	35	4.15
N.Y.U.	36	4.14
USC (Los Angeles)	37	4.13
CALIFORNIA, IRVINE	38	4.12
MASSACHUSETTS (Amherst)	39	4.11
FLORIDA (Gainesville)	40	4.09

A RATING OF GRADUATE PROGRAMS IN PUBLIC ADMINISTRATION
Leading Institutions

Nineteen institutions with scores in the 4.0-5.0 range, in rank order

INSTITUTION	Rank	Score
SYRACUSE	1	4.91
HARVARD	2	4.89
INDIANA (Bloomington)	3	4.86
U.S.C. (Los Angeles)	4	4.83
CALIFORNIA, BERKELEY	5	4.82
TEXAS (Austin)	6	4.79
PRINCETON	7	4.76
PITTSBURGH (Pittsburgh)	8	4.71
MICHIGAN (Ann Arbor)	9	4.69
GEORGIA (Athens)	10	4.66
CARNEGIE-MELLON	11	4.64
MINNESOTA (Minneapolis)	12	4.60
OHIO STATE (Columbus)	13	4.54
AMERICAN (D.C.)	14	4.50
NORTH CAROLINA (Chapel Hill)	15	4.45
SUNY (Albany)	16	4.41
GEORGE WASHINGTON	17	4.33
FLORIDA STATE	18	4.28
KANSAS (Lawrence)	19	4.22

A RATING OF GRADUATE PROGRAMS IN RADIO/TV/FILM
Leading Institutions

Ten institutions with scores in the 4.0-5.0 range, in rank order

INSTITUTION	Rank	Score
USC (Los Angeles)	1	4.88
UCLA	2	4.86
N.Y.U.	3	4.85
NORTHWESTERN (Evanston)	4	4.82
INDIANA (Bloomington)	5	4.78
FLORIDA STATE	6	4.75
COLUMBIA (N.Y.)	7	4.74
TEXAS (Austin)	8	4.70
NORTH CAROLINA (Chapel Hill)	9	4.66
TEMPLE (Philadelphia)	10	4.63

A RATING OF GRADUATE PROGRAMS IN RUSSIAN
Leading Institutions

Ten institutions with scores in the 4.0-5.0 range, in rank order

INSTITUTION	Rank	Score
HARVARD	1	4.87
COLUMBIA (N.Y.)	2	4.85
CORNELL (N.Y.)	3	4.81
PENNSYLVANIA	4	4.77
WASHINGTON (Seattle)	5	4.72
ILLINOIS (Urbana)	6	4.69
NORTH CAROLINA (Chapel Hill)	7	4.66
BROWN	8	4.58
MICHIGAN STATE	9	4.54
OHIO STATE (Columbus)	10	4.49

A RATING OF GRADUATE PROGRAMS IN SENSATION AND PERCEPTION-PSYCHOLOGY
Leading Institutions

Twenty-four institutions with scores in the 4.0-5.0 range, in rank order

INSTITUTION	Rank	Score
STANFORD	1	4.53
MICHIGAN (Ann Arbor)	2	4.52
DUKE	3	4.48
PENNSYLVANIA	4	4.46
MINNESOTA (Minneapolis)	5	4.45
OHIO STATE (Columbus)	6	4.42
WISCONSIN (Madison)	7	4.39
WASHINGTON (Seattle)	8	4.38
TEXAS (Austin)	9	4.37
COLUMBIA (N.Y.)	10	4.36
PURDUE (Lafayette)	11	4.32
JOHNS HOPKINS	12	4.30
VIRGINIA (Charlottesville)	13	4.27
ROCHESTER (N.Y.)	14	4.23
SUNY (Buffalo)	15	4.22
FLORIDA (Gainesville)	16	4.21
CASE WESTERN RESERVE	17	4.20
ILLINOIS (Chicago)	18	4.16
CALIFORNIA, SANTA BARBARA	19	4.14
SUNY (Stony Brook)	20	4.13
CALIFORNIA, DAVIS	21	4.12
TULANE	22	4.11
INDIANA (Bloomington)	23	4.10
LOYOLA (Chicago)	24	4.06

A RATING OF GRADUATE PROGRAMS IN SLAVIC LANGUAGES
Leading Institutions

Sixteen institutions with scores in the 4.0-5.0 range, in rank order

INSTITUTION	Rank	Score
HARVARD	1	4.89
COLUMBIA (N.Y.)	2	4.86
INDIANA (Bloomington)	3	4.83
CORNELL (N.Y.)	4	4.79
WISCONSIN (Madison)	5	4.76
WASHINGTON (Seattle)	6	4.74
ILLINOIS (Urbana)	7	4.70
MICHIGAN (Ann Arbor)	8	4.68
CALIFORNIA, BERKELEY	9	4.65
STANFORD	10	4.60
OHIO STATE (Columbus)	11	4.58
CHICAGO	12	4.54
NORTH CAROLINA (Chapel Hill)	13	4.52
UCLA	14	4.47
BROWN	15	4.45
YALE	16	4.40

A RATING OF GRADUATE PROGRAMS IN SOCIAL PSYCHOLOGY
Leading Institutions

Thirty-two institutions with scores in the 4.0-5.0 range, in rank order

INSTITUTION	Rank	Score
STANFORD	1	4.68
MICHIGAN (Ann Arbor)	2	4.66
YALE	3	4.65
HARVARD	4	4.63
UCLA	5	4.60
PENNSYLVANIA	6	4.59
CARNEGIE-MELLON	7	4.58
CALIFORNIA, BERKELEY	8	4.56
MINNESOTA (Minneapolis)	9	4.54
CORNELL (N.Y.)	10	4.52
WISCONSIN (Madison)	11	4.48
COLUMBIA (N.Y.)	12	4.46
TEXAS (Austin)	13	4.43
WASHINGTON (Seattle)	14	4.42
INDIANA (Bloomington)	15	4.40
VIRGINIA (Charlottesville)	16	4.39
OREGON (Eugene)	17	4.36
OHIO STATE (Columbus)	18	4.33
NORTHWESTERN (Evanston)	19	4.32
COLORADO (Boulder)	20	4.31
NORTH CAROLINA (Chapel Hill)	21	4.30
PURDUE (Lafayette)	22	4.27
JOHNS HOPKINS	23	4.25
DUKE	24	4.22
N.Y.U.	25	4.21
IOWA (Iowa City)	26	4.20
PENN STATE (University Park)	27	4.18
ROCHESTER (N.Y.)	28	4.17
RUTGERS (New Brunswick)	29	4.14
USC (Los Angeles)	30	4.12
SUNY (Stony Brook)	31	4.11
FLORIDA (Gainesville)	32	4.09

A RATING OF GRADUATE PROGRAMS IN SOCIAL WELFARE/SOCIAL WORK
Leading Institutions

Thirty-one institutions with scores in the 4.0-5.0 range, in rank order

INSTITUTION	Rank	Score
CHICAGO	1	4.69
COLUMBIA (N.Y.)	2	4.68
MICHIGAN (Ann Arbor)	3	4.64
WISCONSIN (Madison)	4	4.62
PENNSYLVANIA	5	4.58
CASE WESTERN RESERVE	6	4.55
BRANDEIS	7	4.52
PITTSBURGH (Pittsburgh)	8	4.49
WASHINGTON (St. Louis)	9	4.44
MINNESOTA (Minneapolis)	10	4.42
OHIO STATE (Columbus)	11	4.40
CALIFORNIA, BERKELEY	12	4.38
YESHIVA (N.Y.)	13	4.36
RUTGERS (New Brunswick)	14	4.34
USC(Los Angeles)	15	4.32
CATHOLIC U. (D.C.)	16	4.30
MICHIGAN STATE	17	4.28
SAINT LOUIS U.	18	4.26
TEXAS (Austin)	19	4.24
TULANE	20	4.22
UTAH (Salt Lake City)	21	4.20
DENVER	22	4.19
UCLA	23	4.18
FLORIDA STATE	24	4.17
CUNY (Hunter College)	25	4.16
ILLINOIS (Chicago Circle)	26	4.15
MARYLAND (Baltimore)	27	4.14
SMITH COLLEGE (Massachusetts)	28	4.13
WASHINGTON (Seattle)	29	4.12
HOWARD (D.C.)	30	4.11
BRYN MAWR	31	4.10

A RATING OF GRADUATE PROGRAMS IN SOCIOLOGY
Leading Institutions

Thirty-two institutions with scores in the 4.0-5.0 range, in rank order

INSTITUTION	Rank	Score
WISCONSIN (Madison)	1	4.87
MICHIGAN (Ann Arbor)	2	4.85
CHICAGO	3	4.82
HARVARD	4	4.79
NORTH CAROLINA (Chapel Hill)	5	4.76
PENNSYLVANIA	6	4.73
STANFORD	7	4.71
WASHINGTON (Seattle)	8	4.66
UCLA	9	4.64
NORTHWESTERN (Evanston)	10	4.62
INDIANA (Bloomington)	11	4.60
TEXAS (Austin)	12	4.58
ARIZONA (Tucson)	13	4.55
PRINCETON	14	4.52
COLUMBIA	15	4.51
JOHNS HOPKINS	16	4.50
YALE	17	4.48
DUKE	18	4.46
PENN STATE (University Park)	19	4.43
MINNESOTA (Minneapolis)	20	4.42
CALIFORNIA, SAN DIEGO	21	4.38
SUNY (Stony Brook)	22	4.35
CALIFORNIA, BERKELEY	23	4.32
OHIO STATE (Columbus)	24	4.27
CALIFORNIA, SANTA BARBARA	25	4.26
VANDERBILT	26	4.22
ILLINOIS (Urbana)	27	4.20
SUNY (Albany)	28	4.16
RUTGERS (New Brunswick)	29	4.13
WASHINGTON STATE	30	4.10
MARYLAND (College Park)	31	4.08
N.Y.U.	32	4.06

A RATING OF GRADUATE PROGRAMS IN SPANISH
Leading Institutions

Thirty institutions with scores in the 4.0-5.0 range, in rank order

INSTITUTION	Rank	Score
DUKE	1	4.87
COLUMBIA (N.Y.)	2	4.85
PRINCETON	3	4.81
BROWN	4	4.76
PENNSYLVANIA	5	4.73
CORNELL (N.Y.)	6	4.70
WISCONSIN (Madison)	7	4.66
VIRGINIA (Charlottesville)	8	4.63
HARVARD '	9	4.61
CALIFORNIA, BERKELEY	10	4.58
TEXAS (Austin)	11	4.55
MICHIGAN (Ann Arbor)	12	4.53
STANFORD	13	4.51
UCLA	14	4.49
INDIANA (Bloomington)	15	4.46
CALIFORNIA, IRVINE	16	4.42
CALIFORNIA, SAN DIEGO	17	4.41
CUNY (Graduate School)	18	4.38
CALIFORNIA, DAVIS	19	4.36
KANSAS (Lawrence)	20	4.35
ILLINOIS (Urbana)	21	4.32
N.Y.U.	22	4.30
PENN STATE (University Park)	23	4.27
CALIFORNIA, SANTA BARBARA	24	4.23
PITTSBURGH (Pittsburgh)	25	4.20
MINNESOTA (Minneapolis)	26	4.18
WASHINGTON (St. Louis)	27	4.14
NORTH CAROLINA (Chapel Hill)	28	4.12
GEORGETOWN (D.C.)	29	4.08
KENTUCKY	30	4.05

A RATING OF GRADUATE PROGRAMS IN
SPEECH PATHOLOGY/AUDIOLOGY
Leading Institutions

Twenty-one institutions with scores in the 4.0-5.0 range, in rank order

INSTITUTION	Rank	Score
NORTHWESTERN (Evanston)	1	4.80
IOWA (Iowa City)	2	4.79
MINNESOTA (Minneapolis)	3	4.78
OHIO STATE (Columbus)	4	4.73
PENN STATE (University Park)	5	4.70
PURDUE (Lafayette)	6	4.66
INDIANA (Bloomington)	7	4.65
WASHINGTON (Seattle)	8	4.64
WISCONSIN (Madison)	9	4.60
WAYNE STATE (Detroit)	10	4.58
ILLINOIS (Urbana)	11	4.55
MICHIGAN STATE	12	4.52
CASE WESTERN RESERVE	13	4.49
TEXAS (Austin)	14	4.46
UTAH (Salt Lake City)	15	4.45
SUNY (Buffalo)	16	4.42
N.Y.U.	17	4.39
COLORADO (Boulder)	18	4.38
PITTSBURGH (Pittsburgh)	19	4.35
TEMPLE (Philadelphia)	20	4.30
BOSTON U.	21	4.27

A RATING OF GRADUATE PROGRAMS IN STATISTICS
Leading Institutions

Thirty institutions with scores in the 4.0-5.0 range, in rank order

INSTITUTION	Rank	Score
STANFORD	1	4.93
CALIFORNIA, BERKELEY	2	4.92
CHICAGO	3	4.91
CORNELL (N.Y.)	4	4.89
HARVARD	5	4.86
WASHINGTON (Seattle)	6	4.83
PURDUE (Lafayette)	7	4.80
WISCONSIN (Madison)	8	4.78
UCLA	9	4.75
MINNESOTA (Minneapolis)	10	4.73
NORTH CAROLINA (Chapel Hill)	11	4.72
TEXAS A&M (College Station)	12	4.71
CARNEGIE-MELLON	13	4.68
IOWA STATE (Ames)	14	4.66
PENN STATE (University Park)	15	4.64
RUTGERS (New Brunswick)	16	4.62
YALE	17	4.58
JOHNS HOPKINS	18	4.55
NORTH CAROLINA STATE (Raleigh)	19	4.52
COLUMBIA (N.Y.)	20	4.51
MICHIGAN (Ann Arbor)	21	4.49
ILLINOIS (Urbana)	22	4.45
PENNSYLVANIA	23	4.43
OHIO STATE (Columbus)	24	4.40
MICHIGAN STATE U.	25	4.38
IOWA (Iowa City)	26	4.35
FLORIDA STATE	27	4.33
FLORIDA (Gainesville)	28	4.27
PITTSBURGH (Pittsburgh)	29	4.25
NORTHWESTERN (Evanston)	30	4.21

A RATING OF GRADUATE PROGRAMS IN TOXICOLOGY
Leading Institutions

Thirty-four institutions with scores in the 4.0-5.0 range, in rank order

INSTITUTION	Rank	Score
JOHNS HOPKINS	1	4.91
DUKE	2	4.90
VANDERBILT	3	4.89
NORTH CAROLINA (Chapel Hill)	4	4.86
M.I.T.	5	4.85
WISCONSIN (Madison)	6	4.82
MICHIGAN (Ann Arbor)	7	4.81
N.Y.U.	8	4.80
HARVARD	9	4.76
COLUMBIA (N.Y.)	10	4.73
KANSAS (Lawrence)	11	4.71
CALIFORNIA, DAVIS	12	4.68
MICHIGAN STATE U.	13	4.66
ALABAMA (Birmingham)	14	4.63
CORNELL (N.Y.)	15	4.61
ROCHESTER (N.Y.)	16	4.58
WASHINGTON (Seattle)	17	4.55
TEXAS U. OF (Houston Science Center)	18	4.54
U. OF MEDICINE AND DENTISTRY OF NEW JERSEY	19	4.52
DARTMOUTH	20	4.49
NORTHWESTERN (Evanston)	21	4.48
CASE WESTERN RESERVE	22	4.45
IOWA STATE (Ames)	23	4.43
OHIO STATE (Columbus)	24	4.42
TEXAS U. OF (Medical Branch at Galveston)	25	4.40
UTAH (Salt Lake City)	26	4.36
CALIFORNIA, IRVINE	27	4.34
PURDUE (Lafayette)	28	4.33
RUTGERS (New Brunswick)	29	4.30
OREGON STATE	30	4.29
SUNY (Buffalo)	31	4.26
FLORIDA (Gainesville)	32	4.25
ARIZONA (Tucson)	33	4.21
TEXAS A&M (College Station)	34	4.18

The GOURMAN REPORT
PART II

PROFESSIONAL PROGRAMS

A Rating of International Law Schools

A Rating of Law Schools in Canada

A Rating of U.S.A. Law Schools

A RATING OF LAW SCHOOLS

INTERNATIONAL UNIVERSITIES
Leading Institutions

Fifty-three institutions with scores in the 4.0-5.0 range, in rank order

INSTITUTION	COUNTRY	Rank	Score
PARIS (All Law Campuses)	France	1	4.92
OXFORD	United Kingdom	2	4.91
CAMBRIDGE	United Kingdom	3	4.90
HEIDELBERG	Federal Republic of Germany	4	4.87
LYON III	France	5	4.86
MUNICH	Federal Republic of Germany	6	4.83
MONTPELLIER I	France	7	4.82
BRUSSELS	Belgium	8	4.81
GÖTTINGEN	Federal Republic of Germany	9	4.78
ERLANGEN-NÜRNBERG	Federal Republic of Germany	10	4.77
AIX-MARSEILLE II	France	11	4.76
EDINBURGH	United Kingdom (Scotland)	12	4.75
BORDEAUX I	France	13	4.74
BONN	Federal Republic of Germany	14	4.73
LILLE II	France	15	4.72
DIJON	France	16	4.71
NANCY II	France	17	4.68
BESANCON	France	18	4.66
GRENOBLE II	France	19	4.64
CLERMONT-FERRAND	France	20	4.62
ROUEN	France	21	4.60
REIMS	France	22	4.58
COLOGNE	Federal Republic of Germany	23	4.57
RENNES I	France	24	4.55
VIENNA	Austria	25	4.53
KIEL	Federal Republic of Germany	26	4.50
STOCKHOLM	Sweden	27	4.49
NICE	France	28	4.48
CAEN	France	29	4.47
POITIERS	France	30	4.44
TOULOUSE I	France	31	4.42
LIMOGES	France	32	4.40
NANTES	France	33	4.39
COPENHAGEN	Denmark	34	4.38
MAINZ	Federal Republic of Germany	35	4.35
ORLEANS	France	36	4.34
SAINT-ETIENNE	France	37	4.33
TOKYO	Japan	38	4.32
FREIBURG	Federal Republic of Germany	39	4.31
TÜEBINGEN	Federal Republic of Germany	40	4.30
INNSBRUCK	Austria	41	4.29
MÜNSTER	Federal Republic of Germany	42	4.27
WÜRZBURG	Federal Republic of Germany	43	4.26
DUBLIN	Ireland	44	4.25
HEBREW	Israel	45	4.23

INTERNATIONAL UNIVERSITIES (Continued)
Leading Institutions

Fifty-three institutions with scores in the 4.0-5.0 range, in rank order

INSTITUTION	COUNTRY	Rank	Score
MADRID	Spain	46	4.22
MARBURG	Federal Republic of Germany	47	4.20
GENEVA	Switzerland	48	4.19
LONDON	United Kingdom	49	4.16
FRIBOURG	Switzerland	50	4.15
ROME	Italy	51	4.14
AMSTERDAM	Netherlands	52	4.11
ATHENS	Greece	53	4.05

A RATING OF LAW SCHOOLS IN CANADA

Leading Institutions

INSTITUTION	Rank	Score
UNIVERSITY OF TORONTO	1	4.70
UNIVERSITY OF BRITISH COLUMBIA	2	4.66
McGILL UNIVERSITY	3	4.64
YORK UNIVERSITY	4	4.55
UNIVERSITY OF OTTAWA	5	3.96
DALHOUSIE UNIVERSITY	6	3.60
UNIVERSITY OF MANITOBA	7	3.58
UNIVERSITY OF ALBERTA	8	3.51
QUEEN'S UNIVERSITY	9	3.40
UNIVERSITY OF VICTORIA	10	3.36
UNIVERSITY OF WINDSOR	11	3.20
UNIVERSITY OF CALGARY	12	3.18
UNIVERSITY OF WESTERN ONTARIO	13	3.15
UNIVERSITY OF SASKATCHEWAN	14	3.10

A RATING OF LAW SCHOOLS

U.S.A. LAW SCHOOLS
Very Strong

Twenty institutions with scores in the 4.6-5.0 range, in rank order

INSTITUTION	Rank	Score
HARVARD UNIVERSITY	1	4.92
THE UNIVERSITY OF MICHIGAN (Ann Arbor)	2	4.91
YALE UNIVERSITY	3	4.90
THE UNIVERSITY OF CHICAGO	4	4.89
UNIVERSITY OF CALIFORNIA, BERKELEY (Boalt Hall)	5	4.88
STANFORD UNIVERSITY	6	4.87
COLUMBIA UNIVERSITY (N.Y.)	7	4.86
DUKE UNIVERSITY	8	4.84
UNIVERSITY OF PENNSYLVANIA	9	4.82
CORNELL (N.Y.)	10	4.80
NEW YORK UNIVERSITY	11	4.79
UNIVERSITY OF TEXAS (Austin)	12	4.77
UNIVERSITY OF CALIFORNIA, LOS ANGELES	13	4.76
NORTHWESTERN (Chicago)	14	4.74
VANDERBILT	15	4.73
UNIVERSITY OF VIRGINIA	16	4.72
GEORGETOWN (D.C.)	17	4.68
UNIVERSITY OF NOTRE DAME	18	4.67
UNIVERSITY OF MINNESOTA (Minneapolis)	19	4.63
UNIVERSITY OF CALIFORNIA, SAN FRANCISCO (Hastings)	20	4.61

U.S.A. LAW SCHOOLS (Continued)
Strong

Twenty-three institutions with scores in the 4.0-4.5 range, in rank order

INSTITUTION	Rank	Score
IOWA (Iowa City)	21	4.49
UNIVERSITY OF WISCONSIN (Madison)	22	4.47
BOSTON UNIVERSITY	23	4.45
FORDHAM UNIVERSITY (N.Y.)	24	4.43
UNIVERSITY OF NORTH CAROLINA (Chapel Hill)	25	4.42
UNIVERSITY OF WASHINGTON (Seattle)	26	4.41
UNIVERSITY OF SOUTHERN CALIFORNIA	27	4.39
UNIVERSITY OF CALIFORNIA, DAVIS	28	4.36
TULANE UNIVERSITY	29	4.35
INDIANA UNIVERSITY (Bloomington)	30	4.33
BOSTON COLLEGE	31	4.32
THE GEORGE WASHINGTON UNIVERSITY	32	4.30
McGEORGE SCHOOL OF LAW	33	4.28
THE OHIO STATE UNIVERSITY (Columbus)	34	4.26
SOUTHERN METHODIST UNIVERSITY	35	4.25
ALBANY LAW SCHOOL (Union University)	36	4.23
LOYOLA UNIVERSITY (Los Angeles)	37	4.21
UNIVERSITY OF ILLINOIS (Urbana)	38	4.20
STATE UNIVERSITY OF NEW YORK AT BUFFALO	39	4.19
MARQUETTE UNIVERSITY	40	4.18
WASHINGTON (St. Louis)	41	4.17
UNIVERSITY OF UTAH	42	4.16
HOFSTRA UNIVERSITY (N.Y.)	43	4.15

A RATING OF LAW SCHOOLS

U.S.A. LAW SCHOOLS (Continued)
Good

Thirty-one institutions with scores in the 3.6-3.9 range, in rank order

INSTITUTION	Rank	Score
ITT CHICAGO-KENT COLLEGE OF LAW	44	3.90
THE CATHOLIC UNIVERSITY OF AMERICA	45	3.89
TEMPLE UNIVERSITY	46	3.88
UNIVERSITY OF GEORGIA (Athens)	47	3.87
UNIVERSITY OF SAN DIEGO	48	3.86
PEPPERDINE UNIVERSITY	49	3.85
UNIVERSITY OF SAN FRANCISCO	50	3.84
EMORY UNIVERSITY	51	3.83
CARDOZA SCHOOL OF LAW (N.Y.)	52	3.82
UNIVERSITY OF DENVER	53	3.81
AMERICAN UNIVERSITY (D.C.)	54	3.80
UNIVERSITY OF SANTA CLARA	55	3.79
UNIVERSITY OF FLORIDA (Gainesville)	56	3.78
BRIGHAM YOUNG UNIVERSITY	57	3.77
SYRACUSE UNIVERSITY	58	3.76
UNIVERSITY OF PITTSBURGH (Pittsburgh)	59	3.75
CASE WESTERN RESERVE	60	3.74
RUTGERS UNIVERSITY THE STATE U. OF NEW JERSEY (Newark)	61	3.73
UNIVERSITY OF MISSOURI (Columbia)	62	3.72
UNIVERSITY OF KANSAS	63	3.71
ST. JOHN'S UNIVERSITY (N.Y.)	64	3.70
RUTGERS UNIVERSITY THE STATE U. OF NEW JERSEY (Camden)	65	3.69
UNIVERSITY OF HOUSTON	66	3.68
UNIVERSITY OF OREGON	67	3.67
WAYNE STATE UNIVERSITY (Michigan)	68	3.66
SAINT LOUIS UNIVERSITY	69	3.65
VILLANOVA UNIVERSITY	70	3.64
UNIVERSITY OF MARYLAND (Baltimore)	71	3.63
BROOKLYN LAW SCHOOL	72	3.62
WILLIAMETTE UNIVERSITY	73	3.61
VALPARAISO UNIVERSITY	74	3.60

U.S.A. LAW SCHOOLS (Continued)
Acceptable Plus

Forty-three institutions with scores in the 3.0-3.5 range, in rank order

INSTITUTION	Rank	Score
UNIVERSITY OF COLORADO (Boulder)	75	3.49
LOYOLA UNIVERSITY (Chicago)	76	3.48
GONZAGA UNIVERSITY	77	3.47
DE PAUL UNIVERSITY	78	3.46
UNIVERSITY OF DETROIT MERCY	79	3.45
COLLEGE OF WILLIAM & MARY	80	3.44
SETON HALL UNIVERSITY	81	3.43
GOLDEN GATE UNIVERSITY	82	3.42
FLORIDA STATE UNIVERSITY	83	3.41
UNIVERSITY OF OKLAHOMA (Norman)	84	3.40
SOUTHWESTERN UNIVERSITY (Los Angeles)	85	3.39
LOUISIANA STATE UNIVERSITY (Baton Rouge)	86	3.38
UNIVERSITY OF CONNECTICUT (Hartford)	87	3.37
UNIVERSITY OF MISSOURI (Kansas City)	88	3.36
NEW YORK LAW SCHOOL	89	3.35
UNIVERSITY OF MIAMI (Florida)	90	3.34
DETROIT COLLEGE OF LAW	91	3.33
UNIVERSITY OF ARIZONA (Tucson)	92	3.32
WASHBURN UNIVERSITY SCHOOL OF LAW	93	3.31
BAYLOR UNIVERSITY	94	3.30
ARIZONA STATE UNIVERSITY	95	3.29
UNIVERSITY OF LOUISVILLE	96	3.28
UNIVERSITY OF CINCINNATI	97	3.27
DICKINSON SCHOOL OF LAW	98	3.26
UNIVERSITY OF KENTUCKY	99	3.25
UNIVERSITY OF MISSISSIPPI	100	3.24
UNIVERSITY OF ALABAMA	101	3.23
UNIVERSITY OF NEBRASKA (Lincoln)	102	3.22
DRAKE UNIVERSITY	103	3.21
THE UNIVERSITY OF TULSA	104	3.20
DUQUESNE UNIVERSITY	105	3.19
WEST VIRGINIA UNIVERSITY	106	3.18
TEXAS TECH UNIVERSITY	107	3.17
LEWIS & CLARK COLLEGE	108	3.16
SOUTHERN ILLINOIS UNIVERSITY (Carbondale)	109	3.15
INDIANA UNIVERSITY (Indianapolis)	110	3.14
WAKE FOREST UNIVERSITY	111	3.13
SUFFOLK UNIVERSITY (Massachusetts)	112	3.12
NORTHEASTERN UNIVERSITY (Massachusetts)	113	3.11
CREIGHTON UNIVERSITY	114	3.10
CLEVELAND-MARSHALL COLLEGE OF LAW	115	3.09
NEW ENGLAND SCHOOL OF LAW	116	3.08
CALIFORNIA WESTERN SCHOOL OF LAW	117	3.07

A RATING OF LAW SCHOOLS

U.S.A. LAW SCHOOLS (Continued)
Adequate

Fifty-eight institutions with scores in the 2.1-2.9 range, in rank order

INSTITUTION	Rank	Score
UNIVERSITY OF TENNESSEE (Knoxville)	118	2.94
MERCER UNIVERSITY	119	2.93
WASHINGTON & LEE UNIVERSITY	120	2.92
UNIVERSITY OF SOUTH CAROLINA	121	2.91
WILLIAM MITCHELL COLLEGE OF LAW	122	2.90
THOMAS M. COOLEY LAW SCHOOL	123	2.89
THE UNIVERSITY OF AKRON	124	2.88
UNIVERSITY OF PUGET SOUND (Washington)	125	2.87
HOWARD UNIVERSITY (D.C.)	126	2.86
UNIVERSITY OF ARKANSAS (Fayetteville)	127	2.85
UNIVERSITY OF NEW MEXICO (Albuquerque)	128	2.84
UNIVERSITY OF MONTANA (Missoula)	129	2.83
CAPITAL UNIVERSITY	130	2.81
HAMLINE UNIVERSITY (Minnesota)	131	2.80
SOUTH TEXAS COLLEGE OF LAW	132	2.79
UNIVERSITY OF IDAHO	133	2.78
SAMFORD UNIVERSITY	134	2.77
OKLAHOMA UNIVERSITY	135	2.76
WESTERN NEW ENGLAND COLLEGE (Massachusetts)	136	2.75
UNIVERSITY OF WYOMING	137	2.74
STETSON UNIVERSITY	138	2.72
WIDENER UNIVERSITY SCHOOL OF LAW	139	2.71
UNIVERSITY OF RICHMOND	140	2.69
UNIVERSITY OF MEMPHIS	141	2.68
NOVA SOUTHEASTERN UNIVERSITY (Florida)	142	2.66
FRANKLIN PIERCE COLLEGE	143	2.65
OHIO NORTHERN UNIVERSITY	144	2.63
UNIVERSITY OF BALTIMORE	145	2.61
UNIVERSITY OF HAWAII (Manoa)	146	2.60
UNIVERSITY OF DAYTON	147	2.59
UNIVERSITY OF MAINE (Portland)	148	2.56
WHITTIER COLLEGE OF LAW (Los Angeles)	149	2.53
ST. MARY'S UNIVERSITY (Texas)	150	2.52
VERMONT LAW SCHOOL	151	2.50
LOYOLA UNIVERSITY (New Orleans)	152	2.49
UNIVERSITY OF TOLEDO	153	2.47
UNIVERSITY OF SOUTH DAKOTA	154	2.43
UNIVERSITY OF ARKANSAS (Little Rock)	155	2.41
NORTHERN ILLINOIS UNIVERSITY	156	2.39

U.S.A. LAW SCHOOLS (Continued)
Adequate

Fifty-eight institutions with scores in the 2.1-2.9 range, in rank order

INSTITUTION	Rank	Score
PACE UNIVERSITY (N.Y.)	157	2.36
UNIVERSITY OF NORTH DAKOTA	158	2.34
TEXAS SOUTHERN UNIVERSITY	159	2.33
UNIVERSITY OF PUERTO RICO	160	2.32
GEORGE MASON UNIVERSITY	161	2.31
NORTHERN KENTUCKY UNIVERSITY	162	2.30
BRIDGEPORT SCHOOL OF LAW AT QUINNIDAC COLLEGE	163	2.29
CATHOLIC UNIVERSITY OF PUERTO RICO	164	2.28
NORTH CAROLINA CENTRAL UNIVERSITY	165	2.26
CAMPBELL UNIVERSITY (North Carolina)	166	2.24
INTER-AMERICAN UNIVERSITY OF PUERTO RICO	167	2.23
MISSISSIPPI COLLEGE SCHOOL OF LAW	168	2.22
TOURO COLLEGE OF LAW (N.Y.)	169	2.21
GEORGIA STATE UNIVERSITY (Atlanta)	170	2.20
CUNY LAW SCHOOL AT QUEENS COLLEGE	171	2.19
SOUTHERN UNIVERSITY (Baton Rouge)	172	2.18
THE JOHN MARSHALL LAW SCHOOL (Illinois)	173	2.14
WIDENER UNIVERSITY (Pennsylvania)	174	2.13
DISTRICT OF COLUMBIA SCHOOL OF LAW (D.C.)	175	2.10

The GOURMAN REPORT
PART III

A RATING OF DENTAL SCHOOLS IN CANADA
Leading Institutions

Ten institutions with scores in the 4.0-5.0 range, in rank order

INSTITUTION	Rank	Score
McGILL UNIVERSITY	1	4.91
UNIVERSITY OF TORONTO	2	4.88
UNIVERSITY OF BRITISH COLUMBIA	3	4.86
UNIVERSITÉ DE MONTREAL	4	4.78
UNIVERSITÉ LAVAL	5	4.71
UNIVERSITY OF MANITOBA	6	4.68
UNIVERSITY OF WESTERN ONTARIO	7	4.59
UNIVERSITY OF ALBERTA	8	4.52
DALHOUSIE UNIVERSITY	9	4.47
UNIVERSITY OF SASKATCHEWAN	10	4.36

A RATING OF U.S.A. DENTAL SCHOOLS
Leading Institutions

Fifty-four institutions with scores in the 4.0-5.0 range, in rank order

INSTITUTION	Rank	Score
HARVARD (Boston)	1	4.93
CALIFORNIA (San Francisco)	2	4.92
MICHIGAN (Ann Arbor)	3	4.91
COLUMBIA (New York)	4	4.90
PENNSYLVANIA (Philadelphia)	5	4.88
UCLA (Los Angeles)	6	4.86
TUFTS (Boston)	7	4.85
NORTHWESTERN (Chicago)	8	4.83
WASHINGTON (Seattle)	9	4.79
OHIO STATE (Columbus)	10	4.77
MINNESOTA (Minneapolis)	11	4.76
ILLINOIS (Chicago)	12	4.72
N.Y.U. (New York)	13	4.64
SUNY (Buffalo)	14	4.58
PITTSBURGH (Pittsburgh)	15	4.55
CREIGHTON (Omaha)	16	4.53
SOUTHERN CALIFORNIA (Los Angeles)	17	4.51
MARQUETTE (Milwaukee)	18	4.48
CASE WESTERN RESERVE (Cleveland)	19	4.45
INDIANA (Indianapolis)	20	4.43
NORTH CAROLINA (Chapel Hill)	21	4.42
TEMPLE (Philadelphia)	22	4.41
IOWA (Iowa City)	23	4.38
SUNY (Stony Brook)	24	4.36
BAYLOR (Dallas)	25	4.35
TEXAS (Houston)	26	4.34
OREGON HEALTH SCIENCES UNIVERSITY (Portland)	27	4.33
LOUISVILLE (Louisville)	28	4.32
BOSTON U. (Boston)	29	4.31
PACIFIC (San Francisco)	30	4.30
LOMA LINDA (Loma Linda)	31	4.29
TEXAS (San Antonio)	32	4.28
MISSOURI (Kansas City)	33	4.27
LOUISIANA STATE (New Orleans)	34	4.26
ALABAMA (Birmingham)	35	4.25
TENNESSEE (Memphis)	36	4.24
DETROIT-MERCY (Detroit)	37	4.23
CONNECTICUT (Farmington)	38	4.22
MEDICAL UNIVERSITY OF SOUTH CAROLINA (Charleston)	39	4.21
WEST VIRGINIA (Morgantown)	40	4.18
MARYLAND (Baltimore)	41	4.17
NEBRASKA (Lincoln)	42	4.16
VIRGINIA COMMONWEALTH (Richmond)	43	4.15
MEDICAL COLLEGE OF GEORGIA (Augusta)	44	4.14
MEHARRY MEDICAL COLLEGE (Nashville)	45	4.13

A RATING OF U.S.A. DENTAL SCHOOLS (Continued)
Leading Institutions

Fifty-four institutions with scores in the 4.0-5.0 range, in rank order

INSTITUTION	Rank	Score
UNIVERSITY OF MEDICINE AND DENTISTRY OF NEW JERSEY	46	4.11
COLORADO (Denver)	47	4.10
OKLAHOMA (Oklahoma City)	48	4.09
FLORIDA (Gainesville)	49	4.08
KENTUCKY (Lexington)	50	4.07
SOUTHERN ILLINOIS (Alton)	51	4.06
MISSISSIPPI (Jackson)	52	4.05
HOWARD (D.C.)	53	4.04
PUERTO RICO (San Juan)	54	4.03

A RATING OF MEDICAL SCHOOLS IN CANADA
Leading Institutions

Sixteen institutions with scores in the 4.0-5.0 range, in rank order

INSTITUTION	Rank	Score
McGILL UNIVERSITY		
Faculty of Medicine	1	4.91
UNIVERSITY OF TORONTO		
Faculty of Medicine	2	4.90
UNIVERSITY OF BRITISH COLUMBIA		
Faculty of Medicine	3	4.85
UNIVERSITY OF MONTREAL		
Faculty of Medicine	4	4.78
McMASTER UNIVERSITY		
School of Medicine	5	4.74
QUEEN'S UNIVERSITY		
Faculty of Medicine	6	4.68
LAVAL UNIVERSITY		
Faculty of Medicine	7	4.62
UNIVERSITY OF MANITOBA		
Faculty of Medicine	8	4.56
UNIVERSITY OF OTTAWA		
School of Medicine	9	4.51
UNIVERSITY OF WESTERN ONTARIO		
Faculty of Medicine	10	4.48
UNIVERSITY OF ALBERTA		
Faculty of Medicine	11	4.46
UNIVERSITY OF CALGARY		
Faculty of Medicine	12	4.43
MEMORIAL UNIVERSITY OF NEWFOUNDLAND		
School of Medicine	13	4.37
DALHOUSIE UNIVERSITY		
Faculty of Medicine	14	4.33
UNIVERSITY OF SHERBROOKE		
Faculty of Medicine	15	4.25
UNIVERSITY OF SASKATCHEWAN		
College of Medicine	16	4.16

A RATING OF MEDICAL SCHOOLS

INTERNATIONAL UNIVERSITIES
Leading Institutions

Fifty-five institutions with scores in the 4.0-5.0 range, in rank order

INSTITUTION	COUNTRY	Rank	Score
PARIS (University Medical and Academic Departments) U. of Paris V, VI, VII, XI, XII, XIII	France	1	4.92
OXFORD	United Kingdom	2	4.91
CAMBRIDGE	United Kingdom	3	4.90
HEIDELBERG	Federal Republic of Germany	4	4.89
MUNICH	Federal Republic of Germany	5	4.88
LYON I	France	6	4.87
VIENNA	Austria	7	4.86
MONTPELLIER I	France	8	4.84
ZURICH	Switzerland	9	4.82
GÖTTINGEN	Federal Republic of Germany	10	4.81
EDINBURGH	United Kingdom (Scotland)	11	4.80
LILLE (U.E.R.) II	France	12	4.78
BRUSSELS	Belgium	13	4.76
DIJON	France	14	4.73
LILLE (Faculte Libre de Medicine)	France	15	4.72
GENEVA	Switzerland	16	4.71
KEIO	Japan	17	4.67
ERLANGEN-NURNBERG	Federal Republic of Germany	18	4.66
TOKYO (Medical & Dental)	Japan	19	4.63
AIX-MARSEILLE II	France	20	4.59
NANCY I	France	21	4.57
NICE I	France	22	4.56
REIMS	France	23	4.55
CLERMONT-FERRAND	France	24	4.54
RENNES I	France	25	4.53
ROUEN	France	26	4.52
BORDEAUX II	France	27	4.46
BONN	Federal Republic of Germany	28	4.37
WÜRZBURG	Federal Republic of Germany	29	4.36
HEBREW	Israel	30	4.33
LONDON (12 Campuses)	United Kingdom	31	4.32
FREIBURG	Federal Republic of Germany	32	4.31
HAMBURG	Federal Republic of Germany	33	4.30
AMIENS	France	34	4.29
BESANCON	France	35	4.28
GRENOBLE I	France	36	4.27
MARBURG	Federal Republic of Germany	37	4.26
TUBINGEN	Federal Republic of Germany	38	4.25
POITIERS	France	39	4.24
LIMOGES	France	40	4.23

A RATING OF MEDICAL SCHOOLS

INTERNATIONAL UNIVERSITIES (Continued)
Leading Institutions

Fifty-five institutions with scores in the 4.0-5.0 range, in rank order

INSTITUTION	COUNTRY	Rank	Score
SAINT-ETIENNE	France	41	4.22
MAINZ	Federal Republic of Germany	42	4.21
STRASBOURG I	France	43	4.20
CAEN	France	44	4.19
STOCKHOLM	Sweden	45	4.18
LOUVAIN	Belgium	46	4.17
AMSTERDAM	Netherlands	47	4.16
ROYAL COLLEGE OF SURGEONS	Ireland	48	4.15
LEIDEN	Netherlands	49	4.13
TOURS	France	50	4.12
TOULOUSE III	France	51	4.11
FRANFURT	Federal Republic of Germany	52	4.10
ANGERS	France	53	4.09
MUNSTER	Federal Republic of Germany	54	4.08
NANTES	France	55	4.06

A RATING OF MEDICAL SCHOOLS

U.S.A. MEDICAL SCHOOLS
Very Strong

Nineteen institutions with scores in the 4.6-5.0 range, in rank order

INSTITUTION	Rank	Score
HARVARD MEDICAL SCHOOL (Boston)	1	4.93
JOHNS HOPKINS UNIVERSITY		
School of Medicine (Baltimore)	2	4.92
UNIVERSITY OF PENNSYLVANIA		
School of Medicine (Philadelphia)	3	4.91
UNIVERSITY OF CALIFORNIA		
School of Medicine (San Francisco)	4	4.90
YALE UNIVERSITY		
School of Medicine (New Haven)	5	4.89
UNIVERSITY OF CHICAGO		
Pritzker School of Medicine (Chicago)	6	4.88
COLUMBIA UNIVERSITY		
College of Physicians & Surgeons (New York)	7	4.86
STANFORD UNIVERSITY		
School of Medicine (Palo Alto)	8	4.85
CORNELL UNIVERSITY		
School of Medicine (New York)	9	4.84
UNIVERSITY OF MICHIGAN		
Medical School (Ann Arbor)	10	4.82
UNIVERSITY OF CALIFORNIA		
School of Medicine (Los Angeles)	11	4.80
DUKE UNIVERSITY		
School of Medicine (Durham)	12	4.78
WASHINGTON UNIVERSITY		
School of Medicine (St. Louis)	13	4.76
NORTHWESTERN UNIVERSITY		
Medical School (Chicago)	14	4.73
UNIVERSITY OF MINNESOTA		
Medical School (Minneapolis)	15	4.71
TULANE UNIVERSITY		
Medical School (New Orleans)	16	4.70
UNIVERSITY OF ROCHESTER		
School of Medicine & Dentistry (Rochester)	17	4.68
VANDERBILT UNIVERSITY		
School of Medicine (Nashville)	18	4.65
NEW YORK UNIVERSITY		
School of Medicine (New York)	19	4.62

A RATING OF MEDICAL SCHOOLS

U.S.A. MEDICAL SCHOOLS (Continued)
Strong

Thirty-two institutions with scores in the 4.0-4.5 range, in rank order

INSTITUTION	Rank	Score
UNIVERSITY OF CALIFORNIA		
School of Medicine (San Diego)	20	4.49
UNIVERSITY OF VIRGINIA		
School of Medicine (Charlottesville)	21	4.48
UNIVERSITY OF NORTH CAROLINA		
School of Medicine (Chapel Hill)	22	4.47
TUFTS UNIVERSITY		
School of Medicine (Boston)	23	4.46
UNIVERSITY OF CALIFORNIA		
School of Medicine (Davis)	24	4.45
BOSTON UNIVERSITY		
School of Medicine (Boston)	25	4.44
INDIANA UNIVERSITY		
School of Medicine (Indianapolis)	26	4.43
UNIVERSITY OF WISCONSIN		
Medical School (Madison)	27	4.42
UNIVERSITY OF ILLINOIS		
College of Medicine (Chicago)	28	4.41
UNIVERSITY OF IOWA		
College of Medicine (Iowa City)	29	4.40
UNIVERSITY OF WASHINGTON		
School of Medicine (Seattle)	30	4.39
GEORGETOWN UNIVERSITY		
School of Medicine (Washington D.C.)	31	4.38
OHIO STATE UNIVERSITY		
College of Medicine (Columbus)	32	4.37
STATE UNIVERSITY OF NEW YORK AT BUFFALO		
School of Medicine	33	4.36
GEORGE WASHINGTON UNIVERSITY		
School of Medicine (Washington D.C.)	34	4.35
UNIVERSITY OF CALIFORNIA		
College of Medicine (Irvine)	35	4.34

A RATING OF MEDICAL SCHOOLS

U.S.A. MEDICAL SCHOOLS (Continued)
Strong

Thirty-two institutions with scores in the 4.0-4.5 range, in rank order

INSTITUTION	Rank	Score
BAYLOR COLLEGE OF MEDICINE (Houston)	36	4.33
BOWMAN GRAY SCHOOL OF MEDICINE (Winston-Salem)	37	4.32
EMORY UNIVERSITY		
School of Medicine (Atlanta)	38	4.31
UNIVERSITY OF PITTSBURGH		
School of Medicine (Pittsburgh)	39	4.30
LOMA LINDA UNIVERSITY		
School of Medicine (Loma Linda)	40	4.29
ALBERT EINSTEIN		
College of Medicine of Yeshiva University (New York)	41	4.27
UNIVERSITY OF LOUISVILLE		
School of Medicine (Louisville)	42	4.26
LOYOLA UNIVERSITY OF CHICAGO		
Strich School of Medicine, Maywood)	43	4.25
SAINT LOUIS UNIVERSITY		
School of Medicine (St. Louis)	44	4.24
DARTMOUTH MEDICAL SCHOOL (Hanover)	45	4.22
UNIVERSITY OF SOUTHERN CALIFORNIA		
School of Medicine (Los Angeles)	46	4.20
UNIVERSITY OF MISSOURI		
School of Medicine (Columbia)	47	4.19
WAYNE STATE UNIVERSITY		
School of Medicine (Detroit)	48	4.18
TEMPLE UNIVERSITY		
School of Medicine (Philadelphia)	49	4.17
STATE UNIVERSITY OF NEW YORK AT STONY BROOK		
School of Medicine	50	4.15
BROWN UNIVERSITY PROGRAM IN MEDICINE (Providence)	51	4.14

A RATING OF MEDICAL SCHOOLS

U.S.A. MEDICAL SCHOOLS (Continued)
Good

Twenty-nine institutions with scores in the 3.6-3.9 range, in rank order

INSTITUTION	Rank	Score
CASE WESTERN RESERVE UNIVERSITY		
School of Medicine (Cleveland)	52	3.90
MOUNT SINAI		
School of Medicine of the City University of New York	53	3.89
UNIVERSITY OF CONNECTICUT		
School of Medicine (Farmington)	54	3.88
UNIVERSITY OF KANSAS		
School of Medicine (Kansas City)	55	3.87
CREIGHTON UNIVERSITY		
School of Medicine (Omaha)	56	3.86
UNIVERSITY OF COLORADO		
School of Medicine (Denver)	57	3.85
UNIVERSITY OF MARYLAND		
School of Medicine (Baltimore)	58	3.84
OREGON HEALTH SCIENCES UNIVERSITY		
School of Medicine (Portland)	59	3.83
ALBANY MEDICAL COLLEGE		
of Union University (Albany)	60	3.82
UNIVERSITY OF UTAH		
College of Medicine (Salt Lake City)	61	3.81
UNIVERSITY OF FLORIDA		
College of Medicine (Gainesville)	62	3.80
MAYO MEDICAL SCHOOL (Rochester)	63	3.79
UNIVERSITY OF MIAMI		
School of Medicine (Miami, Florida)	64	3.78
MICHIGAN STATE UNIVERSITY		
College of Human Medicine (East Lansing)	65	3.77
UNIVERSITY OF TEXAS		
Southwestern Medical School (Dallas)	66	3.76
UNIVERSITY OF MISSOURI KANSAS CITY		
School of Medicine (Kansas City)	67	3.75
UNIVERSITY OF TEXAS MEDICAL BRANCH (Galveston)	68	3.74
UNIVERSITY OF TEXAS MEDICAL SCHOOL (San Antonio)	69	3.73
PENNSYLVANIA STATE UNIVERSITY		
College of Medicine (Hershey)	70	3.72
STATE UNIVERSITY OF NEW YORK HEALTH SCIENCE CENTER		
at Brooklyn	71	3.71
UNIVERSITY OF CINCINNATI		
College of Medicine (Cincinnati)	72	3.70
STATE UNIVERSITY OF NEW YORK HEALTH SCIENCE CENTER		
at Syracuse	73	3.69
LOUISIANA STATE UNIVERSITY		
School of Medicine (New Orleans)	74	3.68
UNIVERSITY OF ALABAMA		
School of Medicine (Birmingham)	75	3.67
UNIVERSITY OF NEBRASKA		
College of Medicine (Omaha)	76	3.66
UNIVERSITY OF KENTUCKY		
College of Medicine (Lexington)	77	3.65
UNIVERSITY OF VERMONT		
College of Medicine (Burlington)	78	3.64
LOUISIANA STATE UNIVERSITY		
School of Medicine (Shreveport)	79	3.63
UNIVERSITY OF TENNESSEE		
College of Medicine (Memphis)	80	3.62

A RATING OF MEDICAL SCHOOLS

U.S.A. MEDICAL SCHOOLS (Continued)
Acceptable Plus

Forty-five institutions with scores in the 3.0-3.5 range, in rank order

INSTITUTION	Rank	Score
NEW YORK MEDICAL COLLEGE (New York)	81	3.50
JEFFERSON MEDICAL COLLEGE		
of Thomas Jefferson University (Philadelphia)	82	3.49
UNIVERSITY OF OKLAHOMA		
School of Medicine (Oklahoma City)	83	3.48
WEST VIRGINIA UNIVERSITY		
School of Medicine (Morgantown)	84	3.47
UNIVERSITY OF TEXAS MEDICAL SCHOOL at Houston	85	3.46
UNIVERSITY OF ARKANSAS		
School of Medicine (Little Rock)	86	3.45
MEDICAL COLLEGE OF PENNSYLVANIA/		
HAHNEMANN UNIVERSITY (Philadelphia)	87	3.44
UMDNJ-NEW JERSEY MEDICAL SCHOOL (Newark)	88	3.43
UNIVERSITY OF ARIZONA		
College of Medicine (Tucson)	89	3.42
UNIVERSITY OF SOUTH FLORIDA		
College of Medicine (Tampa)	90	3.41
MEDICAL UNIVERSITY OF SOUTH CAROLINA		
College of Medicine (Charleston)	91	3.40
UNIVERSITY OF MISSISSIPPI		
School of Medicine (Jackson)	92	3.39
MeHARRY MEDICAL COLLEGE		
School of Medicine (Nashville)	93	3.37
RUSH MEDICAL COLLEGE (Chicago)	94	3.36
MEDICAL COLLEGE OF VIRGINIA (Richmond)	95	3.34
MEDICAL COLLEGE OF GEORGIA (Augusta)	96	3.33
MEDICAL COLLEGE OF OHIO (Toledo)	97	3.32
FINCH UNIVERSITY OF HEALTH SCIENCES/		
The Chicago Medical School (North Chicago)	98	3.31
HOWARD UNIVERSITY		
College of Medicine (Washington D.C.)	99	3.30
UNIVERSITY OF NEW MEXICO		
School of Medicine (Albuquerque)	100	3.29
SOUTHERN ILLINOIS UNIVERSITY		
School of Medicine (Springfield)	101	3.28
TEXAS TECH UNIVERSITY		
School of Medicine (Lubbock)	102	3.27
UMDNJ-RUTGERS MEDICAL SCHOOL (Piscataway)	103	3.26
UNIVERSITY OF HAWAII		
School of Medicine (Honolulu)	104	3.25

A RATING OF MEDICAL SCHOOLS

U.S.A. MEDICAL SCHOOLS (Continued)
Acceptable Plus

Forty-five institutions with scores in the 3.0-3.5 range, in rank order

INSTITUTION	Rank	Score
UNIVERSITY OF MASSACHUSETTS		
Medical School (Worcester)	105	3.24
MEDICAL COLLEGE OF WISCONSIN (Milwaukee)	106	3.23
UNIVERSITY OF PUERTO RICO		
School of Medicine (San Juan)	107	3.22
UNIVERSITY OF SOUTH CAROLINA		
School of Medicine (Columbia)	108	3.21
UNIVERSITY OF NEVADA		
School of Medical Science (Reno)	109	3.20
UNIFORMED SERVICES UNIVERSITY OF THE HEALTH SCIENCES		
F. Edward Herbert School of Medicine (Bethesda)	110	3.18
UNIVERSITY OF NORTH DAKOTA		
School of Medicine (Grand Forks)	111	3.17
UNIVERSITY OF SOUTH DAKOTA		
School of Medicine (Vermillion)	112	3.16
NORTHEASTERN OHIO UNIVERSITIES		
College of Medicine (Rootstown)	113	3.15
EAST CAROLINA UNIVERSITY		
School of Medicine (Greenville)	114	3.14
MARSHALL UNIVERSITY		
School of Medicine (Huntington)	115	3.13
EASTERN VIRGINIA MEDICAL SCHOOL (Norfolk)	116	3.12
EAST TENNESSEE STATE UNIVERSITY		
College of Medicine (Johnson City)	117	3.11
UNIVERSITY OF SOUTH CAROLINA		
College of Medicine (Mobile)	118	3.10
TEXAS A&M UNIVERSITY		
College of Medicine (College Station)	119	3.09
VIRGINIA COMMONWEALTH UNIVERSITY		
Medical College of Virginia (Richmond)	120	3.08
WRIGHT STATE UNIVERSITY		
School of Medicine (Dayton)	121	3.07
MOREHOUSE SCHOOL OF MEDICINE (Atlanta)	122	3.06
MERCER UNIVERSITY		
School of Medicine (Macon)	123	3.05
PONCE SCHOOL OF MEDICINE (Ponce)	124	3.04
UNIVERSIDAD CENTRAL DEL CARIBE		
School of Medicine (Cayey)	125	3.03

A RATING OF GRADUATE PROGRAMS IN VETERINARY MEDICINE/SCIENCES
Leading Institutions

Twenty-six institutions with scores in the 4.0-5.0 range, in rank order

INSTITUTION	Rank	Score
CALIFORNIA, DAVIS	1	4.92
CORNELL (N.Y.)	2	4.90
PENNSYLVANIA	3	4.85
OHIO STATE (Columbus)	4	4.80
COLORADO STATE	5	4.79
MICHIGAN STATE	6	4.77
IOWA STATE (Ames)	7	4.73
MINNESOTA (Minneapolis)	8	4.68
PURDUE (Lafayette)	9	4.66
MISSOURI (Columbia)	10	4.64
TEXAS A&M (College Station)	11	4.62
WISCONSIN (Madison)	12	4.59
ILLINOIS (Urbana)	13	4.57
TUFTS	14	4.53
KANSAS STATE	15	4.52
GEORGIA (Athens)	16	4.46
LSU (Baton Rouge)	17	4.42
NORTH CAROLINA STATE (Raleigh)	18	4.37
V.P.I. & STATE U.	19	4.30
AUBURN U. (Auburn)	20	4.27
FLORIDA (Gainesville)	21	4.20
OREGON STATE	22	4.17
WASHINGTON STATE (Pullman)	23	4.11
MISSISSIPPI STATE U.	24	4.08
OKLAHOMA STATE	25	4.04
TENNESSEE (Knoxville)	26	4.01

The GOURMAN REPORT
PART IV

PROFESSIONAL PROGRAMS

A Rating of U.S.A. Nursing Schools

A Rating of U.S.A. Optometry Schools

A Rating of Pharmacy Schools in Canada

A Rating of U.S.A. Pharmacy Schools

A Rating of U.S.A. Public Health Schools

A RATING OF GRADUATE PROGRAMS IN NURSING
Leading Institutions

Thirty institutions with scores in the 4.6-5.0 range, in rank order

INSTITUTION	Rank	Score
CALIFORNIA, SAN FRANCISCO	1	4.93
CASE WESTERN RESERVE	2	4.92
MICHIGAN (Ann Arbor)	3	4.91
N.Y.U.	4	4.90
WASHINGTON (Seattle)	5	4.89
PENNSYLVANIA	6	4.88
ILLINOIS (Chicago)	7	4.87
PITTSBURGH (Pittsburgh)	8	4.86
WAYNE STATE (Detroit)	9	4.85
CATHOLIC U. (D.C.)	10	4.84
YALE	11	4.83
COLUMBIA (N.Y.)	12	4.82
MINNESOTA (Minneapolis)	13	4.81
INDIANA (Indianapolis)	14	4.80
TEXAS (Austin)	15	4.79
OHIO STATE (Columbus)	16	4.78
WISCONSIN (Madison)	17	4.77
COLORADO (Denver)	18	4.76
UCLA	19	4.75
VANDERBILT	20	4.74
UTAH (Salt Lake City)	21	4.73
SUNY (Buffalo)	22	4.72
CUNY (Hunter)	23	4.70
COLUMBIA (Teachers College) (N.Y.)	24	4.68
NORTH CAROLINA (Chapel Hill)	25	4.67
NORTH CAROLINA (Chapel Hill) School of Public Health	26	4.66
THE HEALTH SCIENCES UNIVERSITY (Portland)	27	4.63
MARYLAND (Baltimore)	28	4.62
ROCHESTER (N.Y.)	29	4.61
RUSH U. (Chicago)	30	4.60

A RATING OF GRADUATE PROGRAMS IN NURSING (Continued)
Leading Institutions

Twenty-three institutions with scores in the 4.0-4.5 range, in rank order

INSTITUTION	Rank	Score
TEXAS HEALTH SCIENCE CENTER (San Antonio)	31	4.49
IOWA (Iowa City)	32	4.47
ARIZONA (Tucson)	33	4.46
EMORY	34	4.45
ALABAMA (Birmingham)	35	4.44
ST. LOUIS U.	36	4.41
LOYOLA (Chicago)	37	4.37
KANSAS (Kansas City)	38	4.34
MEDICAL COLLEGE OF GEORGIA	39	4.32
TENNESSEE (Memphis)	40	4.30
FLORIDA (Gainesville)	41	4.28
SYRACUSE	42	4.26
LSU (New Orleans)	43	4.24
LOMA LINDA (California)	44	4.22
CINCINNATI	45	4.21
MARQUETTE	46	4.19
VIRGINIA (Charlottesville)	47	4.17
PENN STATE (University Park)	48	4.15
CONNECTICUT (Storrs)	49	4.13
KENTUCKY	50	4.10
BOSTON COLLEGE	51	4.08
VIRGINIA COMMONWEALTH	52	4.03
ADELPHI (N.Y.)	53	4.00

A RATING OF GRADUATE PROGRAMS IN NURSING (Continued)
Leading Institutions

Twenty institutions with scores in the 3.6-3.9 range, in rank order

INSTITUTION	Rank	Score
TEXAS WOMAN'S U.	54	3.88
ARIZONA STATE	55	3.86
MISSOURI (Columbia)	56	3.85
ARKANSAS (Little Rock)	57	3.82
NEBRASKA (Omaha)	58	3.81
OKLAHOMA (Oklahoma City)	59	3.79
NORTHERN ILLINOIS	60	3.77
RUTGERS (Newark)	61	3.76
SOUTH CAROLINA (Columbia)	62	3.75
SUNY (Binghampton)	63	3.73
TEXAS HEALTH SCIENCE CENTER (Houston)	64	3.72
DE PAUL	65	3.71
DELAWARE (Newark)	66	3.70
WISCONSIN (Milwaukee)	67	3.68
B.Y.U.	68	3.67
CALIFORNIA STATE (Los Angeles)	69	3.65
THE SAGE COLLEGES	70	3.64
SOUTHERN MISSISSIPPI	71	3.63
CALIFORNIA STATE (Fresno)	72	3.61
PUERTO RICO (San Juan)	73	3.60

A RATING OF GRADUATE PROGRAMS IN OPTOMETRY
Leading Institutions

Seventeen institutions with scores in the 4.0-5.0 range, in rank order

INSTITUTION	Rank	Score
UNIVERSITY OF CALIFORNIA, BERKELEY		
School of Optometry	1	4.93
THE OHIO STATE UNIVERSITY		
College of Optometry	2	4.92
INDIANA UNIVERSITY		
School of Optometry	3	4.90
SOUTHERN CALIFORNIA COLLEGE		
School of Optometry	4	4.88
UNIVERSITY OF HOUSTON		
College of Optometry	5	4.84
UNIVERSITY OF ALABAMA AT BIRMINGHAM		
College of Optometry	6	4.83
SUNY STATE		
College of Optometry	7	4.75
UNIVERSITY OF MISSOURI – ST. LOUIS		
College of Optometry	8	4.74
PENNSYLVANIA		
College of Optometry	9	4.72
FERRIS STATE		
College of Optometry	10	4.66
NEW ENGLAND		
College of Optometry	11	4.60
PACIFIC UNIVERSITY		
College of Optometry	12	4.58
ILLINOIS COLLEGE		
School of Optometry	13	4.53
SOUTHERN COLLEGE		
College of Optometry	14	4.37
NORTHEASTERN STATE UNIVERSITY		
College of Optometry	15	4.33
INTER AMERICAN UNIVERSITY OF PUERTO RICO		
School of Optometry	16	4.14
NOVA SOUTHEASTERN UNIVERSITY		
College of Optometry	17	4.12

A RATING OF PHARMACY SCHOOLS IN CANADA

CANADIAN PHARMACY SCHOOLS
Leading Institutions

Eight institutions with scores in the 4.0-5.0 range, in rank order

INSTITUTION	Rank	Score
UNIVERSITY OF TORONTO	1	4.84
UNIVERSITY OF BRITISH COLUMBIA	2	4.81
UNIVERSITY OF MONTREAL	3	4.73
UNIVERSITY OF LAVAL	4	4.68
UNIVERSITY OF MANITOBA	5	4.60
UNIVERSITY OF ALBERTA	6	4.50
DALHOUSIE UNIVERSITY	7	4.45
UNIVERSITY OF SASKATCHEWAN	8	4.37

A RATING OF PHARMACY SCHOOLS

U.S.A. PHARMACY SCHOOLS
Leading Institutions

Fifty-nine institutions with scores in the 4.0-5.0 range, in rank order

INSTITUTION	Rank	Score
CALIFORNIA, SAN FRANCISCO	1	4.93
NORTH CAROLINA (Chapel Hill)	2	4.92
WASHINGTON (Seattle)	3	4.91
WISCONSIN (Madison)	4	4.90
COLORADO (Denver)	5	4.88
IOWA (Iowa City)	6	4.86
MINNESOTA (Minneapolis)	7	4.85
MICHIGAN (Ann Arbor)	8	4.83
TEXAS (Austin)	9	4.81
USC (Los Angeles)	10	4.79
KENTUCKY (Lexington)	11	4.78
MEDICAL U. OF SOUTH CAROLINA (Charleston)	12	4.77
PITTSBURGH (Pittsburgh)	13	4.76
UTAH (Salt Lake City)	14	4.75
CINCINNATI	15	4.73
OREGON STATE (Corvallis)	16	4.71
WEST VIRGINIA (Morgantown)	17	4.69
FLORIDA (Gainesville)	18	4.67
OHIO STATE (Columbus)	19	4.66
TENNESSEE (Memphis)	20	4.65
ILLINOIS (Chicago)	21	4.64
WASHINGTON STATE (Pullman)	22	4.62
MARYLAND (Baltimore)	23	4.60
TEMPLE (Philadelphia)	24	4.58
CONNECTICUT (Storrs)	25	4.56
WAYNE STATE (Detroit)	26	4.55
ALBANY COLLEGE OF UNION U.	27	4.53
KANSAS (Lawrence)	28	4.52
SUNY (Buffalo)	29	4.50
PURDUE (Lafayette)	30	4.49
OKLAHOMA (Oklahoma City)	31	4.48
MISSISSIPPI (University)	32	4.46
ST. JOHN'S U. (Jamaica)	33	4.43
HOUSTON (Houston)	34	4.42
PHILADELPHIA COLLEGE OF PHARMACY & SCIENCE	35	4.40
PUERTO RICO (San Juan)	36	4.38
CREIGHTON (Omaha)	37	4.37
BUTLER U. (Indiana)	38	4.36
RUTGERS THE STATE U. OF NEW JERSEY (New Brunswick)	39	4.35
ARIZONA (Tucson)	40	4.34

A RATING OF PHARMACY SCHOOLS

U.S.A. PHARMACY SCHOOLS
Leading Institutions

Fifty-nine institutions with scores in the 4.0-5.0 range, in rank order

INSTITUTION	Rank	Score
SOUTH CAROLINA (Columbia)	41	4.33
NEBRASKA (Omaha)	42	4.32
RHODE ISLAND (Kingston)	43	4.31
GEORGIA (Athens)	44	4.30
ARKANSAS (Little Rock)	45	4.27
MASSACHUSETTS COLLEGE OF PHARMACY & ALLIED HEALTH SCIENCES	46	4.26
NEW MEXICO (Albuquerque)	47	4.25
DUQUESNE (Pittsburgh)	48	4.24
MISSOURI – KANSAS CITY	49	4.23
PACIFIC, THE UNIVERSITY OF (Stockton)	50	4.22
LONG ISLAND U. (Brooklyn)	51	4.21
VIRGINIA COMMONWEALTH U. MEDICAL COLLEGE OF VIRGINIA	52	4.20
AUBURN (Auburn)	53	4.19
NORTH DAKOTA STATE (Fargo)	54	4.17
NOVA SOUTHEASTERN U. (North Miami Beach)	55	4.15
FERRIS STATE (Big Rapids)	56	4.14
FLORIDA A&M (Tallahassee)	57	4.13
ST. LOUIS COLLEGE OF PHARMACY (St. Louis)	58	4.12
IDAHO STATE (Pocatello)	59	4.10

A RATING OF GRADUATE PROGRAMS IN PUBLIC HEALTH
Leading Institutions

Twenty-six institutions with scores in the 4.0-5.0 range, in rank order

INSTITUTION	Rank	Score
THE JOHNS HOPKINS UNIVERSITY		
School of Hygiene & Public Health	1	4.95
UNIVERSITY OF CALIFORNIA (Berkeley)		
School of Public Health	2	4.94
HARVARD UNIVERSITY		
School of Public Health	3	4.92
UNIVERSITY OF MICHIGAN (Ann Arbor)		
School of Public Health	4	4.91
UNIVERSITY OF CALIFORNIA AT LOS ANGELES (UCLA)		
School of Public Health	5	4.89
YALE UNIVERSITY		
Department of Epidemiology & Public Health	6	4.88
UNIVERSITY OF MINNESOTA		
School of Public Health	7	4.86
UNIVERSITY OF NORTH CAROLINA (Chapel Hill)		
School of Public Health	8	4.84
COLUMBIA UNIVERSITY		
School of Public Health	9	4.82
TULANE UNIVERSITY		
School of Public Health & Tropical Medicine	10	4.80
UNIVERSITY OF WASHINGTON (Seattle)		
School of Public Health & Community Medicine	11	4.76
EMORY UNIVERSITY		
School of Public Health	12	4.74
UNIVERSITY OF PITTSBURGH		
Graduate School of Public Health	13	4.72
UNIVERSITY OF TEXAS–HOUSTON		
School of Public Health	14	4.71
UNIVERSITY OF ALABAMA IN BIRMINGHAM		
Department of Public Health	15	4.68
UNIVERSITY OF OKLAHOMA		
College of Public Health	16	4.66
LOMA LINDA UNIVERSITY		
School of Public Health	17	4.63
UNIVERSITY OF MASSACHUSETTS (Amherst)		
School of Public Health and Health Sciences	18	4.60
BOSTON UNIVERSITY		
School of Public Health	19	4.58
UNIVERSITY OF PUERTO RICO		
School of Public Health	20	4.52
UNIVERSITY OF HAWAII		
School of Public Health	21	4.48
UNIVERSITY OF SOUTH CAROLINA		
School of Public Health	22	4.45
SAINT LOUIS UNIVERSITY		
School of Public Health	23	4.40
UNIVERSITY OF SOUTH FLORIDA		
College of Public Health	24	4.35
UNIVERSITY OF ILLINOIS AT CHICAGO		
School of Public Health	25	4.31
STATE UNIVERSITY OF NEW YORK AT ALBANY		
School of Public Health	26	4.28

The GOURMAN REPORT
PART V

**A RATING OF THE TOP 50
GRADUATE SCHOOLS IN ENGINEERING**

A RATING OF THE TOP 50 GRADUATE SCHOOLS IN ENGINEERING
(All majors evaluated)
Leading Institutions

INSTITUTION	Rank	Score
M.I.T.	1	4.93
CALIFORNIA, BERKELEY	2	4.91
ILLINOIS (Urbana)	3	4.90
STANFORD	4	4.89
CAL TECH	5	4.88
CORNELL (N.Y.)	6	4.86
GEORGIA TECH	7	4.84
PURDUE (Lafayette)	8	4.82
TEXAS (Austin)	9	4.80
MICHIGAN (Ann Arbor)	10	4.79
PENNSYLVANIA	11	4.77
MINNESOTA (Minneapolis)	12	4.74
WISCONSIN (Madison)	13	4.72
CARNEGIE-MELLON	14	4.70
OHIO STATE (Columbus)	15	4.69
PRINCETON	16	4.68
COLUMBIA (N.Y.)	17	4.67
PENN STATE (University Park)	18	4.65
HARVARD	19	4.63
CALIFORNIA, SAN DIEGO	20	4.60
NORTHWESTERN (Evanston)	21	4.57
RICE	22	4.54
RENSSELAER POLYTECHNIC INSTITUTE	23	4.50
WASHINGTON (Seattle)	24	4.48
UCLA	25	4.47
CALIFORNIA, DAVIS	26	4.46
CASE WESTERN RESERVE	27	4.44
TEXAS A&M (College Station)	28	4.42
UNIVERSITY OF SOUTHERN CALIFORNIA	29	4.41
FLORIDA (Gainesville)	30	4.40
NORTH CAROLINA STATE (Raleigh)	31	4.39
VIRGINIA (Charlottesville)	32	4.37
ARIZONA (Tucson)	33	4.36
IOWA STATE (Ames)	34	4.35
UTAH (Salt Lake City)	35	4.34
DELAWARE (Newark)	36	4.33
MARYLAND (College Park)	37	4.32
LEHIGH	38	4.31
CINCINNATI	39	4.29
NOTRE DAME	40	4.27
WASHINGTON (St. Louis)	41	4.26
HOUSTON	42	4.25
YALE	43	4.24
JOHNS HOPKINS	44	4.23
MICHIGAN STATE	45	4.22
MASSACHUSETTS (Amherst)	46	4.21
COLORADO SCHOOL OF MINES	47	4.20
LSU (Baton Rouge)	48	4.19
TENNESSEE (Knoxville)	49	4.17
DREXEL U.	50	4.15

The GOURMAN REPORT
PART VI

**A RATING OF GRADUATE SCHOOLS
IN ENGINEERING**

A RATING OF GRADUATE SCHOOLS IN ENGINEERING

RATING CATEGORIES	Numerical Range
Very Strong	4.51-4.99
Strong	4.01-4.49
Good	3.61-3.99
Acceptable	3.01-3.59

INSTITUTIONS IN ALPHABETICAL ORDER

INSTITUTION	Gourman Ranking	Gourman Score
UNIVERSITY OF AKRON Akron, Ohio	104	3.50
UNIVERSITY OF ALABAMA University, Alabama	90	3.71
UNIVERSITY OF ALABAMA IN BIRMINGHAM Birmingham, Alabama	133	3.11
UNIVERSITY OF ALABAMA IN HUNTSVILLE Huntsville, Alabama	116	3.31
ARIZONA STATE UNIVERSITY Tempe, Arizona	51	4.12
UNIVERSITY OF ARIZONA Tucson, Arizona	33	4.36
UNIVERSITY OF ARKANSAS Fayetteville, Arkansas	73	3.88
AUBURN UNIVERSITY Auburn, Alabama	70	3.93
BOSTON UNIVERSITY Boston, Massachusetts	92	3.67
BRIGHAM YOUNG UNIVERSITY Provo, Utah	131	3.14
BROWN UNIVERSITY Providence, Rhode Island	58	4.08
CALIFORNIA INSTITUTE OF TECHNOLOGY Pasadena, California	5	4.88
UNIVERSITY OF CALIFORNIA, BERKELEY Berkeley, California	2	4.91
UNIVERSITY OF CALIFORNIA, DAVIS Davis, California	26	4.46

A RATING OF GRADUATE SCHOOLS IN ENGINEERING (Continued)

INSTITUTIONS IN ALPHABETICAL ORDER

INSTITUTION	Gourman Ranking	Gourman Score
UNIVERSITY OF CALIFORNIA, IRVINE Irvine, California	93	3.66
UNIVERSITY OF CALIFORNIA, LOS ANGELES (UCLA) Los Angeles, California	25	4.47
UNIVERSITY OF CALIFORNIA, SAN DIEGO La Jolla, California	20	4.60
UNIVERSITY OF CALIFORNIA, SANTA BARBARA Santa Barbara, California	78	3.83
CARNEGIE-MELLON UNIVERSITY Pittsburgh, Pennsylvania	14	4.70
CASE WESTERN RESERVE UNIVERSITY Cleveland, Ohio	27	4.44
CATHOLIC UNIVERSITY OF AMERICA Washington, D.C.	99	3.60
UNIVERSITY OF CENTRAL FLORIDA Orlando, Florida	128	3.18
UNIVERSITY OF CINCINNATI Cincinnati, Ohio	39	4.29
CLARKSON UNIVERSITY Potsdam, New York	86	3.75
CLEMSON UNIVERSITY Clemson, South Carolina	71	3.91
CLEVELAND STATE UNIVERSITY Cleveland, Ohio	127	3.19
COLORADO SCHOOL OF MINES Golden, Colorado	47	4.20
COLORADO STATE UNIVERSITY Fort Collins, Colorado	67	3.98
UNIVERSITY OF COLORADO AT BOULDER Boulder, Colorado	60	4.06
UNIVERSITY OF COLORADO AT DENVER Denver, Colorado	137	3.04

A RATING OF GRADUATE SCHOOLS IN ENGINEERING (Continued)

RATING CATEGORIES	Numerical Range
Very Strong	4.51-4.99
Strong	4.01-4.49
Good	3.61-3.99
Acceptable	3.01-3.59

INSTITUTIONS IN ALPHABETICAL ORDER

INSTITUTION	Gourman Ranking	Gourman Score
COLUMBIA UNIVERSITY New York, New York	17	4.67
UNIVERSITY OF CONNECTICUT Storrs, Connecticut	103	3.53
CORNELL UNIVERSITY Ithaca, New York	6	4.86
DARTMOUTH COLLEGE Hanover, New Hampshire	66	4.00
UNIVERSITY OF DAYTON Dayton, Ohio	101	3.56
UNIVERSITY OF DELAWARE Newark, Delaware	36	4.33
UNIVERSITY OF DETROIT MERCY Detroit, Michigan	134	3.10
DREXEL UNIVERSITY Philadelphia, Pennsylvania	50	4.15
DUKE UNIVERSITY Durham, North Carolina	65	4.01
FLORIDA ATLANTIC UNIVERSITY Boca Raton, Florida	136	3.06
FLORIDA INSTITUTE OF TECHNOLOGY Melbourne, Florida	138	3.02
UNIVERSITY OF FLORIDA Gainesville, Florida	30	4.40
GEORGE WASHINGTON UNIVERSITY Washington, D.C.	87	3.74
GEORGIA INSTITUTE OF TECHNOLOGY Atlanta, Georgia	7	4.84

INSTITUTIONS IN ALPHABETICAL ORDER

INSTITUTION	Gourman Ranking	Gourman Score
HARVARD UNIVERSITY Cambridge, Massachusetts	19	4.63
UNIVERSITY OF HAWAII AT MANOA Honolulu, Hawaii	125	3.21
UNIVERSITY OF HOUSTON Houston, Texas	42	4.25
HOWARD UNIVERSITY Washington, D.C.	135	3.09
UNIVERSITY OF IDAHO Moscow, Idaho	118	3.28
ILLINOIS INSTITUTE OF TECHNOLOGY Chicago, Illinois	81	3.80
UNIVERSITY OF ILLINOIS AT CHICAGO Chicago, Illinois	107	3.44
UNIVERSITY OF ILLINOIS AT URBANA-CHAMPAIGN Urbana, Illinois	3	4.90
IOWA STATE UNIVERSITY Ames, Iowa	34	4.35
UNIVERSITY OF IOWA Iowa City, Iowa	59	4.07
JOHNS HOPKINS UNIVERSITY Baltimore, Maryland	44	4.23
KANSAS STATE UNIVERSITY Manhattan, Kansas	77	3.84
UNIVERSITY OF KANSAS Lawrence, Kansas	55	4.15
UNIVERSITY OF KENTUCKY Lexington, Kentucky	79	3.82
LEHIGH UNIVERSITY Bethlehem, Pennsylvania	38	4.31
LOUISIANA STATE UNIVERSITY Baton Rouge, Louisiana	48	4.19
LOUISIANA TECH UNIVERSITY Ruston, Louisiana	110	3.39

A RATING OF GRADUATE SCHOOLS IN ENGINEERING (Continued)

RATING CATEGORIES	Numerical Range
Very Strong	4.51-4.99
Strong	4.01-4.49
Good	3.61-3.99
Acceptable	3.01-3.59

INSTITUTIONS IN ALPHABETICAL ORDER

INSTITUTION	Gourman Ranking	Gourman Score
UNIVERSITY OF MAINE AT ORONO Orono, Maine	119	3.27
MARQUETTE UNIVERSITY Milwaukee, Wisconsin	132	3.12
UNIVERSITY OF MARYLAND College Park, Maryland	37	4.32
MASSACHUSETTS INSTITUTE OF TECHNOLOGY Cambridge, Massachusetts	1	4.93
UNIVERSITY OF MASSACHUSETTS AMHERST Amherst, Massachusetts	46	4.21
UNIVERSITY OF MASSACHUSETTS LOWELL Lowell, Massachusetts	108	3.42
UNIVERSITY OF MIAMI Coral Gables, Florida	112	3.37
MICHIGAN STATE UNIVERSITY East Lansing, Michigan	45	4.22
MICHIGAN TECHNOLOGICAL UNIVERSITY Houghton, Michigan	84	3.77
UNIVERSITY OF MICHIGAN Ann Arbor, Michigan	10	4.79
UNIVERSITY OF MINNESOTA Minneapolis, Minnesota	12	4.74
MISSISSIPPI STATE UNIVERSITY Mississippi State, Mississippi	88	3.73
UNIVERSITY OF MISSISSIPPI University, Mississippi	121	3.25
UNIVERSITY OF MISSOURI–COLUMBIA Columbia, Missouri	61	4.05
UNIVERSITY OF MISSOURI–ROLLA Rolla, Missouri	57	4.09

A RATING OF GRADUATE SCHOOLS IN ENGINEERING (Continued)

INSTITUTIONS IN ALPHABETICAL ORDER

INSTITUTION	Gourman Ranking	Gourman Score
MONTANA STATE UNIVERSITY Bozeman, Montana	120	3.26
UNIVERSITY OF NEBRASKA–LINCOLN Lincoln, Nebraska	91	3.69
UNIVERSITY OF NEW HAMPSHIRE Durham, New Hampshire	113	3.36
NEW MEXICO STATE UNIVERSITY Las Cruces, New Mexico	129	3.17
UNIVERSITY OF NEW MEXICO Albuquerque, New Mexico	80	3.81
STATE UNIVERSITY OF NEW YORK AT BUFFALO Buffalo, New York	53	4.13
STATE UNIVERSITY OF NEW YORK AT STONY BROOK Stony Brook, New York	72	3.89
CITY COLLEGE OF THE CITY UNIVERSITY OF NEW YORK New York, New York	85	3.76
NORTH CAROLINA STATE UNIVERSITY AT RALEIGH Raleigh, North Carolina	31	4.39
NORTH DAKOTA STATE UNIVERSITY Fargo, North Dakota	124	3.22
NORTHWESTERN UNIVERSITY Evanston, Illinois	21	4.57
UNIVERSITY OF NOTRE DAME Notre Dame, Indiana	40	4.27
OHIO STATE UNIVERSITY Columbus, Ohio	15	4.69
OHIO UNIVERSITY Athens, Ohio	111	3.38
OKLAHOMA STATE UNIVERSITY Stillwater, Oklahoma	69	3.95
UNIVERSITY OF OKLAHOMA Norman, Oklahoma	75	3.86
OLD DOMINION UNIVERSITY Norfolk, Virginia	122	3.24
OREGON STATE UNIVERSITY Corvallis, Oregon	83	3.78

A RATING OF GRADUATE SCHOOLS IN ENGINEERING (Continued)

RATING CATEGORIES	Numerical Range
Very Strong	4.51-4.99
Strong	4.01-4.49
Good	3.61-3.99
Acceptable	3.01-3.59

INSTITUTIONS IN ALPHABETICAL ORDER

INSTITUTION	Gourman Ranking	Gourman Score
PENNSYLVANIA STATE UNIVERSITY University Park, Pennsylvania	18	4.65
UNIVERSITY OF PENNSYLVANIA Philadelphia, Pennsylvania	11	4.77
UNIVERSITY OF PITTSBURGH Pittsburgh, Pennsylvania	52	4.14
POLYTECHNIC UNIVERSITY Brooklyn, New York	62	4.04
PRINCETON UNIVERSITY Princeton, New Jersey	16	4.68
PURDUE UNIVERSITY West Lafayette, Indiana	8	4.82
RENSSELAER POLYTECHNIC INSTITUTE Troy, New York	23	4.50
UNIVERSITY OF RHODE ISLAND Kingston, Rhode Island	115	3.32
RICE UNIVERSITY Houston, Texas	22	4.54
UNIVERSITY OF ROCHESTER Rochester, New York	63	4.03
THE STATE UNIVERSITY OF NEW JERSEY, RUTGERS New Brunswick, New Jersey	56	4.10
UNIVERSITY OF SOUTH CAROLINA Columbia, South Carolina	109	3.40
SOUTH DAKOTA SCHOOL OF MINES AND TECHNOLOGY Rapid City, South Dakota	130	3.15
UNIVERSITY OF SOUTHERN CALIFORNIA Los Angeles, California	29	4.41

INSTITUTIONS IN ALPHABETICAL ORDER

INSTITUTION	Gourman Ranking	Gourman Score
SOUTHERN ILLINOIS UNIVERSITY–CARBONDALE Carbondale, Illinois	117	3.29
SOUTHERN METHODIST UNIVERSITY Dallas, Texas	96	3.63
STANFORD UNIVERSITY Stanford, California	4	4.89
STEVENS INSTITUTE OF TECHNOLOGY Hoboken, New Jersey	68	3.96
SYRACUSE UNIVERSITY Syracuse, New York	64	4.02
UNIVERSITY OF TENNESSEE AT KNOXVILLE Knoxville, Tennessee	49	4.17
TEXAS A&M UNIVERSITY College Station, Texas	28	4.42
TEXAS TECH UNIVERSITY Lubbock, Texas	74	3.87
UNIVERSITY OF TEXAS AT ARLINGTON Arlington, Texas	102	3.54
UNIVERSITY OF TEXAS AT AUSTIN Austin, Texas	9	4.80
UNIVERSITY OF TOLEDO Toledo, Ohio	126	3.20
TUFTS UNIVERSITY Medford, Massachusetts	97	3.62
TULANE UNIVERSITY New Orleans, Louisiana	98	3.60
UNIVERSITY OF TULSA Tulsa, Oklahoma	106	3.45
UTAH STATE UNIVERSITY Logan, Utah	76	3.85
UNIVERSITY OF UTAH Salt Lake City, Utah	35	4.34
VANDERBILT UNIVERSITY Nashville, Tennessee	82	3.79
UNIVERSITY OF VERMONT Burlington, Vermont	139	3.00

RATING CATEGORIES	Numerical Range
Very Strong	4.51-4.99
Strong	4.01-4.49
Good	3.61-3.99
Acceptable	3.01-3.59

INSTITUTIONS IN ALPHABETICAL ORDER

INSTITUTION	Gourman Ranking	Gourman Score
VIRGINIA POLYTECHNIC INSTITUTE AND STATE UNIVERSITY Blacksburg, Virginia	54	4.12
UNIVERSITY OF VIRGINIA Charlottesville, Virginia	32	4.37
WASHINGTON STATE UNIVERSITY Pullman, Washington	89	3.72
WASHINGTON UNIVERSITY St. Louis, Missouri	41	4.26
UNIVERSITY OF WASHINGTON Seattle, Washington	24	4.48
WAYNE STATE UNIVERSITY Detroit, Michigan	94	3.65
WEST VIRGINIA UNIVERSITY Morgantown, West Virginia	105	3.48
WICHITA STATE UNIVERSITY Wichita, Kansas	123	3.23
UNIVERSITY OF WISCONSIN–MADISON Madison, Wisconsin	13	4.72
UNIVERSITY OF WISCONSIN–MILWAUKEE Milwaukee, Wisconsin	95	3.64
WORCESTER POLYTECHNIC INSTITUTE Worcester, Massachusetts	100	3.58
UNIVERSITY OF WYOMING Laramie, Wyoming	114	3.34
YALE UNIVERSITY New Haven, Connecticut	43	4.24

The GOURMAN REPORT
PART VII

A RATING OF EMBA/MANAGEMENT SCHOOLS

A RATING OF GRADUATE PROGRAMS IN EMBA/MANAGEMENT
Leading Institutions

Thirteen institutions with scores in the 4.0-5.0 range, in rank order

INSTITUTION	Rank	Score
PENNSYLVANIA (Wharton)	1	4.90
CHICAGO	2	4.89
COLUMBIA (N.Y.)	3	4.87
UCLA (Anderson)	4	4.85
INDIANA (Bloomington)	5	4.83
NORTHWESTERN (Kellog)	6	4.80
ILLINOIS (Urbana)	7	4.75
N.Y.U. (Stern)	8	4.71
PITTSBURGH (Katz)	9	4.70
TEXAS (Austin)	10	4.67
DUKE (Fuqua)	11	4.62
PURDUE (Krannert)	12	4.57
USC (Los Angeles)	13	4.49

The GOURMAN REPORT
PART VIII

**A RATING OF THE TOP 50
MBA/MANAGEMENT SCHOOLS**

A RATING OF THE TOP 50 MBA/MANAGEMENT SCHOOLS
Leading Institutions

INSTITUTION	Rank	Score
HARVARD	1	4.94
PENNSYLVANIA (Wharton)	2	4.93
STANFORD	3	4.92
M.I.T. (Sloan)	4	4.91
CHICAGO	5	4.90
COLUMBIA	6	4.89
NORTHWESTERN (Kellogg)	7	4.88
UCLA (Anderson)	8	4.87
CALIFORNIA, BERKELEY (Haas)	9	4.86
VIRGINIA (Darden)	10	4.85
INDIANA (Bloomington)	11	4.84
PITTSBURGH (Katz)	12	4.83
DUKE (Fuqua)	13	4.82
CORNELL (Johnson)	14	4.81
N.Y.U. (Stern)	15	4.80
DARTMOUTH (Tuck)	16	4.79
CARNEGIE-MELLON	17	4.78
MICHIGAN (Ann Arbor)	18	4.77
ILLINOIS (Urbana)	19	4.76
NORTH CAROLINA (Kenan-Flager)	20	4.75
TEXAS (Austin)	21	4.74
PURDUE (Krannert)	22	4.73
WASHINGTON (Seattle)	23	4.72
USC (Los Angeles)	24	4.71
TEXAS A&M (College Station)	25	4.70
MICHIGAN STATE (Broad)	26	4.68
WISCONSIN (Madison)	27	4.66
MINNESOTA (Carlson)	28	4.64
CASE WESTERN RESERVE (Weatherhead)	29	4.62
WASHINGTON (Olin) St. Louis	30	4.60
IOWA (Iowa City)	31	4.58
BARUCH (CUNY)	32	4.57
TULANE (Freeman)	33	4.54
PENN STATE (Smeal)	34	4.52
OHIO STATE (Fisher) Columbus	35	4.51
GEORGE WASHINGTON	36	4.50
ROCHESTER (Simon)	37	4.48
LEHIGH	38	4.46
FLORIDA (Gainesville)	39	4.43
HOUSTON	40	4.41
BUFFALO (SUNY)	41	4.40
NOTRE DAME	42	4.37
UTAH (Salt Lake City) (Eccles)	43	4.36
OREGON (Eugene)	44	4.33
ARIZONA STATE	45	4.32
SMU (Cox)	46	4.30
SYRACUSE	47	4.26
EMORY	48	4.24
GEORGIA TECH (Allen)	49	4.21
SOUTH CAROLINA	50	4.18

A RATING OF THE TOP 50 MBA/MANAGEMENT SCHOOLS

RATING CATEGORIES	Numerical Range
Very Strong	4.73-4.99
Strong	4.51-4.72
Good	4.18-4.50

SCHOOL (In Alphabetical Order)	Gourman National Ranking	Gourman National Score
ARIZONA STATE UNIVERSITY .... College of Business Tempe, Arizona	45	4.32
BARUCH COLLEGE – The City University of New York .... School of Business and Public Administration New York, New York	32	4.57
UNIVERSITY OF CALIFORNIA, BERKELEY .... Haas School of Business Administration Berkeley, California	9	4.86
UNIVERSITY OF CALIFORNIA, LOS ANGELES (UCLA) ...... Anderson Graduate School of Management Los Angeles, California	8	4.87
CARNEGIE-MELLON UNIVERSITY .... Graduate School of Industrial Administration Pittsburgh, Pennsylvania	17	4.78
CASE WESTERN RESERVE UNIVERSITY .... Weatherhead School of Management Cleveland, Ohio	29	4.62
UNIVERSITY OF CHICAGO .... Graduate School of Business Chicago, Illinois	5	4.90
COLUMBIA UNIVERSITY .... Graduate School of Business New York, New York	6	4.89
CORNELL UNIVERSITY .... Johnson Graduate School of Management Ithaca, New York	14	4.81
DARTMOUTH COLLEGE .... The Amous Tuck School of Business Administration Hanover, New Hampshire	16	4.79

A RATING OF THE TOP 50 MBA/MANAGEMENT SCHOOLS (Continued)

RATING CATEGORIES	Numerical Range
Very Strong	4.73-4.99
Strong	4.51-4.72
Good	4.18-4.50

SCHOOL (In Alphabetical Order)	Gourman National Ranking	Gourman National Score
DUKE UNIVERSITY . . . . Fuqua School of Business Durham, North Carolina	13	4.82
EMORY UNIVERSITY . . . . Business School Atlanta, Georgia	48	4.24
UNIVERSITY OF FLORIDA . . . . Graduate School of Business Administration Gainesville, Florida	39	4.43
GEORGE WASHINGTON UNIVERSITY . . . . School of Government and Business Administration Washington, D.C.	36	4.50
GEORGIA INSTITUTE OF TECHNOLOGY . . . . Allen College of Management Atlanta, Georgia	49	4.21
HARVARD UNIVERSITY . . . . Graduate School of Business Administration Boston, Massachusetts	1	4.94
UNIVERSITY OF HOUSTON . . . . College of Business Administration Houston, Texas	40	4.41
UNIVERSITY OF ILLINOIS AT URBANA-CHAMPAIGN . . . . College of Commerce and Business Administration Champaign, Illinois	19	4.76
INDIANA UNIVERSITY . . . . The Graduate School of Business Bloomington, Indiana	11	4.84
UNIVERSITY OF IOWA . . . . College of Business Administration Iowa City, Iowa	31	4.58

A RATING OF THE TOP 50 MBA/MANAGEMENT SCHOOLS (Continued)

RATING CATEGORIES	Numerical Range
Very Strong	4.73-4.99
Strong	4.51-4.72
Good	4.18-4.50

SCHOOL (In Alphabetical Order)	Gourman National Ranking	Gourman National Score
LEHIGH UNIVERSITY .... College of Business and Economics Bethlehem, Pennsylvania	38	4.46
MASSACHUSETTS INSTITUTE OF TECHNOLOGY .... Alfred P. Sloan School of Management Cambridge, Massachusetts	4	4.91
UNIVERSITY OF MICHIGAN .... Graduate School of Business Administration Ann Arbor, Michigan	18	4.77
MICHIGAN STATE UNIVERSITY .... Broad School of Management East Lansing, Michigan	26	4.68
UNIVERSITY OF MINNESOTA .... Carlson School of Management Minneapolis, Minnesota	28	4.64
NEW YORK UNIVERSITY .... Stern School of Business New York, New York	15	4.80
UNIVERSITY OF NORTH CAROLINA AT CHAPEL HILL ...... Kenan-Flagler Business School Chapel Hill, North Carolina	20	4.75
NORTHWESTERN UNIVERSITY .... J.L. Kellogg Graduate School of Management Evanston, Illinois	7	4.88
UNIVERSITY OF NOTRE DAME .... College of Business Administration Notre Dame, Indiana	42	4.37
OHIO STATE UNIVERSITY .... Fisher College of Business Columbus, Ohio	35	4.51

A RATING OF THE TOP 50 MBA/MANAGEMENT SCHOOLS (Continued)

RATING CATEGORIES	Numerical Range
Very Strong	4.73-4.99
Strong	4.51-4.72
Good	4.18-4.50

SCHOOL (In Alphabetical Order)	Gourman National Ranking	Gourman National Score
UNIVERSITY OF OREGON .... Graduate School of Management Eugene, Oregon	44	4.33
UNIVERSITY OF PENNSYLVANIA .... The Wharton School Philadelphia, Pennsylvania	2	4.93
PENNSYLVANIA STATE UNIVERSITY .... Smeal College of Business Administration University Park, Pennsylvania	34	4.52
UNIVERSITY OF PITTSBURGH .... Katz Graduate School of Business Pittsburgh, Pennsylvania	12	4.83
PURDUE UNIVERSITY .... Krannert Graduate School of Management West Lafayette, Indiana	22	4.73
UNIVERSITY OF ROCHESTER .... Simon Graduate School of Business Administration Rochester, New York	37	4.48
UNIVERSITY OF SOUTH CAROLINA .... Graduate School of Business Columbia, South Carolina	50	4.18
UNIVERSITY OF SOUTHERN CALIFORNIA .... Graduate School of Business Administration Los Angeles, California	24	4.71
SOUTHERN METHODIST UNIVERSITY .... Edwin L. Cox School of Business Dallas, Texas	46	4.30
STANFORD UNIVERSITY .... Graduate School of Business Stanford, California	3	4.92

A RATING OF THE TOP 50 MBA/MANAGEMENT SCHOOLS (Continued)

RATING CATEGORIES	Numerical Range
Very Strong	4.73-4.99
Strong	4.51-4.72
Good	4.18-4.50

SCHOOL (In Alphabetical Order)	Gourman National Ranking	Gourman National Score
STATE UNIVERSITY OF NEW YORK AT BUFFALO . . . . School of Management Buffalo, New York	41	4.40
SYRACUSE UNIVERSITY . . . . School of Management Syracuse, New York	47	4.26
UNIVERSITY OF TEXAS AT AUSTIN . . . . Graduate School of Business Austin, Texas	21	4.74
TEXAS A&M UNIVERSITY . . . . College of Business Administration College Station, Texas	25	4.70
TULANE UNIVERSITY . . . . A.B. Freeman School of Business New Orleans, Louisiana	33	4.54
UNIVERSITY OF UTAH . . . . Eccles School of Business Salt Lake City, Utah	43	4.36
UNIVERSITY OF VIRGINIA . . . . Colgate Darden Graduate School of Business Administration Charlottesville, Virginia	10	4.85
UNIVERSITY OF WASHINGTON . . . . Graduate School of Business Administration Seattle, Washington	23	4.72
WASHINGTON UNIVERSITY . . . . Olin School of Business St. Louis, Missouri	30	4.60
UNIVERSITY OF WISCONSIN – MADISON . . . . School of Business Madison, Wisconsin	27	4.66

The GOURMAN REPORT
PART IX

**A RATING OF THE TOP 50
DOCTORAL PROGRAMS
IN BUSINESS AND MANAGEMENT**

A RATING OF THE TOP 50 DOCTORAL PROGRAMS IN BUSINESS AND MANAGEMENT OF THE GOURMAN REPORT
Leading Institutions

INSTITUTION	Rank	Score
HARVARD	1	4.94
PENNSYLVANIA (Wharton)	2	4.93
STANFORD	3	4.92
M.I.T. (Sloan)	4	4.91
COLUMBIA	5	4.90
CHICAGO	6	4.89
NORTHWESTERN (Kellogg)	7	4.88
INDIANA (Bloomington)	8	4.87
CALIFORNIA, BERKELEY (Haas)	9	4.86
UCLA (Anderson)	10	4.85
MICHIGAN (Ann Arbor)	11	4.84
PITTSBURGH (Katz)	12	4.83
N.Y.U. (Stern)	13	4.82
TEXAS (Austin)	14	4.81
CORNELL (Johnson)	15	4.80
VIRGINIA (Darden)	16	4.79
PURDUE (Krannert)	17	4.78
NORTH CAROLINA (Kenan-Flagler)	18	4.77
CARNEGIE-MELLON	19	4.76
DUKE (Fuqua)	20	4.75
WASHINGTON (Seattle)	21	4.74
ILLINOIS (Urbana)	22	4.73
TEXAS A&M (College Station)	23	4.72
USC (Los Angeles)	24	4.71
OHIO STATE (Fisher)	25	4.70
WISCONSIN (Madison)	26	4.68
IOWA (Iowa City)	27	4.66
CASE WESTERN RESERVE (Weatherhead)	28	4.65
MICHIGAN STATE (Broad)	29	4.62
MINNESOTA (Carlson)	30	4.60
BARUCH (CUNY)	31	4.58
PENN STATE (Smeal)	32	4.55
WASHINGTON (St. Louis, Olin)	33	4.54
LEHIGH	34	4.53
GEORGE WASHINGTON	35	4.49
ROCHESTER (SIMON)	36	4.48
FLORIDA (Gainesville)	37	4.47
HOUSTON	38	4.44
BUFFALO (SUNY)	39	4.43
ARIZONA STATE	40	4.41
UTAH (Eccles)	41	4.40
TULANE (Freeman)	42	4.36
OREGON (Eugene)	43	4.32
COLORADO (Boulder)	44	4.30
SYRACUSE	45	4.27
GEORGIA TECH (Allen)	46	4.25
LSU (Baton Rouge)	47	4.22
SOUTH CAROLINA (Columbia)	48	4.21
ARIZONA (Tucson)	49	4.20
VANDERBILT (Owen)	50	4.19

A RATING OF THE TOP 50 DOCTORAL PROGRAMS IN BUSINESS AND MANAGEMENT

RATING CATEGORIES	Numerical Range
Very Strong	4.70-4.99
Strong	4.53-4.69
Good	4.19-4.50

SCHOOL (In Alphabetical Order)	Gourman National Ranking	Gourman National Score
UNIVERSITY OF ARIZONA .... College of Business and Public Administration Tucson, Arizona	49	4.20
ARIZONA STATE UNIVERSITY .... College of Business Tempe, Arizona	40	4.41
BARUCH COLLEGE – The City University of New York .... School of Business and Public Administration New York, New York	31	4.58
UNIVERSITY OF CALIFORNIA, BERKELEY .... Haas School of Business Administration Berkeley, California	9	4.86
UNIVERSITY OF CALIFORNIA, LOS ANGELES (UCLA) ...... Anderson GraduateSchool of Management Los Angeles, California	10	4.85
CARNEGIE-MELLON UNIVERSITY .... Graduate School of Industrial Administration Pittsburgh, Pennsylvania	19	4.76
CASE WESTERN RESERVE UNIVERSITY .... Weatherhead School of Management Cleveland, Ohio	28	4.65
UNIVERSITY OF CHICAGO .... Graduate School of Business Chicago, Illinois	6	4.89
UNIVERSITY OF COLORADO .... Graduate School of Business Administration Boulder, Colorado	44	4.30
COLUMBIA UNIVERSITY .... Graduate School of Business New York, New York	5	4.90

A RATING OF THE TOP 50 DOCTORAL PROGRAMS IN BUSINESS AND MANAGEMENT (Continued)

RATING CATEGORIES	Numerical Range
Very Strong	4.70-4.99
Strong	4.53-4.69
Good	4.19-4.50

SCHOOL (In Alphabetical Order)	Gourman National Ranking	Gourman National Score
CORNELL UNIVERSITY . . . . Johnson Graduate School of Management Ithaca, New York	15	4.80
DUKE UNIVERSITY . . . . Fuqua School of Business Durham, North Carolina	20	4.75
UNIVERSITY OF FLORIDA . . . . Graduate School of Business Administration Gainesville, Florida	37	4.47
GEORGE WASHINGTON UNIVERSITY . . . . School of Government and Business Administration Washington, D.C.	35	4.49
GEORGIA INSTITUTE OF TECHNOLOGY . . . . Allen College of Management Atlanta, Georgia	46	4.25
HARVARD UNIVERSITY . . . . Graduate School of Business Administration Boston, Massachusetts	1	4.94
UNIVERSITY OF HOUSTON . . . . College of Business Administration Houston, Texas	38	4.44
UNIVERSITY OF ILLINOIS AT URBANA-CHAMPAIGN . . . . College of Commerce and Business Administration Champaign, Illinois	22	4.73
INDIANA UNIVERSITY . . . . The Graduate School of Business Bloomington, Indiana	8	4.87
UNIVERSITY OF IOWA . . . . College of Business Administration Iowa City, Iowa	27	4.66

A RATING OF THE TOP 50 DOCTORAL PROGRAMS IN BUSINESS AND MANAGEMENT (Continued)

RATING CATEGORIES	Numerical Range
Very Strong	4.70-4.99
Strong	4.53-4.69
Good	4.19-4.50

SCHOOL (In Alphabetical Order)	Gourman National Ranking	Gourman National Score
LEHIGH UNIVERSITY .... College of Business and Economics Bethlehem, Pennsylvania	34	4.53
LOUISIANA STATE UNIVERSITY .... College of Business Administration Baton Rouge, Louisiana	47	4.22
MASSACHUSETTS INSTITUTE OF TECHNOLOGY .... Alfred P. Sloan School of Management Cambridge, Massachusetts	4	4.91
UNIVERSITY OF MICHIGAN .... Graduate School of Business Administration Ann Arbor, Michigan	11	4.84
MICHIGAN STATE UNIVERSITY .... Broad School of Management East Lansing, Michigan	29	4.62
UNIVERSITY OF MINNESOTA .... Carlson School of Management Minneapolis, Minnesota	30	4.60
NEW YORK UNIVERSITY .... Stern School of Business New York, New York	13	4.82
UNIVERSITY OF NORTH CAROLINA AT CHAPEL HILL ...... Kenan-Flagler Busienss School Chapel Hill, North Carolina	18	4.77
NORTHWESTERN UNIVERSITY .... J.L. Kellogg Graduate School of Management Evanston, Illinois	7	4.88
OHIO STATE UNIVERSITY .... Fisher College of Business Columbus, Ohio	25	4.70

A RATING OF THE TOP 50 DOCTORAL PROGRAMS IN BUSINESS AND MANAGEMENT (Continued)

RATING CATEGORIES	Numerical Range
Very Strong	4.70-4.99
Strong	4.53-4.69
Good	4.19-4.50

SCHOOL (In Alphabetical Order)	Gourman National Ranking	Gourman National Score
UNIVERSITY OF OREGON . . . . Graduate School of Management Eugene, Oregon	43	4.32
UNIVERSITY OF PENNSYLVANIA . . . . The Wharton School Philadelphia, Pennsylvania	2	4.93
PENNSYLVANIA STATE UNIVERSITY . . . . Smeal College of Business Administration University Park, Pennsylvania	32	4.55
UNIVERSITY OF PITTSBURGH . . . . Katz Graduate School of Business Pittsburgh, Pennsylvania	12	4.83
PURDUE UNIVERSITY . . . . Krannert Graduate School of Management West Lafayette, Indiana	17	4.78
UNIVERSITY OF ROCHESTER . . . . Simon Graduate School of Business Administration Rochester, New York	36	4.48
UNIVERSITY OF SOUTH CAROLINA . . . . Graduate School of Business Columbia, South Carolina	48	4.21
UNIVERSITY OF SOUTHERN CALIFORNIA . . . . Graduate School of Business Administration Los Angeles, California	24	4.71
STANFORD UNIVERSITY . . . . Graduate School of Business Stanford, California	3	4.92
STATE UNIVERSITY OF NEW YORK AT BUFFALO . . . . School of Management Buffalo, New York	39	4.43

A RATING OF THE TOP 50 DOCTORAL PROGRAMS IN BUSINESS AND MANAGEMENT (Continued)

RATING CATEGORIES	Numerical Range
Very Strong	4.70-4.99
Strong	4.53-4.69
Good	4.19-4.50

SCHOOL (In Alphabetical Order)	Gourman National Ranking	Gourman National Score
SYRACUSE UNIVERSITY . . . . School of Management Syracuse, New York	45	4.27
UNIVERSITY OF TEXAS AT AUSTIN . . . . Graduate School of Business Austin, Texas	14	4.81
TEXAS A&M UNIVERSITY . . . . College of Business Administration College Station, Texas	23	4.72
TULANE UNIVERSITY . . . . A.B. Freeman School of Business New Orleans, Louisiana	42	4.36
UNIVERSITY OF UTAH . . . . Eccles School of Business Salt Lake City, Utah	41	4.40
VANDERBILT UNIVERSITY . . . . Owen Graduate School of Management Nashville, Tennessee	50	4.19
UNIVERSITY OF VIRGINIA . . . . Colgate Darden Graduate School of Business Administration Charlottesville, Virginia	16	4.79
UNIVERSITY OF WASHINGTON . . . . Graduate School of Business Administration Seattle, Washington	21	4.74
WASHINGTON UNIVERSITY . . . . Olin School of Business St. Louis, Missouri	33	4.54
UNIVERSITY OF WISCONSIN–MADISON . . . . School of Business Milwaukee, Wisconsin	26	4.68

The GOURMAN REPORT
PART X

**A RATING OF
LEADING INTERNATIONAL UNIVERSITIES**

A RATING OF GRADUATE QUALITY INSTITUTIONS

INTERNATIONAL UNIVERSITIES
Leading Institutions

Forty-nine institutions with scores in the 4.0-5.0 range, in rank order

INSTITUTION	COUNTRY	Rank	Score
PARIS (All Campuses)	France	1	4.92
OXFORD	United Kingdom	2	4.91
CAMBRIDGE	United Kingdom	3	4.90
HEIDELBERG	Federal Republic of Germany	4	4.89
MONTPELLIER I, II, III	France	5	4.85
MUNICH	Federal Republic of Germany	6	4.83
LYON I, II, III	France	7	4.81
LILLE I, II, III	France	8	4.80
EDINBURGH	United Kingdom (Scotland)	9	4.79
VIENNA	Austria	10	4.77
AIX-MARSEILLE I, II, III	France	11	4.75
BRUSSELS	Belgium	12	4.73
ZÜRICH	Switzerland	13	4.71
GÖTTINGEN	Federal Republic of Germany	14	4.70
BORDEAUX I, II, III	France	15	4.68
NANCY I, II	France	16	4.65
TORONTO	Canada	17	4.63
McGILL	Canada	18	4.60
GENEVA	Switzerland	19	4.59
TÜEBINGEN	Federal Republic of Germany	20	4.56
ERLANGEN-NÜRNBERG	Federal Republic of Germany	21	4.54
GRENOBLE I, II, III	France	22	4.53
DIJON	France	23	4.52
MARBURG	Federal Republic of Germany	24	4.49
RENNES I, II	France	25	4.45
TOULOUSE I, II, III	France	26	4.44
ROUEN	France	27	4.42
CLERMONT-FERRAND	France	28	4.41
BONN	Federal Republic of Germany	29	4.36
COLOGNE	Federal Republic of Germany	30	4.35
NICE	France	31	4.33
HEBREW	Israel	32	4.32
FRANKFURT	Federal Republic of Germany	33	4.30
LOUVAIN	Belgium	34	4.24
STOCKHOLM	Sweden	35	4.20
MÜNSTER	Federal Republic of Germany	36	4.17
COPENHAGEN	Denmark	37	4.16
MAINZ	Federal Republic of Germany	38	4.15
WÜRZBURG	Federal Republic of Germany	39	4.14
BESANCON	France	40	4.13
AMSTERDAM	Netherlands	41	4.12
LONDON	United Kingdom	42	4.11
TOKYO	Japan	43	4.10
NANTES	France	44	4.09
POITIERS	France	45	4.08
ORLEANS	France	46	4.07
CAEN	France	47	4.05
BOLOGNA	Italy	48	4.04
MADRID	Spain	49	4.03

The GOURMAN REPORT

PART XI

CRIMINAL JUSTICE/CRIMINOLOGY
GRADUATE PROGRAMS
NOT ON THE APPROVED LIST OF
THE GOURMAN REPORT

CRIMINAL JUSTICE/CRIMINOLOGY GRADUATE PROGRAMS
Not On The Approved List of The Gourman Report

IN ALPHABETICAL ORDER

INSTITUTION	STATE
ALBANY STATE COLLEGE	Georgia
AMERICAN INTERNATIONAL COLLEGE	Massachusetts
AMERICAN UNIVERSITY	Washington D.C.
ARIZONA STATE UNIVERSITY (Tempe)	Arizona
ARMSTRONG STATE COLLEGE	Georgia
AUBURN (Montgomery)	Alabama
BOSTON UNIVERSITY	Massachusetts
BUFFALO STATE COLLEGE	New York
CALIFORNIA STATE UNIVERSITY (Fresno)	California
CALIFORNIA STATE UNIVERSITY (Long Beach)	California
CALIFORNIA STATE UNIVERSITY (Los Angeles)	California
CALIFORNIA STATE UNIVERSITY (Sacramento)	California
CALIFORNIA STATE UNIVERSITY (San Bernardino)	California
CENTRAL MISSOURI STATE UNIVERSITY	Missouri
CHICAGO STATE UNIVERSITY	Illinois
CITY UNIVERSITY OF NEW YORK THE GRADUATE SCHOOL	New York
CLAREMONT GRADUATE SCHOOL	California
CLARK ATLANTIC UNIVERSITY	Georgia
EASTERN KENTUCKY UNIVERSITY	Kentucky
EASTERN MICHIGAN UNIVERSITY	Michigan
EAST TENNESSEE STATE UNIVERSITY	Tennessee
FLORIDA INTERNATIONAL UNIVERSITY	Florida
FLORIDA STATE UNIVERSITY (Tallahassee)	Florida
GEORGE WASHINGTON UNIVERSITY	Washington D.C.
GEORGIA STATE UNIVERSITY (Atlanta)	Georgia
GRAMBLING STATE UNIVERSITY	Louisiana
ILLINOIS STATE UNIVERSITY (Normal)	Illinois
INDIANA STATE UNIVERSITY (Terre Haute)	Indiana
INDIANA UNIVERSITY (Bloomington)	Indiana
INDIANA UNIVERSITY NORTHWEST (Gary)	Indiana
INDIANA UNIVERSITY OF PENNSYLVANIA	Pennsylvania
INDIANA UNIVERSITY –SOUTH BEND	Indiana
JACKSONVILLE STATE UNIVERSITY	Alabama

CRIMINAL JUSTICE/CRIMINOLOGY GRADUATE PROGRAMS
Not On The Approved List of The Gourman Report (Continued)

IN ALPHABETICAL ORDER

INSTITUTION	STATE
JERSEY CITY STATE COLLEGE	New Jersey
JOHN JAY COLLEGE OF CRIMINAL JUSTICE OF THE (CUNY)	New York
KENT STATE UNIVERSITY	Ohio
LONG ISLAND UNIVERSITY (C.W. Post Campus)	New York
L.S.U. (Baton Rouge)	Louisiana
MARSHALL UNIVERSITY	West Virginia
MICHIGAN STATE UNIVERSITY	Michigan
MIDDLE TENNESSEE STATE UNIVERSITY	Tennessee
MOREHEAD STATE UNIVERSITY	Kentucky
NEW MEXICO STATE UNIVERSITY	New Mexico
NORTH CAROLINA CENTRAL UNIVERSITY	North Carolina
NORTHEASTERN UNIVERSITY	Massachusetts
NORTHEAST LOUISIANA UNIVERSITY	Louisiana
OHIO STATE UNIVERSITY (Columbus)	Ohio
OKLAHOMA CITY UNIVERSITY	Oklahoma
OKLAHOMA STATE	Oklahoma
PENN STATE (University Park)	Pennsylvania
PORTLAND STATE UNIVERSITY	Oregon
RADFORD UNIVERSITY	Virginia
RUTGERS, THE STATE UNIVERSITY OF NEW JERSEY (Newark)	New Jersey
ST. CLOUD STATE UNIVERSITY	Minnesota
SAINT JOSEPH'S UNIVERSITY	Pennsylvania
SAM HOUSTON STATE UNIVERSITY	Texas
SAN JOSE STATE UNIVERSITY	California
SHIPPENSBURGH UNIVERSITY OF PENNSYLVANIA	Pennsylvania
SOUTHEAST MISSOURI STATE UNIVERSITY	Missouri
SOUTHERN ILLINOIS UNIVERSITY (Carbondale)	Illinois
SOUTHWEST TEXAS STATE UNIVERSITY	Texas
SUNY (Albany)	New York
TEMPLE UNIVERSITY (Philadelphia)	Pennsylvania
TENNESSEE STATE UNIVERSITY	Tennessee
UNIVERSITY OF ALABAMA (Birmingham)	Alabama
UNIVERSITY OF ALABAMA (Tuscaloosa)	Alabama)

IN ALPHABETICAL ORDER

INSTITUTION	STATE
UNIVERSITY OF ARKANSAS (Little Rock)	Arkansas
UNIVERSITY OF BALTIMORE	Maryland
UNIVERSITY OF CALIFORNIA (Irvine)	California
UNIVERSITY OF CENTRAL FLORIDA	Florida
UNIVERSITY OF CENTRAL OKLAHOMA	Oklahoma
UNIVERSITY OF CENTRAL TEXAS	Texas
UNIVERSITY OF CINCINNATI	Ohio
UNIVERSITY OF DELAWARE (Newark)	Delaware
UNIVERSITY OF DETROIT MERCY	Michigan
UNIVERSITY OF ILLINOIS (Chicago)	Illinois
UNIVERSITY OF LOUISVILLE	Kentucky
UNIVERSITY OF MARYLAND (College Park)	Maryland
UNIVERSITY OF MASSACHUSETTS LOWELL	Massachusetts
UNIVERSITY OF MEMPHIS	Tennessee
UNIVERSITY OF MISSOURI (Kansas City)	Missouri
UNIVERSITY OF NEBRASKA (Omaha)	Nebraska
UNIVERSITY OF NEW HAVEN	Connecticut
UNIVERSITY OF NORTH CAROLINA (Charlotte)	North Carolina
UNIVERSITY OF NORTH FLORIDA	Florida
UNIVERSITY OF SOUTH CAROLINA (Columbia)	South Carolina
UNIVERSITY OF SOUTHERN MISSISSIPPI	Mississippi
UNIVERSITY OF SOUTH FLORIDA (Tampa)	Florida
UNIVERSITY OF TENNESSEE (Chattanooga)	Tennessee
UNIVERSITY OF TEXAS (Arlington)	Texas
UNIVERSITY OF TEXAS (Tyler)	Texas
UNIVERSITY OF WISCONSIN (Milwaukee)	Wisconsin
VALDOSTA STATE UNIVERSITY	Georgia
VILLANOVA UNIVERSITY	Pennsylvania
VIRGINIA COMMONWEALTH UNIVERSITY	Virginia
WASHINGTON STATE UNIVERSITY (Pullman)	Washington
WAYNE STATE UNIVERSITY	Michigan
WESTCHESTER UNIVERSITY OF PENNSYLVANIA	Pennsylvania
WESTERN ILLINOIS UNIVERSITY	Illinois

CRIMINAL JUSTICE/CRIMINOLOGY GRADUATE PROGRAMS
Not On The Approved List of The Gourman Report (Continued)

IN ALPHABETICAL ORDER

INSTITUTION	STATE
WESTERN MICHIGAN UNIVERSITY	Michigan
WESTFIELD STATE COLLEGE	Massachusetts
WICHITA STATE UNIVERSITY	Kansas
XAVIER UNIVERSITY	Ohio
YOUNGSTOWN STATE UNIVERSITY	Ohio

The GOURMAN REPORT
PART XII

**EDUCATION
NOT ON THE APPROVED LIST
OF THE GOURMAN REPORT**

**EDUCATION DEGREES/MAJORS (at any level)
Not on the Approved List of THE GOURMAN REPORT**

**ELEMENTARY EDUCATION
Not on the Approved List of THE GOURMAN REPORT**

**SECONDARY EDUCATION
Not on the Approved List of THE GOURMAN REPORT**

**TEACHER EDUCATION
Not on the Approved List of THE GOURMAN REPORT**

**GRADUATE DEPARTMENT OF EDUCATION
COLLEGES/UNIVERSITIES
Not on the Approved List of THE GOURMAN REPORT**

**POSTSECONDARY EDUCATION COMMISSION
Not on the Approved List of THE GOURMAN REPORT**

**STATE DEPARTMENT OF EDUCATION
Not on the Approved List of THE GOURMAN REPORT**

EDUCATION DEGREES/MAJORS (AT ANY LEVEL)
Not On The Approved List of The Gourman Report

IN ALPHABETICAL ORDER

STATE		STATE	
ALABAMA	Not Approved	MONTANA	Not Approved
ALASKA	Not Approved	NEBRASKA	Not Approved
ARIZONA	Not Approved	NEVADA	Not Approved
ARKANSAS	Not Approved	NEW HAMPSHIRE	Not Approved
CALIFORNIA	Not Approved	NEW JERSEY	Not Approved
COLORADO	Not Approved	NEW MEXICO	Not Approved
CONNECTICUT	Not Approved	NEW YORK	Not Approved
DELAWARE	Not Approved	NORTH CAROLINA	Not Approved
DISTRICT OF COLUMBIA	Not Approved	NORTH DAKOTA	Not Approved
FLORIDA	Not Approved	OHIO	Not Approved
GEORGIA	Not Approved	OKLAHOMA	Not Approved
HAWAII	Not Approved	OREGON	Not Approved
IDAHO	Not Approved	PENNSYLVANIA	Not Approved
ILLINOIS	Not Approved	RHODE ISLAND	Not Approved
INDIANA	Not Approved	SOUTH CAROLINA	Not Approved
IOWA	Not Approved	SOUTH DAKOTA	Not Approved
KANSAS	Not Approved	TENNESSEE	Not Approved
KENTUCKY	Not Approved	TEXAS	Not Approved
LOUISIANA	Not Approved	UTAH	Not Approved
MAINE	Not Approved	VERMONT	Not Approved
MARYLAND	Not Approved	VIRGINIA	Not Approved
MASSACHUSETTS	Not Approved	WASHINGTON	Not Approved
MICHIGAN	Not Approved	WEST VIRGINIA	Not Approved
MINNESOTA	Not Approved	WISCONSIN	Not Approved
MISSISSIPPI	Not Approved	WYOMING	Not Approved
MISSOURI	Not Approved		

NOTE:

THE GOURMAN REPORT does not approve of Education Degrees/Majors Public and Private Colleges/Universities in each state. Meaningless courses of no substance down grades the major. The major should be abolished by all institutions.

ELEMENTARY EDUCATION
Not On The Approved List of The Gourman Report

IN ALPHABETICAL ORDER

STATE		STATE	
ALABAMA	Not Approved	MONTANA	Not Approved
ALASKA	Not Approved	NEBRASKA	Not Approved
ARIZONA	Not Approved	NEVADA	Not Approved
ARKANSAS	Not Approved	NEW HAMPSHIRE	Not Approved
CALIFORNIA	Not Approved	NEW JERSEY	Not Approved
COLORADO	Not Approved	NEW MEXICO	Not Approved
CONNECTICUT	Not Approved	NEW YORK	Not Approved
DELAWARE	Not Approved	NORTH CAROLINA	Not Approved
DISTRICT OF COLUMBIA	Not Approved	NORTH DAKOTA	Not Approved
FLORIDA	Not Approved	OHIO	Not Approved
GEORGIA	Not Approved	OKLAHOMA	Not Approved
HAWAII	Not Approved	OREGON	Not Approved
IDAHO	Not Approved	PENNSYLVANIA	Not Approved
ILLINOIS	Not Approved	RHODE ISLAND	Not Approved
INDIANA	Not Approved	SOUTH CAROLINA	Not Approved
IOWA	Not Approved	SOUTH DAKOTA	Not Approved
KANSAS	Not Approved	TENNESSEE	Not Approved
KENTUCKY	Not Approved	TEXAS	Not Approved
LOUISIANA	Not Approved	UTAH	Not Approved
MAINE	Not Approved	VERMONT	Not Approved
MARYLAND	Not Approved	VIRGINIA	Not Approved
MASSACHUSETTS	Not Approved	WASHINGTON	Not Approved
MICHIGAN	Not Approved	WEST VIRGINIA	Not Approved
MINNESOTA	Not Approved	WISCONSIN	Not Approved
MISSISSIPPI	Not Approved	WYOMING	Not Approved
MISSOURI	Not Approved		

NOTE:

Preparation for Elementary Education in both Public and Private Colleges/Universities in each state not on the approved list of THE GOURMAN REPORT.

SECONDARY EDUCATION
Not On The Approved List of The Gourman Report

IN ALPHABETICAL ORDER

STATE		STATE	
ALABAMA	Not Approved	MONTANA	Not Approved
ALASKA	Not Approved	NEBRASKA	Not Approved
ARIZONA	Not Approved	NEVADA	Not Approved
ARKANSAS	Not Approved	NEW HAMPSHIRE	Not Approved
CALIFORNIA	Not Approved	NEW JERSEY	Not Approved
COLORADO	Not Approved	NEW MEXICO	Not Approved
CONNECTICUT	Not Approved	NEW YORK	Not Approved
DELAWARE	Not Approved	NORTH CAROLINA	Not Approved
DISTRICT OF COLUMBIA	Not Approved	NORTH DAKOTA	Not Approved
FLORIDA	Not Approved	OHIO	Not Approved
GEORGIA	Not Approved	OKLAHOMA	Not Approved
HAWAII	Not Approved	OREGON	Not Approved
IDAHO	Not Approved	PENNSYLVANIA	Not Approved
ILLINOIS	Not Approved	RHODE ISLAND	Not Approved
INDIANA	Not Approved	SOUTH CAROLINA	Not Approved
IOWA	Not Approved	SOUTH DAKOTA	Not Approved
KANSAS	Not Approved	TENNESSEE	Not Approved
KENTUCKY	Not Approved	TEXAS	Not Approved
LOUISIANA	Not Approved	UTAH	Not Approved
MAINE	Not Approved	VERMONT	Not Approved
MARYLAND	Not Approved	VIRGINIA	Not Approved
MASSACHUSETTS	Not Approved	WASHINGTON	Not Approved
MICHIGAN	Not Approved	WEST VIRGINIA	Not Approved
MINNESOTA	Not Approved	WISCONSIN	Not Approved
MISSISSIPPI	Not Approved	WYOMING	Not Approved
MISSOURI	Not Approved		

NOTE:

Preparation for Secondary Education in both Public and Private Colleges/Universities in each state not on the approved list of THE GOURMAN REPORT.

TEACHER EDUCATION
Not On The Approved List of The Gourman Report

IN ALPHABETICAL ORDER

STATE		STATE	
ALABAMA	Not Approved	MONTANA	Not Approved
ALASKA	Not Approved	NEBRASKA	Not Approved
ARIZONA	Not Approved	NEVADA	Not Approved
ARKANSAS	Not Approved	NEW HAMPSHIRE	Not Approved
CALIFORNIA	Not Approved	NEW JERSEY	Not Approved
COLORADO	Not Approved	NEW MEXICO	Not Approved
CONNECTICUT	Not Approved	NEW YORK	Not Approved
DELAWARE	Not Approved	NORTH CAROLINA	Not Approved
DISTRICT OF COLUMBIA	Not Approved	NORTH DAKOTA	Not Approved
FLORIDA	Not Approved	OHIO	Not Approved
GEORGIA	Not Approved	OKLAHOMA	Not Approved
HAWAII	Not Approved	OREGON	Not Approved
IDAHO	Not Approved	PENNSYLVANIA	Not Approved
ILLINOIS	Not Approved	RHODE ISLAND	Not Approved
INDIANA	Not Approved	SOUTH CAROLINA	Not Approved
IOWA	Not Approved	SOUTH DAKOTA	Not Approved
KANSAS	Not Approved	TENNESSEE	Not Approved
KENTUCKY	Not Approved	TEXAS	Not Approved
LOUISIANA	Not Approved	UTAH	Not Approved
MAINE	Not Approved	VERMONT	Not Approved
MARYLAND	Not Approved	VIRGINIA	Not Approved
MASSACHUSETTS	Not Approved	WASHINGTON	Not Approved
MICHIGAN	Not Approved	WEST VIRGINIA	Not Approved
MINNESOTA	Not Approved	WISCONSIN	Not Approved
MISSISSIPPI	Not Approved	WYOMING	Not Approved
MISSOURI	Not Approved		

NOTE:

Teacher Education preparation in both Public and Private Colleges/Universities in each state not on the approved list of THE GOURMAN REPORT.

GRADUATE DEPARTMENT OF EDUCATION COLLEGES/ UNIVERSITIES Not On The Approved List of The Gourman Report

IN ALPHABETICAL ORDER

STATE		STATE	
ALABAMA	Not Approved	MONTANA	Not Approved
ALASKA	Not Approved	NEBRASKA	Not Approved
ARIZONA	Not Approved	NEVADA	Not Approved
ARKANSAS	Not Approved	NEW HAMPSHIRE	Not Approved
CALIFORNIA	Not Approved	NEW JERSEY	Not Approved
COLORADO	Not Approved	NEW MEXICO	Not Approved
CONNECTICUT	Not Approved	NEW YORK	Not Approved
DELAWARE	Not Approved	NORTH CAROLINA	Not Approved
DISTRICT OF COLUMBIA	Not Approved	NORTH DAKOTA	Not Approved
FLORIDA	Not Approved	OHIO	Not Approved
GEORGIA	Not Approved	OKLAHOMA	Not Approved
HAWAII	Not Approved	OREGON	Not Approved
IDAHO	Not Approved	PENNSYLVANIA	Not Approved
ILLINOIS	Not Approved	RHODE ISLAND	Not Approved
INDIANA	Not Approved	SOUTH CAROLINA	Not Approved
IOWA	Not Approved	SOUTH DAKOTA	Not Approved
KANSAS	Not Approved	TENNESSEE	Not Approved
KENTUCKY	Not Approved	TEXAS	Not Approved
LOUISIANA	Not Approved	UTAH	Not Approved
MAINE	Not Approved	VERMONT	Not Approved
MARYLAND	Not Approved	VIRGINIA	Not Approved
MASSACHUSETTS	Not Approved	WASHINGTON	Not Approved
MICHIGAN	Not Approved	WEST VIRGINIA	Not Approved
MINNESOTA	Not Approved	WISCONSIN	Not Approved
MISSISSIPPI	Not Approved	WYOMING	Not Approved
MISSOURI	Not Approved		

NOTE:

THE GOURMAN REPORT does not approve of the Graduate Department of Education Public and Private Colleges/Universities in each state. The Department of Education should be abolished by each institution.

POSTSECONDARY EDUCATION COMMISSION
Not On The Approved List of The Gourman Report

IN ALPHABETICAL ORDER

STATE		STATE	
ALABAMA	Not Approved	MONTANA	Not Approved
ALASKA	Not Approved	NEBRASKA	Not Approved
ARIZONA	Not Approved	NEVADA	Not Approved
ARKANSAS	Not Approved	NEW HAMPSHIRE	Not Approved
CALIFORNIA	Not Approved	NEW JERSEY	Not Approved
COLORADO	Not Approved	NEW MEXICO	Not Approved
CONNECTICUT	Not Approved	NEW YORK	Not Approved
DELAWARE	Not Approved	NORTH CAROLINA	Not Approved
DISTRICT OF COLUMBIA	Not Approved	NORTH DAKOTA	Not Approved
FLORIDA	Not Approved	OHIO	Not Approved
GEORGIA	Not Approved	OKLAHOMA	Not Approved
HAWAII	Not Approved	OREGON	Not Approved
IDAHO	Not Approved	PENNSYLVANIA	Not Approved
ILLINOIS	Not Approved	RHODE ISLAND	Not Approved
INDIANA	Not Approved	SOUTH CAROLINA	Not Approved
IOWA	Not Approved	SOUTH DAKOTA	Not Approved
KANSAS	Not Approved	TENNESSEE	Not Approved
KENTUCKY	Not Approved	TEXAS	Not Approved
LOUISIANA	Not Approved	UTAH	Not Approved
MAINE	Not Approved	VERMONT	Not Approved
MARYLAND	Not Approved	VIRGINIA	Not Approved
MASSACHUSETTS	Not Approved	WASHINGTON	Not Approved
MICHIGAN	Not Approved	WEST VIRGINIA	Not Approved
MINNESOTA	Not Approved	WISCONSIN	Not Approved
MISSISSIPPI	Not Approved	WYOMING	Not Approved
MISSOURI	Not Approved		

NOTE:

THE GOURMAN REPORT does not approve of the Postsecondary Commission or any Commission in each state. Their recommendations on higher education does not meet the standard of complex issues of education with reference to colleges and universities. There is a definite omission of leadership which affect good judgment on action taken by the Commission.

STATE DEPARTMENT OF EDUCATION
Not On The Approved List of The Gourman Report

IN ALPHABETICAL ORDER

STATE		STATE	
ALABAMA	Not Approved	MONTANA	Not Approved
ALASKA	Not Approved	NEBRASKA	Not Approved
ARIZONA	Not Approved	NEVADA	Not Approved
ARKANSAS	Not Approved	NEW HAMPSHIRE	Not Approved
CALIFORNIA	Not Approved	NEW JERSEY	Not Approved
COLORADO	Not Approved	NEW MEXICO	Not Approved
CONNECTICUT	Not Approved	NEW YORK	Not Approved
DELAWARE	Not Approved	NORTH CAROLINA	Not Approved
DISTRICT OF COLUMBIA	Not Approved	NORTH DAKOTA	Not Approved
FLORIDA	Not Approved	OHIO	Not Approved
GEORGIA	Not Approved	OKLAHOMA	Not Approved
HAWAII	Not Approved	OREGON	Not Approved
IDAHO	Not Approved	PENNSYLVANIA	Not Approved
ILLINOIS	Not Approved	RHODE ISLAND	Not Approved
INDIANA	Not Approved	SOUTH CAROLINA	Not Approved
IOWA	Not Approved	SOUTH DAKOTA	Not Approved
KANSAS	Not Approved	TENNESSEE	Not Approved
KENTUCKY	Not Approved	TEXAS	Not Approved
LOUISIANA	Not Approved	UTAH	Not Approved
MAINE	Not Approved	VERMONT	Not Approved
MARYLAND	Not Approved	VIRGINIA	Not Approved
MASSACHUSETTS	Not Approved	WASHINGTON	Not Approved
MICHIGAN	Not Approved	WEST VIRGINIA	Not Approved
MINNESOTA	Not Approved	WISCONSIN	Not Approved
MISSISSIPPI	Not Approved	WYOMING	Not Approved
MISSOURI	Not Approved		

NOTE:

THE GOURMAN REPORT does not approve of the State Department of Education in each state with reference to their requirements for teacher certification.

The GOURMAN REPORT
PART XIII

**DEPARTMENTS OF GRADUATE EDUCATION
NOT ON THE APPROVED LIST OF
THE GOURMAN REPORT**

DEPARTMENTS OF GRADUATE EDUCATION
Not On The Approved List of The Gourman Report

RATING CATEGORIES	Numerical Range
Very Strong	4.51-4.99
Strong	4.01-4.49
Good	3.61-3.99
Acceptable Plus	3.01-3.59
Adequate	2.51-2.99
Marginal	2.01-2.49

Not Sufficient for Graduate Programs   0.

Department of Graduate Education INSTITUTION	Gourman Overall Academic Score (Combined Areas/Fields)	Administration (Attitude and Policy) (Quality of Leadership at All Levels of Administration)	Curriculum (Attractiveness of Program)	Faculty Effectiveness	Faculty (Quality of Research/ Scholarship)	Library Resources
Abilene Christian University .... Abilene, TX	0.38	0.35	0.	0.	0.	0.31
Adams State College .... Alamosa, CO	0.39	0.36	0.	0.	0.	0.32
Adelphi University .... Garden City, NY	0.45	0.37	0.	0.	0.	0.34
Alabama Agricultural and Mechanical University .... Normal, AL	0.31	0.32	0.	0.	0.	0.28
Alabama State University ...... Montgomery, AL	0.30	0.31	0.	0.	0.	0.27
Alaska Pacific University .... Anchorage, AK	0.31	0.29	0.	0.	0.	0.25
Albany State College .... Albany, GA	0.29	0.28	0.	0.	0.	0.22
Alcorn State University .... Lorman, MS	0.28	0.27	0.	0.	0.	0.19
Alfred University .... Alfred, NY	0.32	0.30	0.	0.	0.	0.31
American International College .. Springfield, MA	0.31	0.30	0.	0.	0.	0.30
American University .... Washington, D.C.	0.60	0.53	0.	0.	0.	0.49
Andrews University .... Berrien Springs, MI	0.37	0.36	0.	0.	0.	0.30
Angelo State University .... San Angelo, TX	0.41	0.40	0.	0.	0.	0.34
Appalachian State University ... Boone, NC	0.41	0.39	0.	0.	0.	0.32
Arizona State University .... Tempe, AZ	0.73	0.68	0.	0.	0.	0.78
Arkansas State University ...... State University, AR	0.32	0.31	0.	0.	0.	0.31

DEPARTMENTS OF GRADUATE EDUCATION
Not On The Approved List of The Gourman Report (Continued)

Department of Graduate Education INSTITUTION	Gourman Overall Academic Score (Combined Areas/Fields)	Administration (Attitude and Policy) (Quality of Leadership at All Levels of Administration)	Curriculum (Attractiveness of Program)	Faculty Effectiveness	Faculty (Quality of Research/ Scholarship)	Library Resources
Arkansas Tech University ...... Russellville, AR	0.33	0.32	0.	0.	0.	0.28
Auburn University .... Auburn, AL	0.52	0.51	0.	0.	0.	0.46
Auburn University at Montgomery Montgomery, AL	0.28	0.29	0.	0.	0.	0.28
Austin Peay State University .... Clarksville, TN	0.34	0.33	0.	0.	0.	0.29
Azusa Pacific University .... Azusa, CA	0.35	0.34	0.	0.	0.	0.30
Ball State University .... Muncie, IN	0.51	0.46	0.	0.	0.	0.41
Barry University .... Miami Shores, FL	0.33	0.31	0.	0.	0.	0.31
Baylor University .... Waco, TX	0.51	0.50	0.	0.	0.	0.45
Bemidji State University .... Bemidji, MN	0.36	0.37	0.	0.	0.	0.37
Bloomsburgh University of Pennsylvania .... Bloomsburgh, PA	0.39	0.37	0.	0.	0.	0.35
Boise State University .... Boise, ID	0.38	0.39	0.	0.	0.	0.36
Boston College .... Chestnut Hill, MA	0.48	0.46	0.	0.	0.	0.43
Boston University .... Boston, MA	0.68	0.64	0.	0.	0.	0.56
Bowie State University .... Bowie, MD	0.26	0.25	0.	0.	0.	0.19
Bowling Green State University . Bowling Green, OH	0.52	0.48	0.	0.	0.	0.49
Bradley University .... Peoria, IL	0.50	0.47	0.	0.	0.	0.49
Bridgewater State College ..... Bridgewater, MA	0.39	0.36	0.	0.	0.	0.38
Brigham Young University ...... Provo, UT	0.54	0.52	0.	0.	0.	0.51
Bucknell University .... Lewisburg, PA	0.34	0.33	0.	0.	0.	0.33
Butler University .... Indianapolis, IN	0.47	0.45	0.	0.	0.	0.48
California Lutheran College ..... Thousand Oaks, CA	0.46	0.44	0.	0.	0.	0.47
California Polytechnic State University, San Luis Obispo .... San Luis Obispo, CA	0.49	0.51	0.	0.	0.	0.49

DEPARTMENTS OF GRADUATE EDUCATION
Not On The Approved List of The Gourman Report (Continued)

RATING CATEGORIES	Numerical Range
Very Strong	4.51-4.99
Strong	4.01-4.49
Good	3.61-3.99
Acceptable Plus	3.01-3.59
Adequate	2.51-2.99
Marginal	2.01-2.49

Not Sufficient for Graduate Programs   0.

Department of Graduate Education INSTITUTION	Gourman Overall Academic Score (Combined Areas/Fields)	Administration (Attitude and Policy) (Quality of Leadership at All Levels of Administration)	Curriculum (Attractiveness of Program)	Faculty Effectiveness	Faculty (Quality of Research/ Scholarship)	Library Resources
California State University, Bakersfield Bakersfield, CA	0.45	0.46	0.	0.	0.	0.29
California State Polytechnic University, Pomona . . . . Pomona, CA	0.46	0.48	0.	0.	0.	0.41
California State University, Chico Chico, CA	0.48	0.49	0.	0.	0.	0.48
California State University, Dominguez Hills . . . . Carson, CA	0.49	0.46	0.	0.	0.	0.47
California State University, Fresno Fresno, CA	0.52	0.49	0.	0.	0.	0.48
California State University, Fullerton Fullerton, CA	0.51	0.48	0.	0.	0.	0.38
California State University, Hayward Hayward, CA	0.47	0.46	0.	0.	0.	0.42
California State University, Long Beach . . . . Long Beach, CA	0.47	0.42	0.	0.	0.	0.46
California State University, Los Angeles . . . . Los Angeles, CA	0.38	0.37	0.	0.	0.	0.39
California State University, Northridge . . . . Northridge, CA	0.48	0.40	0.	0.	0.	0.41
California State University, Sacramento . . . . Sacramento, CA	0.48	0.49	0.	0.	0.	0.45
California State University, San Bernardino . . . . San Bernardino, CA	0.49	0.50	0.	0.	0.	0.46
California State University, Stanislaus . . . . Turlock, CA	0.45	0.46	0.	0.	0.	0.37

Department of Graduate Education INSTITUTION	Gourman Overall Academic Score (Combined Areas/Fields)	Administration (Attitude and Policy) (Quality of Leadership at All Levels of Administration)	Curriculum (Attractiveness of Program)	Faculty Effectiveness	Faculty (Quality of Research/ Scholarship)	Library Resources
California University of Pennsylvania California, PA	0.38	0.36	0.	0.	0.	0.35
Canisius College . . . . Buffalo, NY	0.36	0.35	0.	0.	0.	0.37
Catholic University of America . . Washington, D.C.	0.54	0.49	0.	0.	0.	0.52
Central Connecticut State University New Britain, CT	0.45	0.42	0.	0.	0.	0.41
Central Michigan University . . . . Mount Pleasant, MI	0.47	0.46	0.	0.	0.	0.38
Central Missouri State University Warrensburg, MO	0.45	0.42	0.	0.	0.	0.39
Central State University . . . . Edmond, OK	0.32	0.28	0.	0.	0.	0.26
Central Washington University . . Ellensburg, WA	0.43	0.39	0.	0.	0.	0.37
Chapman University . . . . Orange, CA	0.41	0.39	0.	0.	0.	0.35
Cheyney University of Pennsylvania Cheyney, PA	0.37	0.35	0.	0.	0.	0.34
Chicago State University . . . . Chicago, IL	0.38	0.40	0.	0.	0.	0.38
City University of New York, Bernard M. Baruch College . . . . . New York, NY	0.34	0.33	0.	0.	0.	0.32
City University of New York, Brooklyn College . . . . Brooklyn, NY	0.49	0.45	0.	0.	0.	0.48
City University of New York, City College . . . . New York, NY	0.52	0.46	0.	0.	0.	0.46
City University of New York, College of Staten Island . . . . Staten Island, NY	0.32	0.31	0.	0.	0.	0.31
City University of New York, Herbert H. Lehman College . . . . Bronx, NY	0.34	0.33	0.	0.	0.	0.32
City University of New York, Hunter College . . . . New York, NY	0.51	0.47	0.	0.	0.	0.48
City University of New York, Queens College . . . . Flushing, NY	0.51	0.46	0.	0.	0.	0.49
Claremont Graduate School . . . . Claremont, CA	0.44	0.46	0.	0.	0.	0.36

RATING CATEGORIES	Numerical Range
Very Strong	4.51-4.99
Strong	4.01-4.49
Good	3.61-3.99
Acceptable Plus	3.01-3.59
Adequate	2.51-2.99
Marginal	2.01-2.49

Not Sufficient for Graduate Programs   0.

Department of Graduate Education INSTITUTION	Gourman Overall Academic Score (Combined Areas/Fields)	Administration (Attitude and Policy) (Quality of Leadership at All Levels of Administration)	Curriculum (Attractiveness of Program)	Faculty Effectiveness	Faculty (Quality of Research/ Scholarship)	Library Resources
Clarion University of Pennsylvania Clarion, PA	0.36	0.35	0.	0.	0.	0.34
Clark University .... Worcester, MA	0.46	0.45	0.	0.	0.	0.41
Clemson University .... Clemson, SC	0.49	0.44	0.	0.	0.	0.47
Cleveland State University ..... Cleveland, OH	0.44	0.43	0.	0.	0.	0.45
College of William and Mary .... Williamsburg, VA	0.43	0.44	0.	0.	0.	0.43
Colorado State University ...... Fort Collins, CO	0.50	0.46	0.	0.	0.	0.47
Cornell University .... Ithaca, NY	0.88	0.83	0.	0.	0.	0.81
Creighton University .... Omaha, NE	0.41	0.39	0.	0.	0.	0.37
Delta State University .... Cleveland, MS	0.27	0.26	0.	0.	0.	0.22
De Paul University .... Chicago, IL	0.49	0.46	0.	0.	0.	0.48
Drake University .... Des Moines, IA	0.47	0.45	0.	0.	0.	0.48
Drury College .... Springfield, MO	0.27	0.28	0.	0.	0.	0.28
Duquesne University .... Pittsburgh, PA	0.45	0.43	0.	0.	0.	0.41
East Carolina University .... Greenville, NC	0.42	0.41	0.	0.	0.	0.42
East Central University .... Ada, OK	0.39	0.37	0.	0.	0.	0.31
Eastern Connecticut State University Willimantic, CT	0.41	0.39	0.	0.	0.	0.38
Eastern Illinois University ...... Charleston, IL	0.43	0.41	0.	0.	0.	0.39

Department of Graduate Education INSTITUTION	Gourman Overall Academic Score (Combined Areas/Fields)	Administration (Attitude and Policy) (Quality of Leadership at All Levels of Administration)	Curriculum (Attractiveness of Program)	Faculty Effectiveness	Faculty (Quality of Research/ Scholarship)	Library Resources
Eastern Kentucky University .... Richmond, KY	0.44	0.38	0.	0.	0.	0.38
Eastern Michigan University .... Ypsilanti, MI	0.45	0.43	0.	0.	0.	0.41
Eastern New Mexico University . Portales, NM	0.43	0.38	0.	0.	0.	0.39
Eastern Washington University .. Cheney, WA	0.47	0.43	0.	0.	0.	0.41
East Stroudsburg University of Pennsylvania .... East Stroudsburg, PA	0.37	0.35	0.	0.	0.	0.38
East Tennessee State University Johnson City, TN	0.39	0.38	0.	0.	0.	0.39
East Texas State University .... Commerce, TX	0.37	0.36	0.	0.	0.	0.38
Edinboro University of Pennsylvania Edinboro, PA	0.35	0.34	0.	0.	0.	0.36
Emporia State University .... Emporia, KS	0.39	0.35	0.	0.	0.	0.37
Fairfield University .... Fairfield, CT	0.39	0.35	0.	0.	0.	0.38
Fairleigh Dickinson University, Teaneck-Hackensack Campus .. Teaneck, NJ	0.46	0.42	0.	0.	0.	0.40
Fayetteville State University .... Fayetteville, NC	0.36	0.33	0.	0.	0.	0.35
Florida Agricultural and Mechanical University .... Tallahassee, FL	0.31	0.30	0.	0.	0.	0.33
Florida Atlantic University ...... Boca Raton, FL	0.32	0.31	0.	0.	0.	0.32
Florida International University .. Miami, FL	0.31	0.30	0.	0.	0.	0.31
Florida State University .... Tallahassee, FL	0.62	0.58	0.	0.	0.	0.60
Fordham University .... Bronx, NY	0.56	0.52	0.	0.	0.	0.53
Fort Hays University .... Hays, KS	0.38	0.36	0.	0.	0.	0.32
Framingham State College ..... Framingham, MA	0.39	0.35	0.	0.	0.	0.34
Frostburg State University ...... Frostburg, MD	0.28	0.25	0.	0.	0.	0.26
Gannon University .... Erie, PA	0.29	0.28	0.	0.	0.	0.28

DEPARTMENTS OF GRADUATE EDUCATION
Not On The Approved List of The Gourman Report (Continued)

RATING CATEGORIES	Numerical Range
Very Strong	4.51-4.99
Strong	4.01-4.49
Good	3.61-3.99
Acceptable Plus	3.01-3.59
Adequate	2.51-2.99
Marginal	2.01-2.49

Not Sufficient for Graduate Programs   0.

Department of Graduate Education INSTITUTION	Gourman Overall Academic Score (Combined Areas/Fields)	Administration (Attitude and Policy) (Quality of Leadership at All Levels of Administration)	Curriculum (Attractiveness of Program)	Faculty Effectiveness	Faculty (Quality of Research/ Scholarship)	Library Resources
George Mason University . . . . . . Fairfax, VA	0.32	0.33	0.	0.	0.	0.34
George Washington University . . Washington D.C.	0.67	0.63	0.	0.	0.	0.62
Georgia College . . . . Milledgeville, GA	0.30	0.27	0.	0.	0.	0.29
Georgia Southern University . . . . Statesboro, GA	0.30	0.26	0.	0.	0.	0.28
Georgia State University . . . . Atlanta, GA	0.41	0.35	0.	0.	0.	0.36
Gonzaga University . . . . Spokane, WA	0.48	0.47	0.	0.	0.	0.47
Governors State University . . . . . Park Forest South, IL	0.38	0.39	0.	0.	0.	0.39
Grand Valley State University . . . Allendale, MI	0.37	0.36	0.	0.	0.	0.37
Hampton University . . . . Hampton, VA	0.28	0.26	0.	0.	0.	0.22
Hardin-Simmons University . . . . . Abilene, TX	0.36	0.34	0.	0.	0.	0.34
Harvard University . . . . Cambridge, MA	0.91	0.89	0.	0.	0.	0.90
Henderson State University . . . . Arkadelphia, AR	0.27	0.26	0.	0.	0.	0.28
Hofstra University . . . . Hempstead, NY	0.50	0.45	0.	0.	0.	0.49
Howard University . . . . Washington D.C.	0.35	0.33	0.	0.	0.	0.34
Humboldt State University . . . . . . Arcata, CA	0.36	0.35	0.	0.	0.	0.33
Idaho State University . . . . Pocatello, ID	0.37	0.34	0.	0.	0.	0.36
Illinois State University . . . . Normal, IL	0.49	0.45	0.	0.	0.	0.46

DEPARTMENTS OF GRADUATE EDUCATION
Not On The Approved List of The Gourman Report (Continued)

Department of Graduate Education INSTITUTION	Gourman Overall Academic Score (Combined Areas/Fields)	Administration (Attitude and Policy) (Quality of Leadership at All Levels of Administration)	Curriculum (Attractiveness of Program)	Faculty Effectiveness	Faculty (Quality of Research/ Scholarship)	Library Resources
Indiana State University at Terre Haute Terre Haute, IN	0.48	0.44	0.	0.	0.	0.47
Indiana University South Bend .. South Bend, IN	0.40	0.41	0.	0.	0.	0.45
Indiana University, Bloomington . Bloomington, IN	0.86	0.85	0.	0.	0.	0.91
Indiana University of Pennsylvania Indiana, PA	0.38	0.35	0.	0.	0.	0.35
Indiana University – Purdue University Fort Wayne .. Fort Wayne, IN	0.49	0.45	0.	0.	0.	0.39
Indiana University – Purdue University Indianapolis .. Indianapolis, IN	0.50	0.49	0.	0.	0.	0.48
Iowa State University .... Ames, IA	0.58	0.57	0.	0.	0.	0.59
Jackson State University .... Jackson, MS	0.29	0.25	0.	0.	0.	0.18
Jacksonville State University .... Jacksonville, AL	0.30	0.24	0.	0.	0.	0.19
Jacksonville University .... Jacksonville, FL	0.39	0.35	0.	0.	0.	0.30
James Madison University ..... Harrisonburg, VA	0.36	0.32	0.	0.	0.	0.35
Jersey City State College ...... Jersey City, NJ	0.37	0.36	0.	0.	0.	0.36
John Carroll University .... University Heights, OH	0.30	0.31	0.	0.	0.	0.30
Johns Hopkins University ...... Baltimore, MD	0.71	0.68	0.	0.	0.	0.70
Kansas State University .... Manhattan, KS	0.58	0.57	0.	0.	0.	0.56
Kean College of New Jersey .... Union, NJ	0.39	0.36	0.	0.	0.	0.34
Keene State College .... Keene, NH	0.27	0.25	0.	0.	0.	0.20
Kent State University .... Kent, OH	0.51	0.50	0.	0.	0.	0.50
Kutztown University of Pennsylvania Kutztown, PA	0.36	0.33	0.	0.	0.	0.31
Lamar University .... Beaumont, TX	0.37	0.34	0.	0.	0.	0.33
Lehigh University .... Bethlehem, PA	0.40	0.42	0.	0.	0.	0.41
Loma Linda University .... Loma Linda, CA	0.36	0.35	0.	0.	0.	0.35

DEPARTMENTS OF GRADUATE EDUCATION
Not On The Approved List of The Gourman Report (Continued)

RATING CATEGORIES	Numerical Range
Very Strong	4.51-4.99
Strong	4.01-4.49
Good	3.61-3.99
Acceptable Plus	3.01-3.59
Adequate	2.51-2.99
Marginal	2.01-2.49
Not Sufficient for Graduate Programs	0.

Department of Graduate Education INSTITUTION	Gourman Overall Academic Score (Combined Areas/Fields)	Administration (Attitude and Policy) (Quality of Leadership at All Levels of Administration)	Curriculum (Attractiveness of Program)	Faculty Effectiveness	Faculty (Quality of Research/ Scholarship)	Library Resources
Long Island University, Brooklyn Center . . . . Brooklyn, NY	0.35	0.36	0.	0.	0.	0.30
Long Island University, C.W. Post Campus . . . . Greenvale, NY	0.43	0.41	0.	0.	0.	0.41
Louisiana State University and Agricultural and Mechanical College Baton Rouge, LA	0.57	0.55	0.	0.	0.	0.58
Louisiana State University in Shreveport . . . . Shreveport, LA	0.31	0.32	0.	0.	0.	0.29
Louisiana Tech University . . . . . . Ruston, LA	0.32	0.33	0.	0.	0.	0.30
Loyola College . . . . Baltimore, MD	0.29	0.28	0.	0.	0.	0.26
Loyola Marymount University . . . Los Angeles, CA	0.40	0.39	0.	0.	0.	0.36
Loyola University, New Orleans . New Orleans, LA	0.39	0.38	0.	0.	0.	0.35
Loyola University of Chicago . . . . Chicago, IL	0.42	0.40	0.	0.	0.	0.41
Lynchburg College . . . . Lynchburg, VA	0.31	0.28	0.	0.	0.	0.30
Mankato State University . . . . . . Mankato, MN	0.32	0.29	0.	0.	0.	0.29
Mansfield University of Pennsylvania Mansfield, PA	0.36	0.35	0.	0.	0.	0.37
Marquette University . . . . Milwaukee, WI	0.50	0.49	0.	0.	0.	0.47
Marshall University . . . . Huntington, WV	0.38	0.36	0.	0.	0.	0.35
Mercer University . . . . Macon, GA	0.28	0.26	0.	0.	0.	0.26

Department of Graduate Education INSTITUTION	Gourman Overall Academic Score (Combined Areas/Fields)	Administration (Attitude and Policy) (Quality of Leadership at All Levels of Administration)	Curriculum (Attractiveness of Program)	Faculty Effectiveness	Faculty (Quality of Research/ Scholarship)	Library Resources
Mercer University in Atlanta .... Atlanta, GA	0.25	0.25	0.	0.	0.	0.23
Miami University .... Oxford, OH	0.41	0.38	0.	0.	0.	0.37
Michigan State University ...... East Lansing, MI	0.78	0.75	0.	0.	0.	0.79
Middle Tennessee State University Murfreesboro, TN	0.46	0.43	0.	0.	0.	0.45
Midwestern State University .... Wichita Falls, TX	0.40	0.38	0.	0.	0.	0.39
Millersville University of Pennsylvania Millersville, PA	0.36	0.35	0.	0.	0.	0.33
Mississippi State University ..... Mississippi State, MS	0.46	0.44	0.	0.	0.	0.41
Montana State University – Billings Billings, MT	0.20	0.17	0.	0.	0.	0.15
Montana State University ...... Bozeman, MT	0.43	0.42	0.	0.	0.	0.40
Montana State University – Northern Havre, MT	0.18	0.15	0.	0.	0.	0.12
Montclair State College .... Upper Monclair, NJ	0.39	0.38	0.	0.	0.	0.37
Moorhead State University ..... Moorhead, MN	0.39	0.35	0.	0.	0.	0.34
Morehead State University ..... Morehead, KY	0.31	0.30	0.	0.	0.	0.30
Morgan State University .... Baltimore, MD	0.28	0.26	0.	0.	0.	0.21
Murray State University .... Murray, KY	0.31	0.30	0.	0.	0.	0.29
National Louis University .... Evanston, IL	0.40	0.38	0.	0.	0.	0.41
New Mexico Highlands University Las Vegas, NM	0.26	0.27	0.	0.	0.	0.25
New Mexico State University ... Las Cruces, NM	0.42	0.41	0.	0.	0.	0.41
New York University .... New York, NY	0.80	0.78	0.	0.	0.	0.83
Niagara University .... Niagara University, NY	0.30	0.29	0.	0.	0.	0.25
Nicholls State University .... Thibodaux, LA	0.31	0.30	0.	0.	0.	0.27
Norfolk State University .... Norfolk, VA	0.29	0.28	0.	0.	0.	0.20
North Adams State College ..... North Adams, MA	0.30	0.30	0.	0.	0.	0.29

RATING CATEGORIES	Numerical Range
Very Strong	4.51-4.99
Strong	4.01-4.49
Good	3.61-3.99
Acceptable Plus	3.01-3.59
Adequate	2.51-2.99
Marginal	2.01-2.49

Not Sufficient for Graduate Programs   0.

Department of Graduate Education INSTITUTION	Gourman Overall Academic Score (Combined Areas/Fields)	Administration (Attitude and Policy) (Quality of Leadership at All Levels of Administration)	Curriculum (Attractiveness of Program)	Faculty Effectiveness	Faculty (Quality of Research/ Scholarship)	Library Resources
North Carolina Agricultural and Technical State University ...... Greensboro, NC	0.25	0.26	0.	0.	0.	0.21
North Carolina Central University Durham, NC	0.26	0.27	0.	0.	0.	0.20
North Carolina State University at Raleigh .... Raleigh, NC	0.49	0.48	0.	0.	0.	0.48
North Dakota State University ... Fargo, ND	0.38	0.39	0.	0.	0.	0.36
Northeastern Illinois University .. Chicago, IL	0.43	0.42	0.	0.	0.	0.43
Northeastern State University ... Tahlequah, OK	0.30	0.30	0.	0.	0.	0.29
Northeastern University .... Boston, MA	0.45	0.42	0.	0.	0.	0.45
Northeast Louisiana University .. Monroe, LA	0.38	0.37	0.	0.	0.	0.36
Northeast Missouri State University Kirksville, MO	0.32	0.31	0.	0.	0.	0.31
Northern Arizona University .... Flagstaff, AZ	0.35	0.36	0.	0.	0.	0.35
Northern Illinois University ..... DeKalb, IL	0.43	0.42	0.	0.	0.	0.41
Northern Kentucky University ... Highland Heights, KY	0.30	0.31	0.	0.	0.	0.29
Northern Michigan University ... Marquette, MI	0.39	0.40	0.	0.	0.	0.39
Northern State University ...... Aberdeen, SD	0.28	0.26	0.	0.	0.	0.21
Northwestern Oklahoma State University .... Alva, OK	0.29	0.31	0.	0.	0.	0.28

DEPARTMENTS OF GRADUATE EDUCATION
Not On The Approved List of The Gourman Report (Continued)

Department of Graduate Education INSTITUTION	Gourman Overall Academic Score (Combined Areas/Fields)	Administration (Attitude and Policy) (Quality of Leadership at All Levels of Administration)	Curriculum (Attractiveness of Program)	Faculty Effectiveness	Faculty (Quality of Research/ Scholarship)	Library Resources
Northwestern State University of Louisiana . . . . Natchitoches, LA	0.31	0.32	0.	0.	0.	0.29
Northwestern University . . . . Evanston, IL	0.79	0.82	0.	0.	0.	0.83
Northwest Missouri State University Maryville, MO	0.36	0.34	0.	0.	0.	0.32
Norwich University . . . . Northfield, VT	0.28	0.26	0.	0.	0.	0.27
Nova University . . . . Fort Lauderdale, FL	0.32	0.30	0.	0.	0.	0.31
Oakland University . . . . Rochester, MI	0.29	0.30	0.	0.	0.	0.23
Ohio State University . . . . Columbus, OH	0.79	0.81	0.	0.	0.	0.80
Ohio University . . . . Athens, OH	0.57	0.58	0.	0.	0.	0.56
Oklahoma State University . . . . . Stillwater, OK	0.40	0.39	0.	0.	0.	0.42
Old Dominion University . . . . Norfolk, VA	0.43	0.42	0.	0.	0.	0.42
Oral Roberts University . . . . Tulsa, OK	0.25	0.23	0.	0.	0.	0.18
Oregon State University . . . . Corvallis, OR	0.59	0.58	0.	0.	0.	0.57
Pace University . . . . New York, NY	0.43	0.41	0.	0.	0.	0.42
Pacific Lutheran University . . . . . Tacoma, WA	0.31	0.32	0.	0.	0.	0.30
Pacific University . . . . Forest Grove, OR	0.30	0.31	0.	0.	0.	0.29
Pennsylvania State University – Capitol Campus . . . . Middletown, PA	0.22	0.21	0.	0.	0.	0.19
Pennsylvania State University – University Park Campus . . . . University Park, PA	0.61	0.62	0.	0.	0.	0.64
Pepperdine University . . . . Malibu, CA	0.38	0.34	0.	0.	0.	0.31
Pittsburg State University . . . . . . Pittsburg, KS	0.32	0.32	0.	0.	0.	0.28
Portland State University . . . . Portland, OR	0.34	0.35	0.	0.	0.	0.33
Prairie View A&M University . . . . Prairie View, TX	0.26	0.22	0.	0.	0.	0.20
Purdue University . . . . West Lafayette, IN	0.70	0.72	0.	0.	0.	0.74

RATING CATEGORIES	Numerical Range
Very Strong	4.51-4.99
Strong	4.01-4.49
Good	3.61-3.99
Acceptable Plus	3.01-3.59
Adequate	2.51-2.99
Marginal	2.01-2.49

Not Sufficient for Graduate Programs   0.

Department of Graduate Education INSTITUTION	Gourman Overall Academic Score (Combined Areas/Fields)	Administration (Attitude and Policy) (Quality of Leadership at All Levels of Administration)	Curriculum (Attractiveness of Program)	Faculty Effectiveness	Faculty (Quality of Research/ Scholarship)	Library Resources
Purdue University – Calumet ... Hammond, IN	0.31	0.32	0.	0.	0.	0.25
Radford University .... Radford, VA	0.33	0.34	0.	0.	0.	0.28
Roosevelt University .... Chicago, IL	0.48	0.50	0.	0.	0.	0.50
Rutgers University, New Brunswick New Brunswick, NJ	0.65	0.68	0.	0.	0.	0.67
Saginaw Valley State University . University Center, MI	0.23	0.22	0.	0.	0.	0.25
St. Bonaventure University ..... St. Bonaventure, NY	0.30	0.31	0.	0.	0.	0.30
St. Cloud State University ...... St. Cloud, MN	0.31	0.33	0.	0.	0.	0.32
St. John's University .... Jamaica, NY	0.44	0.43	0.	0.	0.	0.41
Saint Louis University .... St. Louis, MO	0.46	0.47	0.	0.	0.	0.47
Samford University .... Birmingham, AL	0.30	0.31	0.	0.	0.	0.29
Sam Houston State University .. Huntsville, TX	0.32	0.32	0.	0.	0.	0.31
San Diego State University ..... San Diego, CA	0.45	0.44	0.	0.	0.	0.41
San Francisco State University .. San Francisco, CA	0.45	0.44	0.	0.	0.	0.45
San Jose State University ...... San Jose, CA	0.44	0.43	0.	0.	0.	0.44
Seattle University .... Seattle, WA	0.40	0.41	0.	0.	0.	0.41
Seton Hall University .... South Orange, NJ	0.39	0.43	0.	0.	0.	0.42
Shippensburg University of Pennsylvania .... Shippensburg, PA	0.35	0.34	0.	0.	0.	0.31

DEPARTMENTS OF GRADUATE EDUCATION
Not On The Approved List of The Gourman Report (Continued)

Department of Graduate Education INSTITUTION	Gourman Overall Academic Score (Combined Areas/Fields)	Administration (Attitude and Policy) (Quality of Leadership at All Levels of Administration)	Curriculum (Attractiveness of Program)	Faculty Effectiveness	Faculty (Quality of Research/ Scholarship)	Library Resources
Simmons College . . . . Boston, MA	0.36	0.37	0.	0.	0.	0.35
Slippery Rock University of Pennsylvania . . . . Slippery Rock, PA	0.32	0.33	0.	0.	0.	0.32
Smith College . . . . Northampton, MA	0.33	0.34	0.	0.	0.	0.33
Sonoma State University . . . . Rohnert Park, CA	0.36	0.35	0.	0.	0.	0.34
South Dakota State University . . Brookings, SD	0.37	0.36	0.	0.	0.	0.33
Southeastern Louisiana University Hammond, LA	0.32	0.29	0.	0.	0.	0.30
Southeast Missouri State University Cape Girardeau, MO	0.30	0.35	0.	0.	0.	0.31
Southern Connecticut State University New Haven, CT	0.32	0.36	0.	0.	0.	0.34
Southern Illinois University at Carbondale . . . . Carbondale, IL	0.61	0.65	0.	0.	0.	0.66
Southern Illinois University at Edwardsville . . . . Edwardsville, IL	0.50	0.51	0.	0.	0.	0.52
Southern University and Agricultural and Mechanical College . . . . Baton Rouge, LA	0.28	0.27	0.	0.	0.	0.28
Southwestern Oklahoma State University . . . . Weatherford, OK	0.31	0.30	0.	0.	0.	0.28
Southwest Missouri State University Springfield, MO	0.30	0.29	0.	0.	0.	0.27
Southwest Texas State University San Marcos, TX	0.32	0.31	0.	0.	0.	0.30
Stanford University . . . . Stanford, CA	0.87	0.90	0.	0.	0.	0.89
State University of New York at Albany Albany, NY	0.53	0.54	0.	0.	0.	0.52
State University of New York at Binghamton . . . . Binghamton, NY	0.54	0.55	0.	0.	0.	0.54
State University of New York at Buffalo Buffalo, NY	0.65	0.64	0.	0.	0.	0.68
State University of New York College at Brockport . . . . Brockport, NY	0.30	0.31	0.	0.	0.	0.29

RATING CATEGORIES	Numerical Range
Very Strong	4.51-4.99
Strong	4.01-4.49
Good	3.61-3.99
Acceptable Plus	3.01-3.59
Adequate	2.51-2.99
Marginal	2.01-2.49
Not Sufficient for Graduate Programs	0.

Department of Graduate Education INSTITUTION	Gourman Overall Academic Score (Combined Areas/Fields)	Administration (Attitude and Policy) (Quality of Leadership at All Levels of Administration)	Curriculum (Attractiveness of Program)	Faculty Effectiveness	Faculty (Quality of Research/ Scholarship)	Library Resources
State University of New York College at Buffalo . . . . Buffalo, NY	0.31	0.32	0.	0.	0.	0.30
State University of New York College at Cortland . . . . Cortland, NY	0.29	0.31	0.	0.	0.	0.31
State University of New York College at Fredonia . . . . Fredonia, NY	0.34	0.33	0.	0.	0.	0.32
State University of New York College at Geneseo . . . . Geneseo, NY	0.35	0.34	0.	0.	0.	0.33
State University of New York College at New Paltz . . . . New Paltz, NY	0.36	0.35	0.	0.	0.	0.34
State University of New York College at Oneonta . . . . Oneonta, NY	0.33	0.30	0.	0.	0.	0.32
State University of New York College at Oswego . . . . Oswego, NY	0.34	0.29	0.	0.	0.	0.33
State University of New York College at Plattsburgh . . . . Plattsburgh, NY	0.30	0.31	0.	0.	0.	0.32
State University of New York College at Potsdam . . . . Potsdam, NY	0.35	0.33	0.	0.	0.	0.35
Stephen F. Austin State University Nacogdoches, TX	0.36	0.34	0.	0.	0.	0.32
Stetson University . . . . Deland, FL	0.30	0.29	0.	0.	0.	0.30
Suffolk University . . . . Boston, MA	0.35	0.31	0.	0.	0.	0.34
Sul Ross State University . . . . . . Alpine, TX	0.30	0.29	0.	0.	0.	0.30

Department of Graduate Education INSTITUTION	Gourman Overall Academic Score (Combined Areas/Fields)	Administration (Attitude and Policy) (Quality of Leadership at All Levels of Administration)	Curriculum (Attractiveness of Program)	Faculty Effectiveness	Faculty (Quality of Research/ Scholarship)	Library Resources
Syracuse University Syracuse, NY	0.71	0.74	0.	0.	0.	0.76
Tarleton State University Stephenville, TX	0.41	0.46	0.	0.	0.	0.45
Teachers College, Columbia University New York, NY	0.79	0.75	0.	0.	0.	0.80
Temple University Philadelphia, PA	0.73	0.76	0.	0.	0.	0.79
Tennessee State University Nashville, TN	0.30	0.28	0.	0.	0.	0.26
Tennessee Technological University Cookeville, TN	0.29	0.30	0.	0.	0.	0.24
Texas A&M International University Laredo, TX	0.28	0.29	0.	0.	0.	0.23
Texas A&M University College Station, TX	0.61	0.63	0.	0.	0.	0.62
Texas A&M University–Corpus Christi Corpus, TX	0.21	0.20	0.	0.	0.	0.20
Texas A&M University–Kingsville Kingsville, TX	0.22	0.21	0.	0.	0.	0.18
Texas Christian University Fort Worth, TX	0.30	0.33	0.	0.	0.	0.33
Texas Southern University Houston, TX	0.27	0.25	0.	0.	0.	0.20
Texas Tech University Lubbock, TX	0.48	0.45	0.	0.	0.	0.48
Texas Woman's University Denton, TX	0.33	0.35	0.	0.	0.	0.31
Towson State University Baltimore, MD	0.28	0.27	0.	0.	0.	0.23
Trenton State College Trenton, NJ	0.34	0.34	0.	0.	0.	0.31
Trinity University San Antonio, TX	0.30	0.31	0.	0.	0.	0.28
Troy State University Troy, AL	0.33	0.32	0.	0.	0.	0.29
Tufts University Medford, MA	0.49	0.53	0.	0.	0.	0.47
Tulane University New Orleans, LA	0.46	0.51	0.	0.	0.	0.50
Tuskegee University Tuskegee, AL	0.21	0.22	0.	0.	0.	0.16
United States International University San Diego, CA	0.30	0.26	0.	0.	0.	0.24

RATING CATEGORIES	Numerical Range
Very Strong	4.51-4.99
Strong	4.01-4.49
Good	3.61-3.99
Acceptable Plus	3.01-3.59
Adequate	2.51-2.99
Marginal	2.01-2.49

Not Sufficient for Graduate Programs   0.

Department of Graduate Education INSTITUTION	Gourman Overall Academic Score (Combined Areas/Fields)	Administration (Attitude and Policy) (Quality of Leadership at All Levels of Administration)	Curriculum (Attractiveness of Program)	Faculty Effectiveness	Faculty (Quality of Research/ Scholarship)	Library Resources
University of Akron . . . . Akron, OH	0.31	0.27	0.	0.	0.	0.29
University of Alabama . . . . University, AL	0.51	0.48	0.	0.	0.	0.46
University of Alabama in Birmingham Birmingham, AL	0.30	0.32	0.	0.	0.	0.29
University of Alaska, Anchorage . Anchorage, AK	0.26	0.23	0.	0.	0.	0.17
University of Alaska, Fairbanks . . Fairbanks, AK	0.31	0.32	0.	0.	0.	0.28
University of Arizona . . . . Tucson, AZ	0.63	0.62	0.	0.	0.	0.61
University of Arkansas . . . . Fayetteville, AR	0.52	0.50	0.	0.	0.	0.52
University of Arkansas at Little Rock Little Rock, AR	0.30	0.29	0.	0.	0.	0.29
University of Bridgeport . . . . Bridgeport, CT	0.34	0.33	0.	0.	0.	0.32
University of California, Berkeley Berkeley, CA	0.87	0.86	0.	0.	0.	0.91
University of California, Davis . . . Davis, CA	0.61	0.62	0.	0.	0.	0.64
University of California, Los Angeles Los Angeles, CA	0.84	0.86	0.	0.	0.	0.85
University of California, Riverside Riverside, CA	0.49	0.48	0.	0.	0.	0.50
University of California, Santa Barbara Santa Barbara, CA	0.69	0.65	0.	0.	0.	0.71
University of Central Arkansas . . Conway, AR	0.29	0.28	0.	0.	0.	0.27
University of Central Florida . . . . Orlando, FL	0.30	0.27	0.	0.	0.	0.20
University of Chicago . . . . Chicago, IL	0.94	0.93	0.	0.	0.	0.91

DEPARTMENTS OF GRADUATE EDUCATION
Not On The Approved List of The Gourman Report (Continued)

Department of Graduate Education INSTITUTION	Gourman Overall Academic Score (Combined Areas/Fields)	Administration (Attitude and Policy) (Quality of Leadership at All Levels of Administration)	Curriculum (Attractiveness of Program)	Faculty Effectiveness	Faculty (Quality of Research/ Scholarship)	Library Resources
University of Cincinnati .... Cincinnati, OH	0.62	0.61	0.	0.	0.	0.60
University of Colorado at Boulder Boulder, CO	0.65	0.66	0.	0.	0.	0.65
University of Colorado at Colorado Springs .... Colorado Springs, CO	0.31	0.29	0.	0.	0.	0.22
University of Colorado at Denver Denver, CO	0.41	0.40	0.	0.	0.	0.36
University of Connecticut ...... Storrs, CT	0.66	0.65	0.	0.	0.	0.64
University of Dallas .... Irving, TX	0.31	0.29	0.	0.	0.	0.27
University of Dayton .... Dayton, OH	0.32	0.35	0.	0.	0.	0.31
University of Delaware .... Newark, DE	0.49	0.46	0.	0.	0.	0.45
University of Denver .... Denver, CO	0.53	0.51	0.	0.	0.	0.50
University of Detroit Mercy ..... Detroit, MI	0.36	0.37	0.	0.	0.	0.36
University of Evansville .... Evansville, IN	0.34	0.36	0.	0.	0.	0.35
University of Florida .... Gainesville, FL	0.61	0.60	0.	0.	0.	0.58
University of Georgia .... Athens, GA	0.62	0.61	0.	0.	0.	0.62
University of Hartford .... West Hartford, CT	0.31	0.28	0.	0.	0.	0.29
University of Hawaii at Manoa ... Honolulu, HI	0.36	0.35	0.	0.	0.	0.33
University of Houston – Clear Lake Houston, TX	0.27	0.28	0.	0.	0.	0.26
University of Houston .... Houston, TX	0.49	0.50	0.	0.	0.	0.49
University of Idaho .... Moscow, ID	0.41	0.43	0.	0.	0.	0.43
University of Illinois at Chicago .. Chicago, IL	0.76	0.72	0.	0.	0.	0.75
University of Illinois at Springfield Springfield, IL	0.32	0.31	0.	0.	0.	0.31
University of Illinois at Urbana-Champaign .... Urbana, IL	0.82	0.84	0.	0.	0.	0.84
University of Iowa .... Iowa City, IA	0.77	0.79	0.	0.	0.	0.80

RATING CATEGORIES	Numerical Range
Very Strong	4.51-4.99
Strong	4.01-4.49
Good	3.61-3.99
Acceptable Plus	3.01-3.59
Adequate	2.51-2.99
Marginal	2.01-2.49
Not Sufficient for Graduate Programs	0.

Department of Graduate Education INSTITUTION	Gourman Overall Academic Score (Combined Areas/Fields)	Administration (Attitude and Policy) (Quality of Leadership at All Levels of Administration)	Curriculum (Attractiveness of Program)	Faculty Effectiveness	Faculty (Quality of Research/ Scholarship)	Library Resources
University of Kansas .... Lawrence, KS	0.62	0.63	0.	0.	0.	0.64
University of Kentucky .... Lexington, KY	0.49	0.48	0.	0.	0.	0.48
University of Louisville .... Louisville, KY	0.42	0.41	0.	0.	0.	0.40
University of Maine at Orono .... Orono, ME	0.33	0.34	0.	0.	0.	0.34
University of Maryland at College Park College Park, MD	0.58	0.61	0.	0.	0.	0.63
University of Maryland, Baltimore County .... Catonsville, MD	0.27	0.25	0.	0.	0.	0.19
University of Massachusetts Amherst Amherst, MA	0.48	0.49	0.	0.	0.	0.50
University of Massachusetts Boston Boston, MA	0.30	0.29	0.	0.	0.	0.25
University of Massachusetts Lowell Lowell, MA	0.30	0.28	0.	0.	0.	0.29
The University of Memphis ..... Memphis, TN	0.49	0.48	0.	0.	0.	0.47
University of Miami .... Coral Gables, FL	0.33	0.34	0.	0.	0.	0.33
University of Michigan .... Ann Arbor, MI	0.92	0.91	0.	0.	0.	0.90
University of Minnesota, Duluth . Duluth, MN	0.28	0.29	0.	0.	0.	0.25
University of Minnesota, Twin Cities Minneapolis, MN	0.81	0.83	0.	0.	0.	0.84
University of Mississippi .... University, MS	0.41	0.44	0.	0.	0.	0.44
University of Missouri – Columbia Columbia, MO	0.59	0.61	0.	0.	0.	0.61
University of Missouri – Kansas City Kansas City, MO	0.49	0.50	0.	0.	0.	0.48

Department of Graduate Education INSTITUTION	Gourman Overall Academic Score (Combined Areas/Fields)	Administration (Attitude and Policy) (Quality of Leadership at All Levels of Administration)	Curriculum (Attractiveness of Program)	Faculty Effectiveness	Faculty (Quality of Research/ Scholarship)	Library Resources
University of Missouri – St. Louis St. Louis, MO	0.26	0.27	0.	0.	0.	0.27
University of Montana . . . . Missoula, MT	0.31	0.33	0.	0.	0.	0.33
University of Montevallo . . . . Montevallo, AL	0.28	0.24	0.	0.	0.	0.21
University of Nebraska at Kearney Kearney, NE	0.27	0.22	0.	0.	0.	0.23
University of Nebraska at Omaha Omaha, NE	0.30	0.29	0.	0.	0.	0.25
University of Nebraska – Lincoln . Lincoln, NE	0.54	0.56	0.	0.	0.	0.51
University of Nevada – Las Vegas Las Vegas, NV	0.33	0.34	0.	0.	0.	0.32
University of Nevada – Reno . . . Reno, NV	0.31	0.33	0.	0.	0.	0.31
University of New Hampshire . . . Durham, NH	0.46	0.45	0.	0.	0.	0.42
University of New Mexico . . . . . . Albuquerque, NM	0.49	0.50	0.	0.	0.	0.49
University of New Orleans . . . . . . New Orleans, LA	0.30	0.31	0.	0.	0.	0.29
University of North Alabama . . . . Florence, AL	0.29	0.32	0.	0.	0.	0.28
University of North Carolina at Chapel Hill . . . . Chapel Hill, NC	0.64	0.65	0.	0.	0.	0.63
University of North Carolina at Charlotte . . . . Charlotte, NC	0.32	0.33	0.	0.	0.	0.35
University of North Carolina at Greensboro . . . . Greensboro, NC	0.41	0.42	0.	0.	0.	0.40
University of North Carolina at Wilmington . . . . Wilmington, NC	0.20	0.19	0.	0.	0.	0.15
University of North Dakota . . . . . Grand Forks, ND	0.35	0.34	0.	0.	0.	0.30
University of Northern Colorado . Greeley, CO	0.38	0.39	0.	0.	0.	0.34
University of Northern Iowa . . . . . Cedar Falls, IA	0.33	0.34	0.	0.	0.	0.32
University of North Florida . . . . . . Jacksonville, FL	0.31	0.32	0.	0.	0.	0.31
University of North Texas . . . . . . Denton, TX	0.43	0.42	0.	0.	0.	0.40

DEPARTMENTS OF GRADUATE EDUCATION
Not On The Approved List of The Gourman Report (Continued)

RATING CATEGORIES	Numerical Range
Very Strong	4.51-4.99
Strong	4.01-4.49
Good	3.61-3.99
Acceptable Plus	3.01-3.59
Adequate	2.51-2.99
Marginal	2.01-2.49
Not Sufficient for Graduate Programs	0.

Department of Graduate Education INSTITUTION	Gourman Overall Academic Score (Combined Areas/Fields)	Administration (Attitude and Policy) (Quality of Leadership at All Levels of Administration)	Curriculum (Attractiveness of Program)	Faculty Effectiveness	Faculty (Quality of Research/ Scholarship)	Library Resources
University of Oklahoma .... Norman, OK	0.58	0.59	0.	0.	0.	0.58
University of Oregon .... Eugene, OR	0.60	0.64	0.	0.	0.	0.63
University of Pennsylvania ..... Philadelphia, PA	0.74	0.66	0.	0.	0.	0.70
University of Pittsburgh .... Pittsburgh, PA	0.72	0.73	0.	0.	0.	0.71
University of Portland .... Portland, OR	0.36	0.31	0.	0.	0.	0.30
University of Puget Sound ...... Tacoma, WA	0.32	0.33	0.	0.	0.	0.31
University of Redlands .... Redlands, CA	0.31	0.32	0.	0.	0.	0.29
University of Rhode Island ..... Kingston, RI	0.36	0.34	0.	0.	0.	0.33
University of Richmond .... Richmond, VA	0.34	0.33	0.	0.	0.	0.30
University of Rochester .... Rochester, NY	0.62	0.66	0.	0.	0.	0.66
University of San Diego .... San Diego, CA	0.31	0.30	0.	0.	0.	0.29
University of San Francisco .... San Francisco, CA	0.39	0.38	0.	0.	0.	0.37
University of Santa Clara ...... Santa Clara, CA	0.29	0.26	0.	0.	0.	0.26
University of Scranton .... Scranton, PA	0.32	0.31	0.	0.	0.	0.26
University of South Alabama ..... Mobile, AL	0.34	0.32	0.	0.	0.	0.31
University of South Carolina .... Columbia, SC	0.46	0.45	0.	0.	0.	0.44
University of South Dakota ..... Vermillion, SD	0.34	0.31	0.	0.	0.	0.32

DEPARTMENTS OF GRADUATE EDUCATION
Not On The Approved List of The Gourman Report (Continued)

Department of Graduate Education INSTITUTION	Gourman Overall Academic Score (Combined Areas/Fields)	Administration (Attitude and Policy) (Quality of Leadership at All Levels of Administration)	Curriculum (Attractiveness of Program)	Faculty Effectiveness	Faculty (Quality of Research/ Scholarship)	Library Resources
University of Southern California . Los Angeles, CA	0.60	0.58	0.	0.	0.	0.63
University of Southern Mississippi Hattiesburg, MS	0.33	0.33	0.	0.	0.	0.30
University of South Florida . . . . . Tampa, FL	0.32	0.34	0.	0.	0.	0.32
University of Southwestern Louisiana Lafayette, LA	0.34	0.32	0.	0.	0.	0.31
University of Tennessee at Chattanooga . . . . Chattanooga, TN	0.31	0.30	0.	0.	0.	0.26
University of Tennessee at Martin Martin, TN	0.29	0.29	0.	0.	0.	0.22
University of Tennessee . . . . Knoxville, TN	0.48	0.49	0.	0.	0.	0.47
University of Texas at Arlington . Austin, TX	0.20	0.18	0.	0.	0.	0.17
University of Texas at Austin . . . . Richardson, TX	0.65	0.61	0.	0.	0.	0.66
University of Texas at El Paso . . El Paso, TX	0.30	0.25	0.	0.	0.	0.24
University of Texas at San Antonio San Antonio, TX	0.28	0.27	0.	0.	0.	0.20
University of Texas at Tyler . . . . . Tyler, TX	0.22	0.23	0.	0.	0.	0.22
University of Texas The Permin Basin Odessa, TX	0.19	0.18	0.	0.	0.	0.16
University of Texas – Pan American Edinburg, TX	0.21	0.22	0.	0.	0.	0.20
University of the District of Columbia Washington, D.C.	0.20	0.21	0.	0.	0.	0.16
University of the Pacific . . . . Stockton, CA	0.47	0.46	0.	0.	0.	0.43
University of Toledo . . . . Toledo, OH	0.34	0.35	0.	0.	0.	0.33
University of Tulsa . . . . Tulsa, OK	0.33	0.36	0.	0.	0.	0.34
University of Utah . . . . Salt Lake City, UT	0.60	0.59	0.	0.	0.	0.61
University of Vermont . . . . Burlington, VT	0.41	0.41	0.	0.	0.	0.42
University of Virginia . . . . Charlottesville, VA	0.51	0.53	0.	0.	0.	0.58
University of Washington . . . . . . Seattle, WA	0.68	0.69	0.	0.	0.	0.71
University of West Florida . . . . . . Pensacola, FL	0.29	0.30	0.	0.	0.	0.30

DEPARTMENTS OF GRADUATE EDUCATION
Not On The Approved List of The Gourman Report (Continued)

RATING CATEGORIES	Numerical Range
Very Strong	4.51-4.99
Strong	4.01-4.49
Good	3.61-3.99
Acceptable Plus	3.01-3.59
Adequate	2.51-2.99
Marginal	2.01-2.49

Not Sufficient for Graduate Programs 0.

Department of Graduate Education INSTITUTION	Gourman Overall Academic Score (Combined Areas/Fields)	Administration (Attitude and Policy) (Quality of Leadership at All Levels of Administration)	Curriculum (Attractiveness of Program)	Faculty Effectiveness	Faculty (Quality of Research/ Scholarship)	Library Resources
University of Wisconsin – Eau Claire Eau Claire, WI	0.29	0.29	0.	0.	0.	0.25
University of Wisconsin – La Crosse La Crosse, WI	0.27	0.26	0.	0.	0.	0.22
University of Wisconsin – Madison Madison, WI	0.73	0.75	0.	0.	0.	0.84
University of Wisconsin – Milwaukee Milwaukee, WI	0.50	0.51	0.	0.	0.	0.59
University of Wisconsin – Oshkosh Oshkosh, WI	0.26	0.27	0.	0.	0.	0.24
University of Wisconsin – Platteville Platteville, WI	0.28	0.26	0.	0.	0.	0.23
University of Wisconsin – River Falls River Falls, WI	0.25	0.24	0.	0.	0.	0.22
University of Wisconsin – Stevens Point . . . . Stevens Point, WI	0.24	0.23	0.	0.	0.	0.21
University of Wisconsin – Stout . . Menomonie, WI	0.21	0.22	0.	0.	0.	0.19
University of Wisconsin – Superior Superior, WI	0.23	0.21	0.	0.	0.	0.20
University of Wisconsin – Whitewater Whitewater, WI	0.26	0.24	0.	0.	0.	0.21
University of Wyoming . . . . Laramie, WY	0.36	0.37	0.	0.	0.	0.35
Utah State University . . . . Logan, UT	0.37	0.38	0.	0.	0.	0.34
Valdosta State College . . . . Valdosta, GA	0.27	0.26	0.	0.	0.	0.24
Vanderbilt University . . . . Nashville, TN	0.52	0.50	0.	0.	0.	0.50
Villanova University . . . . Villanova, PA	0.30	0.31	0.	0.	0.	0.28
Virginia Commonwealth University Richmond, VA	0.48	0.47	0.	0.	0.	0.47

Department of Graduate Education INSTITUTION	Gourman Overall Academic Score (Combined Areas/Fields)	Administration (Attitude and Policy) (Quality of Leadership at All Levels of Administration)	Curriculum (Attractiveness of Program)	Faculty Effectiveness	Faculty (Quality of Research/ Scholarship)	Library Resources
Virginia Polytechnic Institute and State University . . . . Blackburg, VA	0.48	0.49	0.	0.	0.	0.46
Virginia State University . . . . Petersburg, VA	0.20	0.21	0.	0.	0.	0.15
Wake Forest University . . . . Winston-Salem, NC	0.30	0.31	0.	0.	0.	0.30
Washburn University of Topeka . Topeka, KS	0.27	0.25	0.	0.	0.	0.24
Washington State University . . . . Pullman, WA	0.57	0.58	0.	0.	0.	0.56
Washington University . . . . St. Louis, MO	0.61	0.64	0.	0.	0.	0.63
Wayne State University . . . . Detroit, MI	0.66	0.68	0.	0.	0.	0.69
Westchester University of Pennsylvania . . . . Westchester, PA	0.36	0.33	0.	0.	0.	0.30
Western Carolina University . . . . Cullowhee, NC	0.37	0.38	0.	0.	0.	0.36
Western Illinois University . . . . . . Macomb, IL	0.43	0.44	0.	0.	0.	0.42
Western Kentucky University . . . Bowling Green, KY	0.40	0.41	0.	0.	0.	0.41
Western Michigan University . . . . Kalamazoo, MI	0.45	0.46	0.	0.	0.	0.46
Western Washington University . Bellingham, WA	0.41	0.42	0.	0.	0.	0.42
West Texas A&M University . . . . Canyon, TX	0.38	0.39	0.	0.	0.	0.35
West Virginia University . . . . Morgantown, WV	0.44	0.45	0.	0.	0.	0.47
Wichita State University . . . . Wichita, KS	0.27	0.30	0.	0.	0.	0.24
Widener University . . . . Chester, PA	0.30	0.31	0.	0.	0.	0.27
William Patterson College of New Jersey . . . . Wayne, NJ	0.31	0.32	0.	0.	0.	0.28
Winona State University . . . . Winona, MN	0.32	0.30	0.	0.	0.	0.29
Wright State University . . . . Dayton, OH	0.33	0.34	0.	0.	0.	0.31
Xavier University . . . . Cincinnati, OH	0.30	0.29	0.	0.	0.	0.25
Yeshiva University . . . . New York, NY	0.58	0.59	0.	0.	0.	0.56

DEPARTMENTS OF GRADUATE EDUCATION
Not On The Approved List of The Gourman Report (Continued)

RATING CATEGORIES	Numerical Range
Very Strong	4.51-4.99
Strong	4.01-4.49
Good	3.61-3.99
Acceptable Plus	3.01-3.59
Adequate	2.51-2.99
Marginal	2.01-2.49
Not Sufficient for Graduate Programs	0.

Department of Graduate Education / INSTITUTION	Gourman Overall Academic Score (Combined Areas/Fields)	Administration (Attitude and Policy) (Quality of Leadership at All Levels of Administration)	Curriculum (Attractiveness of Program)	Faculty Effectiveness	Faculty (Quality of Research/ Scholarship)	Library Resources
Youngstown State University . . . Youngstown, OH	0.27	0.28	0.	0.	0.	0.26

The GOURMAN REPORT
PART XIV

**A RATING OF THE TOP 50
QUALITY GRADUATE SCHOOLS
IN THE UNITED STATES**

A RATING OF THE TOP 50 QUALITY GRADUATE SCHOOLS

U.S.A. UNIVERSITIES
Leading Institutions

Fifty institutions with scores in the 4.00-5.00 range, in rank order

INSTITUTION	Rank	Score
HARVARD	1	4.94
CALIFORNIA, BERKELEY	2	4.93
MICHIGAN (Ann Arbor)	3	4.92
YALE	4	4.91
STANFORD	5	4.90
CHICAGO	6	4.89
PRINCETON	7	4.88
WISCONSIN (Madison)	8	4.87
UCLA	9	4.86
CORNELL (N.Y.)	10	4.85
COLUMBIA (N.Y.)	11	4.84
CAL TECH	12	4.83
M.I.T.	13	4.82
PENNSYLVANIA	14	4.81
MINNESOTA (Minneapolis)	15	4.80
NORTHWESTERN (Evanston)	16	4.79
ILLINOIS (Urbana)	17	4.78
JOHNS HOPKINS	18	4.77
CALIFORNIA, SAN DIEGO	19	4.76
BROWN	20	4.75
DUKE	21	4.73
INDIANA (Bloomington)	22	4.71
IOWA (Iowa City)	23	4.69
NORTH CAROLINA (Chapel Hill)	24	4.68
VIRGINIA (Charlottesville)	25	4.67
TEXAS (Austin)	26	4.65
WASHINGTON (Seattle)	27	4.63
WASHINGTON (St.Louis)	28	4.61
CARNEGIE-MELLON	29	4.58
CALIFORNIA, DAVIS	30	4.57
PURDUE (Lafayette)	31	4.55
RENSSELAER (N.Y.)	32	4.53
ROCHESTER (N.Y.)	33	4.51
CALIFORNIA, SAN FRANCISCO	34	4.49
RICE	35	4.47
SUNY (Stony Brook)	36	4.45
PENN STATE (University Park)	37	4.43
PITTSBURGH (Pittsburgh)	38	4.41
NOTRE DAME	39	4.40
VANDERBILT	40	4.37
CALIFORNIA, IRVINE	41	4.35
RUTGERS (New Brunswick)	42	4.33
GEORGIA TECH	43	4.31
DARTMOUTH	44	4.30
CASE WESTERN RESERVE	45	4.27
OHIO STATE (Columbus)	46	4.24
TUFTS	47	4.22
SUNY (Buffalo)	48	4.18
TULANE	49	4.16
BRANDEIS	50	4.13

**NOTE: Departments of Education excluded from the overall ratings of graduate schools.
Not approved by THE GOURMAN REPORT**

The GOURMAN REPORT
PART XV

**A RATING OF GRADUATE SCHOOLS
IN THE UNITED STATES**

A Rating of United States Graduate Schools: Academic and Selective

RATING CATEGORIES	Numerical Range
Very Strong	4.51-4.99
Strong	4.01-4.49
Good	3.61-3.99
Acceptable Plus	3.01-3.59
Adequate	2.51-2.99
Marginal	2.01-2.49

Not Sufficient for Graduate Programs   0.

INSTITUTION	Gourman Overall Academic Rating	INSTITUTION	Gourman Overall Academic Rating
Air Force Institute of Technology . . Wright-Patterson AFB, OH	2.80	Bridgewater State College . . . . Bridgewater, MA	0.
Alabama Agricultural and Mechanical University . . . . Normal, AL	2.10	Brigham Young University . . . . Provo, UT	2.70
Alfred University . . . . Alfred, NY	3.10	Brown University . . . . Providence, RI	4.75
American University . . . . Washington, D.C.	3.18	Bryn Mawr College . . . . Bryn Mawr, PA	3.30
Appalachian State University . . . . . Boone, NC	2.01	California Institute of Technology . . Pasadena, CA	4.83
Arizona State University . . . . Tempe, AZ	3.65	California Polytechnic State University, San Luis Obispo . . . . San Luis Obispo, CA	2.60
Arkansas State University . . . . State University, AR	2.02	California State University, Bakerfield Bakersfield, CA	0.
Auburn University . . . . Auburn, AL	3.59	California State Polytechnic University, Pomona . . . . Pomona, CA	2.02
Ball State University . . . . Muncie, IN	2.30	California State University, Chico . . Chico, CA	0.
Baylor University . . . . Waco, TX	3.61	California State University, Dominguez Hills . . . . Carson, CA	0.
Bloomsburg University of Pennsylvania Bloomsburg, PA	0.	California State University, Fresno . Fresno, CA	2.14
Boston College . . . . Chestnut Hill, MA	2.55	California State University, Fullerton Fullerton, CA	2.13
Boston University . . . . Boston, MA	3.91	California State University, Hayward Hayward, CA	0.
Bowling Green State University . . . Bowling Green, OH	2.90	California State University, Long Beach Long Beach, CA	2.12
Bradley University . . . . Peoria, IL	2.40	California State University, Los Angeles Los Angeles, CA	1.89
Brandeis University . . . . Waltham, MA	4.13		

NOTE: *Excluded from THE GOURMAN REPORT –Schools of Education Not Approved*

A Rating of United States Graduate Schools: Academic and Selective (Continued)

INSTITUTION	Gourman Overall Academic Rating	INSTITUTION	Gourman Overall Academic Rating
California State University, Northridge Northridge, CA	1.90	City University of New York, Herbert H. Lehman College Bronx, NY	2.68
California State University, Sacramento Sacramento, CA	2.15	City University of New York, Hunter College New York, NY	3.13
California State University, San Bernardino San Bernardino, CA	2.03	City University of New York, Queens College Flushing, NY	3.15
California State University, Stanislaus Turlock, CA	0.	Claremont Graduate School Claremont, CA	3.52
California University of Pennsylvania California, PA	0.	Clarion University of Pennsylvania Clarion, PA	0.
Carnegie-Mellon University Pittsburgh, PA	4.58	Clarkson University Potsdam, NY	2.76
Case Western Reserve University Cleveland, OH	4.27	Clark University Worcester, MA	3.55
Catholic University of America Washington, D.C.	3.12	Clemson University Clemson, SC	3.10
Central Connecticut State University New Britain, CT	2.07	Cleveland State University Cleveland, OH	2.15
Central Michigan University Mount Pleasant, MI	2.09	College of William & Mary Williamsburg, VA	2.51
Central Missouri State University Warrensburg, MO	2.01	Colorado School of Mines Golden, CO	3.84
Cheyney University of Pennsylvania Cheyney, PA	0.	Colorado State University Fort Collins, CO	2.95
Chicago State University Chicago, IL	0.	Columbia University New York, NY	4.84
City University of New York, Bernard M. Baruch College New York, NY	3.08	Cooper Union for the Advancement of Science and Art New York, NY	2.58
City University of New York, Brooklyn College New York, NY	3.10	Cornell University Ithaca, NY	4.85
City University of New York, City College New York, NY	3.31	Creighton University Omaha, NE	3.09
City University of New York, College of Staten Island Staten Island, NY	0.	Dartmouth College Hanover, NH	4.30
City University of New York, Graduate School & University Center New York, NY	3.88	De Paul University Chicago, IL	2.89
		Drake University Des Moines, IA	2.10

RATING CATEGORIES	Numerical Range
Very Strong	4.51-4.99
Strong	4.01-4.49
Good	3.61-3.99
Acceptable Plus	3.01-3.59
Adequate	2.51-2.99
Marginal	2.01-2.49
Not Sufficient for Graduate Programs	0.

INSTITUTION	Gourman Overall Academic Rating	INSTITUTION	Gourman Overall Academic Rating
Drexel University . . . . Philadelphia, PA	3.62	Fairleigh Dickinson University, Teaneck-Hackensack Campus . . . . Teaneck, NJ	3.06
Duke University . . . . Durham, NC	4.73	Florida Agricultural and Mechanical University . . . . Tallahassee, FL	2.12
Duquesne University . . . . Pittsburgh, PA	2.14	Florida Atlantic University . . . . Boca Raton, FL	2.04
East Carolina University . . . . Greenville, NC	2.53	Florida Institute of Technology . . . . Melbourne, FL	2.05
Eastern Illinois University . . . . Charleston, IL	2.06	Florida International University . . . . Miami, FL	2.06
Eastern Kentucky University . . . . . . Richmond, KY	2.18	Florida State University . . . . Tallahassee, FL	3.52
Eastern Michigan University . . . . . . Ypsilanti, MI	2.31	Fordham University . . . . Bronx, NY	3.37
Eastern New Mexico University . . . Portales, NM	2.04	Fort Hays State University . . . . Hays, KS	2.01
Eastern Washington University . . . . Cheney, WA	2.02	Framingham State College . . . . Framingham, MA	0.
East Stroudsburg University of Pennsylvania . . . . East Stroudburg, PA	0.	George Mason University . . . . Fairfax, VA	2.13
East Tennessee State University . . Johnson City, TN	2.19	Georgetown University . . . . Washington, D.C.	4.04
East Texas State University . . . . . . Commerce, TX	0.	George Washington University . . . . Washington, D.C.	3.68
Edinboro University of Pennsylvania Edinboro, PA	0.	Georgia Institute of Technology . . . Atlanta, GA	4.31
Emory University . . . . Atlanta, GA	3.79	Georgia Southern University . . . . . . Statesboro, GA	2.11
Emporia State University . . . . Emporia, KS	2.18	Georgia State University . . . . Atlanta, GA	2.27
Fairleigh Dickinson University, Florham-Madison Campus . . . . Madison, NJ	3.05	Golden Gate University . . . . San Francisco, CA	2.25

INSTITUTION	Gourman Overall Academic Rating	INSTITUTION	Gourman Overall Academic Rating
Gonzaga University . . . . Spokane, WA	2.96	Kansas State University . . . . Manhattan, KS	3.48
Grand Valley State University . . . . . Allendale, MI	2.01	Kent State University . . . . Kent, OH	2.70
Harvard University . . . . Cambridge, MA	4.94	Kutztown University of Pennsylvania Kutztown, PA	0.
Hofstra University . . . . Hempstead, NY	2.88	Lamar University–Beaumont . . . . . . Beaumont, TX	2.02
Howard University . . . . Washington D.C.	2.68	Lehigh University . . . . Bethlehem, PA	3.41
Humboldt State University . . . . Arcata, CA	2.01	Loma Linda University . . . . Loma Linda, CA	3.29
Idaho State University . . . . Pocatello, ID	2.28	Long Island University, Brooklyn Center Brooklyn, NY	3.27
Illinois Institute of Technology . . . . . Chicago, IL	2.54	Long Island University, C.W. Post Campus . . . . Brookville, NY	3.14
Illinois State University . . . . Normal, IL	2.45	Louisiana State University and Agricultural and Mechanical College Baton Rouge, LA	3.61
Indiana State University at Terre Haute Terre Haute, IN	2.01	Louisiana State University in Shreveport Shreveport, LA	2.01
Indiana University Bloomington . . . . Bloomington, IN	4.71	Louisiana Tech University . . . . Ruston, LA	2.18
Indiana University Kokomo . . . . Kokomo, IN	0.	Loyola University of Chicago . . . . . . Chicago, IL	3.14
Indiana University Northwest . . . . . Gary, IN	0.	Mankato State University . . . . Mankato, MN	2.09
Indiana University of Pennsylvania . Indiana, PA	0.	Mansfield University of Pennsylvania Mansfield, PA	0.
Indiana University–Purdue University Fort Wayne . . . . Fort Wayne, IN	2.04	Marquette University . . . . Milwaukee, WI	3.38
Indiana University–Purdue University Indianapolis . . . . Indianapolis, IN	3.98	Marshall University . . . . Huntington, WV	2.45
Indiana University South Bend . . . . South Bend, IN	0.	Massachusetts Institute of Technology Cambridge, MA	4.82
Indiana University Southeast . . . . . New Albany, IN	0.	Mercer University . . . . Macon, GA	2.45
Iowa State University . . . . Ames, IA	3.64	Miami University . . . . Oxford, OH	2.28
James Madison University . . . . Harrisonburg, VA	2.31	Michigan State University . . . . East Lansing, MI	4.03
Johns Hopkins University . . . . Baltimore, MD	4.77	Michigan Technological University . Houghton, MI	2.93

INSTITUTION	Gourman Overall Academic Rating
Middle Tennessee State University . Murfreesboro, TN	2.16
Millersville University of Pennsylvania Millersville, PA	0.
Milwaukee School of Engineering . . Milwaukee, WI	2.62
Mississippi State University . . . . Mississippi State, MS	2.91
Montana Tech of the University of Montana . . . . Butte, MT	3.19
Montana State University–Billings . . Billings, MT	0.
Montana State University–Northern Havre, MT	0.
Montana State University . . . . Bozeman, MT	2.55
Montclair State University . . . . Upper Montclair, NJ	2.78
Moorhead State University . . . . Moorhead, MN	2.12
Morehead State University . . . . Morehead, KY	2.09
Murray State University . . . . Murray, KY	2.03
Naval Postgraduate School . . . . Monterey, CA	2.85
New Jersey Institute of Technology Newark, NJ	2.88
New Mexico Highlands University . . Las Vegas, NM	0.
New Mexico Institute of Mining and Technology . . . . Socorro, NM	2.95
New Mexico State University . . . . . Las Cruces, NM	2.08
New School for Social Research . . . New York, NY	3.07
New York Institute of Technology, Old Westbury Campus . . . . Old Westbury, NY	2.04
New York University . . . . New York, NY	4.02
North Adams State College . . . . North Adams, MA	0.

INSTITUTION	Gourman Overall Academic Rating
North Carolina Agricultural and Technical State University . . . . Greensboro, NC	2.11
North Carolina Central University . . Durhan, NC	2.01
North Carolina State University at Raleigh . . . . Raleigh, NC	3.42
North Dakota State University . . . . . Fargo, ND	3.01
Northeastern Illinois University . . . . Chicago, IL	2.01
Northeastern University . . . . Boston, MA	2.29
Northeast Louisiana University . . . . Monroe, LA	2.04
Northeast Missouri State University Kirksville, MO	2.09
Northern Arizona University . . . . . . Flagstaff, AZ	2.10
Northern Illinois University . . . . DeKalb, IL	2.51
Northern Michigan University . . . . . Marquette, MI	2.12
Northwestern State University of Louisiana . . . . Natchitoches, LA	2.06
Northwestern University . . . . Evanston, IL	4.79
Nova Southeastern University . . . . . Fort Lauderdale, FL	2.28
Oakland University . . . . Rochester, NY	3.23
Ohio State University . . . . Columbus, OH	4.24
Ohio University . . . . Athens, OH	3.06
Oklahoma State University . . . . Stillwater, OK	2.84
Old Dominion University . . . . Norfolk, VA	2.59
Oregon State University . . . . Corvallis, OR	3.69
Pace University . . . . New York, NY	2.27

A Rating of United States Graduate Schools: Academic and Selective (Continued)

INSTITUTION	Gourman Overall Academic Rating
Pennsylvania State University – University Park Campus University Park, PA	4.43
Pepperdine University Malibu, CA	0.
Polytechnic University, Brooklyn Campus Brooklyn, NY	3.21
Portland State University Portland, OR	2.07
Pratt Institute Brooklyn, NY	2.60
Princeton University Princeton, NJ	4.88
Purdue University West Lafayette, IN	4.55
Purdue University Calumet Hammond, IN	2.01
Purdue University North Central Westville, IN	0.
Radford University Radford, VA	2.19
Rensselaer Polytechnic Institute Troy, NY	4.51
Rice University Houston, TX	4.47
Rochester Institute of Technology Rochester, NY	2.11
Rockefeller University New York, NY	4.02
Roosevelt University Chicago, IL	2.60
Rose-Hulman Institute of Technology Terre Haute, IN	2.51
Rutgers University, Newark Newark, NJ	2.74
Rutgers University, New Brunswick New Brunswick, NJ	4.33
St. Cloud State University St. Cloud, MN	2.01
St. John's University Jamaica, NY	2.50
Saint Louis University St. Louis, MO	3.31

INSTITUTION	Gourman Overall Academic Rating
Samford University Birmingham, AL	2.10
Sam Houston State University Huntsville, TX	2.11
San Diego State University San Diego, CA	2.20
San Francisco State University San Francisco, CA	2.19
San Jose State University San Jose, CA	2.18
Seattle University Seattle, WA	2.52
Seton Hall University South Orange, NJ	2.50
Shippensburg University of Pennsylvania Shippensburg, PA	0.
Simmons College Boston, MA	2.33
Slippery Rock University of Pennsylvania Slippery Rock, PA	0.
Smith College Northhampton, MA	2.67
Sonoma State University Rohnert Park, CA	0.
South Dakota School of Mines and Technology Rapid City, SD	3.15
South Dakota State University Brookings, SD	2.49
Southeastern Louisiana University Hammond, LA	2.01
Southeast Missouri State University Cape Giradeau, MO	2.01
Southern Connecticut State University New Haven, CT	2.05
Southern Illinois University at Carbondale Carbondale, IL	3.27
Southern Illinois University at Edwardsville Edwardsville, IL	2.12

RATING CATEGORIES	Numerical Range
Very Strong	4.51-4.99
Strong	4.01-4.49
Good	3.61-3.99
Acceptable Plus	3.01-3.59
Adequate	2.51-2.99
Marginal	2.01-2.49

Not Sufficient for Graduate Programs   0.

INSTITUTION	Gourman Overall Academic Rating
Southern Methodist University .... Dallas, TX	3.28
Southern University and Agricultural and Mechanical College .... Baton Rouge, LA	2.01
Southwest Missouri State University Springfield, MO	2.16
Southwest Texas State University . San Marcos, TX	2.21
Stanford University .... Stanford, CA	4.90
State University of New York at Albany Albany, NY	3.92
State University of New York at Binghamton .... Binghamton, NY	3.98
State University of New York at Buffalo Buffalo, NY	4.18
State University of New York at Stony Brook .... Stony Brook, NY	4.45
State University of New York College at Brockport .... Brockport, NY	0.
State University of New York College at Buffalo .... Buffalo, NY	0.
State University of New York College at Cortland .... Cortland, NY	0.
State University of New York College at Fredonia .... Fredonia, NY	0.

INSTITUTION	Gourman Overall Academic Rating
State University of New York College at Geneseo .... Geneseo, NY	0.
State University of New York College at New Paltz .... New Paltz, NY	0.
State University of New York College at Oneonta .... Oneonta, NY	0.
State University of New York College at Oswego .... Oswego, NY	0.
State University of New York College at Plattsburgh .... Plattsburgh, NY	0.
State University of New York College at Potsdam .... Potsdam, NY	0.
State University of New York College of Environmental Science & Forestry Syracuse, NY	3.80
Stephen F. Austin State University . Nacogdoches, TX	2.19
Stevens Institute of Technology ... Hoboken, NJ	3.31
Suffolk University .... Boston, MA	2.12
Syracuse University .... Syracuse, NY	3.78
Tarleton State University .... Stephenville, TX	2.02
Teachers College, Columbia University New York, NY	3.32

INSTITUTION	Gourman Overall Academic Rating	INSTITUTION	Gourman Overall Academic Rating
Temple University .... Philadelphia, PA	3.20	University of Arkansas at Little Rock Little Rock, AR	2.19
Tennessee State University ...... Nashville, TN	2.01	University of California, Berkeley .. Berkeley, CA	4.93
Tennessee Technological University Cookeville, TN	2.10	University of California, Davis ..... Davis, CA	4.57
Texas A&M International University Laredo, TX	0.	University of California, Irvine ..... Irvine, CA	4.35
Texas A&M University .... College Station, TX	3.71	University of California, Los Angeles Los Angeles, CA	4.86
Texas A&M University–Corpus Christi Corpus Christi, TX	0.	University of California, Riverside .. Riverside, CA	3.80
Texas A&M University–Kingsville .. Kingsville, TX	0.	University of California, San Diego . La Jolla, CA	4.76
Texas Christian University .... Fort Worth, TX	2.90	University of California, San Francisco San Francisco, CA	4.49
Texas Southern University .... Houston, TX	2.15	University of California, Santa Barbara Santa Barbara, CA	3.95
Texas Tech University .... Lubbock, TX	3.01	University of California, Santa Cruz Santa Cruz, CA	3.50
Texas Woman's University .... Denton, TX	2.79	University of Central Florida ...... Orlando, FL	2.19
Tufts University .... Medford, MA	4.22	University of Chicago .... Chicago, IL	4.89
Tulane University .... New Orleans, LA	4.16	University of Cincinnati .... Cincinnati, OH	3.52
Tuskegee University .... Tuskegee Institute, AL	2.40	University of Colorado at Boulder .. Boulder, CO	3.73
University of Akron .... Akron, OH	2.36	University of Colorado at Colorado Springs .... Colorado Springs, CO	2.01
University of Alabama .... University, AL	3.36	University of Colorado at Denver .. Denver, CO	3.06
University of Alabama in Birmingham Birmingham, AL	3.38	University of Connecticut .... Storrs, CT	3.71
University of Alabama in Huntsville . Huntsville, AL	2.77	University of Dallas .... Irving, TX	2.12
University of Alaska, Anchorage ... Anchorage, AK	2.01	University of Dayton .... Dayton, OH	2.19
University of Alaska, Fairbanks .... Fairbanks, AK	2.60	University of Delaware .... Newark, DE	3.30
University of Arizona .... Tucson, AZ	3.72	University of Denver .... Denver, CO	3.55
University of Arkansas .... Fayetteville, AR	3.15		

A Rating of United States Graduate Schools: Academic and Selective (Continued)

RATING CATEGORIES	Numerical Range
Very Strong	4.51-4.99
Strong	4.01-4.49
Good	3.61-3.99
Acceptable Plus	3.01-3.59
Adequate	2.51-2.99
Marginal	2.01-2.49
Not Sufficient for Graduate Programs	0.

INSTITUTION	Gourman Overall Academic Rating
University of Detroit Mercy .... Detroit, MI	2.33
University of Florida .... Gainesville, FL	3.89
University of Georgia .... Athens, GA	3.51
University of Hartford .... West Hartford, CT	2.55
University of Hawaii at Manoa ..... Honolulu, HI	3.42
University of Houston – Clear Lake . Houston, TX	2.01
University of Houston .... Houston, TX	3.47
University of Idaho .... Moscow, ID	3.05
University of Illinois at Chicago .... Chicago, IL	3.77
University of Illinois at Springfield .. Springfield, IL	2.05
University of Illinois at Urbana-Champaign .... Urbana, IL	4.78
University of Iowa .... Iowa City, IA	4.69
University of Kansas .... Lawrence, KS	3.99
University of Kentucky .... Lexington, KY	3.24
University of Louisville .... Louisville, KY	3.22
University of Maine at Orono ...... Orono, ME	3.19
University of Maryland College Park College Park, MD	3.80

INSTITUTION	Gourman Overall Academic Rating
University of Maryland Graduate School Baltimore .... Baltimore, MD	3.79
University of Massachusetts Amherst Amherst, MA	3.86
University of Massachusetts Boston Boston, MA	2.20
University of Massachusetts Dartmouth North Dartmouth, MA	2.11
University of Massachusetts Lowell Lowell, MA	3.26
University of Memphis .... Memphis, TN	3.05
University of Miami .... Coral Gables, FL	2.99
University of Michigan .... Ann Arbor, MI	4.92
University of Michigan – Dearborn . Dearborn, MI	2.40
University of Minnesota, Duluth ... Duluth, MN	2.60
University of Minnesota, Twin Cities Minneapolis, MN	4.80
University of Mississippi .... University, MS	2.93
University of Missouri – Columbia .. Columbia, MO	3.79
University of Missouri – Kansas City Kansas City, MO	3.36
University of Missouri – Rolla ..... Rolla, MO	3.51
University of Missouri – St. Louis .. St. Louis, MO	3.28
University of Montana – Missoula .. Missoula, MT	3.30

A Rating of United States Graduate Schools: Academic and Selective (Continued)

INSTITUTION	Gourman Overall Academic Rating
University of Montevallo Montevallo, AL	0.
University of Nebraska at Kearney Kearney, NE	2.68
University of Nebraska at Omaha Omaha, NE	3.27
University of Nebraska – Lincoln Lincoln, NE	3.41
University of Nevada – Las Vegas Las Vegas, NV	2.45
University of Nevada – Reno Reno, NV	2.57
University of New Hampshire Durham, NH	2.97
University of New Haven West Haven, CT	2.01
University of New Mexico Albuquerque, NM	3.22
University of New Orleans New Orleans, LA	2.49
University of North Carolina at Chapel Hill Chapel Hill, NC	4.68
University of North Carolina at Charlotte Charlotte, NC	2.34
University of North Carolina at Greensboro Greensboro, NC	2.32
University of North Dakota Grand Forks, ND	3.06
University of Northern Colorado Greeley, CO	2.01
University of Northern Iowa Cedar Falls, IA	2.04
University of North Florida Jacksonville, FL	2.01
University of North Texas Denton, TX	2.84
University of Notre Dame Notre Dame, IN	4.40
University of Oklahoma Norman, OK	3.31
University of Oregon Eugene, OR	3.80

INSTITUTION	Gourman Overall Academic Rating
University of Pennsylvania Philadelphia, PA	4.81
University of Pittsburgh Pittsburgh, PA	4.41
University of Portland Portland, OR	2.01
University of Rhode Island Kingston, RI	2.86
University of Richmond Richmond, VA	2.02
University of Rochester Rochester, NY	4.51
University of San Diego San Diego, CA	2.01
University of San Francisco San francisco, CA	2.11
University of Santa Clara Santa Clara, CA	2.47
University of South Alabama Mobile, AL	2.38
University of South Carolina Columbia, SC	3.27
University of South Dakota Vermillion, SD	2.96
University of Southern California Los Angeles, CA	3.84
University of Southern Mississippi Hattiesburg, MS	2.36
University of South Florida Tampa, FL	3.20
University of Southwestern Louisiana Lafayette, LA	2.21
University of Tennessee at Chattanooga Chattanooga, TN	2.02
University of Tennessee Knoxville, TN	3.60
University of Tennessee at Martin Martin, TN	2.01
University of Texas at Arlington Arlington, TX	2.29
University of Texas at Austin Austin, TX	4.65
University of Texas at Bronsville Bronsville, TX	0.

A Rating of United States Graduate Schools: Academic and Selective (Continued)

RATING CATEGORIES	Numerical Range
Very Strong	4.51-4.99
Strong	4.01-4.49
Good	3.61-3.99
Acceptable Plus	3.01-3.59
Adequate	2.51-2.99
Marginal	2.01-2.49
Not Sufficient for Graduate Programs	0.

INSTITUTION	Gourman Overall Academic Rating	INSTITUTION	Gourman Overall Academic Rating
University of Texas at Dallas . . . . . . Richardson, TX	3.31	University of Wisconsin – La Crosse La Crosse, WI	0.
University of Texas at El Paso . . . . El Paso, TX	2.05	University of Wisconsin – Madison . Madison, WI	4.87
University of Texas at San Antonio . San Antonio, TX	2.39	University of Wisconsin – Milwaukee Milwaukee, WI	3.43
University of Texas at Tyler . . . . Tyler, TX	0.	University of Wisconsin – Oshkosh . Oshkosh, WI	0.
University of Texas of the Permian Basin . . . . Odessa, TX	0.	University of Wisconsin – Parkside . Kenosha, WI	0.
University of Texas – Pan American Edinburg, TX	0.	University of Wisconsin – Platteville Platteville, WI	0.
University of the District of Columbia Washington, D.C.	0.	University of Wisconsin – River Falls River Falls, WI	0.
University of the Pacific . . . . Stockton, CA	2.81	University of Wisconsin – Stevens Point Stevens Point, WI	0.
University of Toledo . . . . Toledo, OH	2.56	University of Wisconsin – Stout . . . . Menomonie, WI	0.
University of Tulsa . . . . Tulsa, OK	2.64	University of Wisconsin – Superior . Superior, WI	0.
University of Utah . . . . Salt Lake City, UT	3.96	University of Wisconsin – Whitewater Whitewater, WI	0.
University of Vermont . . . . Burlington, VT	2.97	University of Wyoming . . . . Laramie, WY	3.11
University of Virginia . . . . Charlottesville, VA	4.67	Utah State University . . . . Logan, UT	2.96
University of Washington . . . . Seattle, WA	4.63	Vanderbilt University . . . . Nashville, TN	4.37
University of West Florida . . . . Pensacola, FL	2.01	Villanova University . . . . Villanova, PA	0.
University of Wisconsin – Eau Claire Eau Claire, WI	0.	Virginia Commonwealth University . Richmond, VA	3.11
University of Wisconsin – Green Bay Green Bay, WI	0.	Virginia Polytechnic Institute and State University . . . . Blacksburg, VA	3.59

INSTITUTION	Gourman Overall Academic Rating	INSTITUTION	Gourman Overall Academic Rating
Wake Forest University Winston-Salem, NC	2.89		
Washington State University Pullman, WA	3.40		
Washington University St. Louis, MO	4.61		
Wayne State University Detroit, MI	3.40		
Wesleyan University Middletown, CT	2.37		
Westchester University of Pennsylvania Westchester, PA	0.		
Western Illinois University Macomb, IL	2.08		
Western Kentucky University Bowling Green, KY	2.15		
Western Michigan University Kalamazoo, MI	2.52		
Western Washington University Bellingham, WA	2.01		
West Texas A&M University Canyon, TX	2.01		
West Virginia University Morgantown, WV	3.19		
Wichita State University Wichita, KS	2.05		
Widener University Chester, PA	2.18		
William Patterson College of New Jersey Wayne, NJ	2.02		
Winona State University Winona, MN	2.01		
Worchester Polytechnic Institute Worchester, MA	2.95		
Wright State University Dayton, OH	2.95		
Yale University New Haven, CT	4.91		
Yeshiva University New York, NY	3.79		
Youngstown State University Youngstown, OH	1.68		

The GOURMAN REPORT
PART XVI

A RATING OF GRADUATE RESEARCH LIBRARIES

A RATING OF GRADUATE RESEARCH LIBRARIES
Leading Institutions

Fifty institutions with scores in the 4.0-5.0 range, in rank order

INSTITUTION	Rank	Score
HARVARD	1	4.93
CALIFORNIA, BERKELEY	2	4.92
MICHIGAN (Ann Arbor)	3	4.91
YALE	4	4.90
STANFORD	5	4.89
CHICAGO	6	4.88
PRINCETON	7	4.87
WISCONSIN (Madison)	8	4.86
UCLA	9	4.85
CORNELL (N.Y.)	10	4.84
COLUMBIA (N.Y.)	11	4.83
CAL TECH	12	4.82
M.I.T.	13	4.81
PENNSYLVANIA	14	4.80
MINNESOTA (Minneapolis)	15	4.79
NORTHWESTERN (Evanston)	16	4.78
ILLINOIS (Urbana)	17	4.77
JOHNS HOPKINS	18	4.76
CALIFORNIA, SAN DIEGO	19	4.75
BROWN	20	4.74
DUKE	21	4.72
INDIANA (Bloomington)	22	4.70
IOWA (Iowa City)	23	4.68
NORTH CAROLINA (Chapel Hill)	24	4.67
VIRGINIA (Charlottesville)	25	4.66
TEXAS (Austin)	26	4.64
WASHINGTON (Seattle)	27	4.62
WASHINGTON (St. Louis)	28	4.60
CARNEGIE-MELLON	29	4.57
CALIFORNIA, DAVIS	30	4.56
PURDUE (Lafayette)	31	4.54
RENNSELAER (N.Y.)	32	4.52
ROCHESTER (N.Y.)	33	4.50
CALIFORNIA, SAN FRANCISCO	34	4.48
RICE	35	4.46
SUNY (Stony Brook)	36	4.44
PENN STATE (University Park)	37	4.42
PITTSBURGH (Pittsburgh)	38	4.40
NOTRE DAME	39	4.39
VANDERBILT	40	4.36
CALIFORNIA, IRVINE	41	4.34
RUTGERS (New Brunswick)	42	4.32
GEORGIA TECH	43	4.30
DARTMOUTH	44	4.29
CASE WESTERN RESERVE	45	4.26
OHIO STATE (Columbus)	46	4.23
TUFTS	47	4.20
SUNY (Buffalo)	48	4.17
TULANE	49	4.15
BRANDEIS	50	4.11

**NOTE: *Departments of Education Research Libraries excluded from the overall ratings.
Not approved by THE GOURMAN REPORT.***

The GOURMAN REPORT
PART XVII

APPENDIXES – INCLUDED IN THE 7TH EDITION

APPENDIX A
A List of Tables

TABLE 1
A Rating of Graduate Programs in the United States

FIELD OF STUDY	Selected Number of Institutions Granting Degree	Total Number of Programs (Curriculum) Evaluated	Total Number of Areas of Study Evaluated	Total Number of Faculty Areas Evaluated	Quality Institutions Listed in the Gourman Report
Aerospace Engineering	38	38	885	370	30
Agricultural Economics	74	74	801	166	34
Agricultural Engineering	39	39	658	143	32
Agricultural Sciences	104	104	2,412	638	32
Agronomy/Soil Sciences	69	69	977	202	26
Anthropology	72	72	964	138	31
Applied Mathematics	131	131	996	242	24
Applied Physics	44	44	407	88	11
Architecture	89	89	833	207	29
Art History	40	40	551	96	20
Astronomy	57	57	865	352	27
Biochemistry	201	201	1,011	450	30
Biomedical Engineering	43	43	736	223	26
Botany	110	110	911	210	40
Business Administration (EMB)[1]	See Table 14.				
Business Administration (MBA)[2]	See Table 15.				
Business Administration (Ph.D./DBA)[3]	See Table 16.				
Cell Biology	184	184	912	214	35
Ceramic Sciences and Engineering	15	15	641	188	9
Chemical Engineering	98	98	933	207	50
Chemistry	173	173	1,016	450	40
Child Development-Psychology	48	48	333	86	14
City/Regional Planning	75	75	220	51	17
Civil Engineering	107	107	975	77	40
Classics	31	31	402	50	30
Clinical Psychology	258	258	851	78	24
Cognitive-Psychology	125	125	306	65	31
Comparative Literature	46	46	222	47	30
Computer Science	119	119	862	58	41
Developmental Psychology	107	107	860	63	26
Drama/Theatre	190	190	1,613	268	32
Economics	113	113	998	303	40
Electrical Engineering	135	135	989	301	35
English	131	131	990	338	37
Entomology	60	60	870	229	31
Environmental Engineering	82	82	691	214	10
Experimental Psychology (General)	135	135	1,122	427	16
Forestry	53	53	839	255	31
French	48	48	309	200	32

APPENDIX A
A List of Tables

TABLE 1
A Rating of Graduate Programs in the United States (Continued)

FIELD OF STUDY	Selected Number of Institutions Granting Degree	Total Number of Programs (Curriculum) Evaluated	Total Number of Areas of Study Evaluated	Total Number of Faculty Areas Evaluated	Quality Institutions Listed in the Gourman Report
Geography	40	40	307	166	30
Georsciences	111	111	1,120	460	39
German	35	35	732	361	31
History	119	119	989	264	37
Horticulture	47	47	709	207	27
Industrial Engineering	44	44	971	211	30
Industrial/Labor Relations	49	49	310	48	8
Industrial/Organizational Psychology	106	106	812	99	17
Inorganic Chemistry	63	63	960	75	16
Journalism	100	100	914	312	22
Landscape Architecture	24	24	359	91	17
Library Science	56	56	864	322	20
Linguistics	43	43	630	209	32
Materials Science	72	72	910	355	36
Mathematics	145	145	1,119	840	47
Mechanical Engineering	117	117	994	219	36
Microbiology	194	194	2,866	631	40
Molecular Genetics	107	107	862	222	36
Music	71	71	840	232	36
Near and Middle Eastern Studies	25	25	244	80	13
Neurosciences	105	105	765	243	35
Nuclear Engineering	38	38	995	416	25
Nutrition	140	140	870	239	38
Occupational Therapy	52	52	978	224	20
Oceanography	30	30	430	120	24
Organic Chemistry	63	63	964	166	13
Personality-Psychology	60	60	627	128	18
Petroleum Engineering	27	27	965	140	14
Pharmacology	130	130	970	215	30
Plant Pathology	44	44	560	208	30
Philosophy	80	80	688	171	40
Physical Chemistry	65	65	793	87	16
Physical Therapy	111	111	891	322	21
Physics	155	155	1,119	460	41
Physiology	148	148	828	261	30
Political Science	104	104	733	388	34

APPENDIX A
A List of Tables

TABLE 1
A Rating of Graduate Programs in the United States (Continued)

FIELD OF STUDY	Selected Number of Institutions Granting Degree	Total Number of Programs (Curriculum) Evaluated	Total Number of Areas of Study Evaluated	Total Number of Faculty Areas Evaluated	Quality Institutions Listed in the Gourman Report
Psychology	190	190	1,114	640	40
Public Administration	60	60	608	211	19
Radio/TV/Film	73	73	541	112	10
Russian	26	26	158	49	10
Sensation and Perception-Psychology	55	55	361	77	24
Slavic Languages	31	31	404	50	16
Social Psychology	118	118	991	234	32
Social Welfare/Social Work	169	169	941	485	31
Sociology	112	112	968	450	32
Spanish	61	61	444	100	30
Speech Pathology/Audiology	226	226	1,150	453	21
Statistics	71	71	984	366	30
Toxicology	85	85	573	88	34

APPENDIX A (Continued)
A List of Tables

TABLE 2
A Rating of Law Schools: Canada

	Canadian Law Schools
Selected Number of Law Schools Evaluated	14
Quality Law Schools Listed in the Gourman Report	14
Total Number of Law Programs Evaluated	14
Total Number of Faculty Areas Evaluated	217
Total Number of Administrative Areas Evaluated	290
Total Number of Curriculum Areas Evaluated	253

TABLE 3
A Rating of Law Schools: International and the United States

	International Law Schools	U.S.A. Law Schools
Selected Number of Law Schools Evaluated	543	175
Quality Law Schools Listed in the Gourman Report	53	175*
Total Number of Law Programs Evaluated	543	175
Total Number of Faculty Areas Evaluated	2,098	983
Total Number of Administrative Areas Evaluated	2,161	1,854
Total Number of Curriculum Areas Evaluated	3,002	1,833

*U.S.A. SCHOOLS OF LAW

Rating Categories	Numerical Range	Number of Institutions
Very Strong	4.6-5.0	20
Strong	4.0-4.5	23
Good	3.6-3.9	31
Acceptable Plus	3.0-3.5	43
Adequate	2.1-2.9	58
	TOTAL	175

TABLE 4
A Rating of Dental Schools in Canada

	Canadian Dental Schools
Selected Number of Dental Schools Evaluated	10
Quality Dental Schools Listed in the Gourman Report	10
Total Number of Dental Programs Evaluated	10
Total Number of Curriculum Areas Evaluated	972
Total Number of Faculty Areas Evaluated	466
Total Number of Administrative Areas Evaluated	500

TABLE 5
A Rating of Dental Schools in the United States

	U.S.A. Dental Schools
Selected Number of Dental Schools Evaluated	54
Quality Dental Schools Listed in the Gourman Report	54
Total Number of Dental Programs Evaluated	54
Total Number of Curriculum Areas Evaluated	1,002
Total Number of Faculty Areas Evaluated	630
Total Number of Administrative Areas Evaluated	848

TABLE 6
A Rating of Medical Schools in Canada

	Canadian Medical Schools
Selected Number of Medical Schools Evaluated	16
Quality Medical Schools Listed in the Gourman Report	16
Total Number of Medical Programs Evaluated	16
Total Number of Faculty Areas Evaluated	225
Total Number of Administrative Areas Evaluated	612
Total Number of Curriculum Areas Evaluated	848

TABLE 7
A Rating of Medical Schools: International and the United States

	International Medical Schools	U.S.A. Medical Schools
Selected Number of Medical Schools Evaluated	712	125
Quality Medical Schools Listed in the Gourman Report	55	125*
Total Number of Medical Programs Evaluated	712	125
Total Number of Faculty Areas Evaluated	1,650	900
Total Number of Administrative Areas Evaluated	2,310	1,071
Total Number of Curriculum Areas Evaluated	5,898	4,680

*U.S.A. SCHOOLS OF MEDICINE

Rating Categories	Numerical Range	Number of Institutions
Very Strong	4.6-5.0	19
Strong	4.0-4.5	32
Good	3.6-3.9	29
Acceptable Plus	3.0-3.5	45
	TOTAL	125

TABLE 8
A Rating of United States Veterinary Schools

	U.S.A. Veterinary Schools
Selected Number of Veterinary Schools Evaluated	27
Quality Veterinary Schools Listed in the Gourman Report	26
Total Number of Veterinary Programs Evaluated	27
Total Number of Curriculum Areas Evaluated	2,010
Total Number of Faculty Areas Evaluated	667
Total Number of Administrative Areas Evaluated	846

APPENDIX A (Continued)
A List of Tables

TABLE 9
A Rating of United States Nursing Schools

	U.S.A Nursing Schools
Selected Number of Nursing Schools Evaluated	73
Quality Nursing Schools Listed in the Gourman Report	73
Total Number of Nursing Programs Evaluated	73
Total Number of Curriculum Areas Evaluated	1,733
Total Number of Faculty Areas Evaluated	675
Total Number of Administrative Areas Evaluated	914

TABLE 10
A Rating of United States Optometry Schools

	U.S.A. Optometry Schools
Selected Number of Optometry Schools Evaluated	17
Quality Optometry Schools Listed in the Gourman Report	17
Total Number of Optometry Programs Evaluated	17
Total Number of Curriculum Areas Evaluated	740
Total Number of Faculty Areas Evaluated	155
Total Number of Administrative Areas Evaluated	488

TABLE 11
A Rating of Pharmacy Schools in Canada

	Canadian Pharmacy Schools
Selected Number of Pharmacy Schools Evaluated	8
Quality Pharmacy Schools Listed in the Gourman Report	8
Total Number of Pharmacy Programs Evaluated	8
Total Number of Curriculum Areas Evaluated	711
Total Number of Faculty Areas Evaluated	153
Total Number of Administrative Areas Evaluated	322

TABLE 12
A Rating of United States Pharmacy Schools

	U.S.A Pharmacy Schools
Selected Number of Pharmacy Schools Evaluated	73
Quality Pharmacy Schools Listed in the Gourman Report	59
Total Number of Pharmacy Programs Evaluated	73
Total Number of Curriculum Areas Evaluated	3,115
Total Number of Faculty Areas Evaluated	860
Total Number of Administrative Areas Evaluated	939

TABLE 13
A Rating of United States Public Health Schools

	U.S.A. Public Health Schools
Selected Number of Public Health Schools Evaluated	28
Quality Public Health Schools Listed in the Gourman Report	26
Total Number of Public Health Programs Evaluated	28
Total Number of Curriculum Areas Evaluated	462
Total Number of Faculty Areas Evaluated	325
Total Number of Administrative Areas Evaluated	422

TABLE 14
A Rating of United States EMBA/Management Schools

	U.S.A. EMBA/Management Schools
Number of Schools Evaluated	20
Number of Schools Listed in the Gourman Report	13
Total Number of Administrative Areas Evaluated	61
Total Number of Curriculum Areas Evaluated	264
Total Number of Faculty Areas Evaluated	70

APPENDIX A (Continued)
A List of Tables

TABLE 15
A Rating of United States MBA/Management Schools

	U.S.A MBA/Management Schools
Number of Schools Evaluated	528
Number of Schools Listed in the Gourman Report	50
Total Number of Administrative Areas Evaluated	1,976
Total Number of Curriculum Areas Evaluated	2,020
Total Number of Faculty Areas Evaluated	981

TABLE 16
A Rating of United States Doctoral Business/Management Schools

	U.S.A. Doctoral/ Bus. Managemnt Schools
Number of Schools Evaluated	135
Number of Schools Listed in the Gourman Report	50
Total Number of Administrative Areas Evaluated	1,001
Total Number of Curriculum Areas Evaluated	988
Total Number of Faculty Areas Evaluated	980

TABLE 17
A Rating of United States Engineering Schools

	U.S.A. Engineering Schools
Number of Schools Evaluated	139
Number of Schools Listed in the Gourman Report	50
Total Number of Administrative Areas Evaluated	974
Total Number of Curriculum Areas Evaluated	1,001
Total Number of Faculty Areas Evaluated	732

APPENDIX B
International Institutions of Law Included in the 7th Edition

COUNTRY AND LAW SCHOOL

AUSTRIA
University of Innsbruck
University of Vienna

BELGIUM
Free University of Brussels

DENMARK
University of Copenhagen

FRANCE
University of Aix-Marseilles II
University of Besancon
University of Bordeaux I
University of Caen
University of Clermont
University of Dijon
University of Social Sciences (Grenoble II)
University of Law and Health Sciences
(Lille II)
University of Limoges
University of Lyon III (Jean Moulin)
University of Montpellier I
University of Nancy I
University of Nantes
University of Nice
University of Orleans
University of Paris (Pantheon-Sorbonne)
University of Law, Economics, and
Social Sciences (Paris II)
University of Paris-Nanterre (Paris X)
University of Paris XII
University of Paris-Nord (Paris XIII)
University of Poitiers
University of Reims
University of Rennes I
University of Rouen
University of Saint-Etienne
University of Social Sciences (Toulouse I)

FEDERAL REPUBLIC OF GERMANY
Rhemish Friedrich-Wilhelm University of
Bonn
University of Cologne
Friedrich Alexander University of
Erlangen-Nuremberg

FEDERAL REPUBLIC OF GERMANY
Albert Ludwig University of Freiburg
Georg August University of Göttingen
Rupert Charles University of Heidelberg
Christian Albrecht University of Kiel
Johannes Gutenberg University of Mainz
Philipps University of Marburg
Ludwig Maximilian University of Munich
University of Munster
Eberhard Karl University of Tubingen
University of Würzburg

GREECE
National and Capodistrian University
of Athens

IRELAND
University of Dublin, Trinity College

ISRAEL
The Hebrew University of Jerusalem

ITALY
University of Rome

JAPAN
The University of Tokyo

NETHERLANDS
University of Amsterdam

SPAIN
University of Madrid

SWEDEN
University of Stockholm

SWITZERLAND
University of Fribourg
University of Geneva

UNITED KINGDOM
University of Cambridge
University of Edinburgh
University of London
University of Oxford

APPENDIX C
Law Schools in Canada Included in the 7th Edition

PROVINCE AND LAW SCHOOL

ALBERTA
University of Alberta
Faculty of Law
Edmonton, Alberta

University of Calgary
Faculty of Law
Calgary, Alberta

BRITISH COLUMBIA
University of British Columbia
Faculty of Law
Vancouver, British Columbia

University of Victoria
Faculty of Law
Victoria, British Columbia

MANITOBA
University of Manitoba
Faculty of Law
Winnipeg, Manitoba

NOVA SCOTIA
Dalhousie University
Faculty of Law
Halifax, Nova Scotia

ONTARIO
University of Ottawa
Common Law Section
Ottawa, Ontario

Queen's University
Faculty of Law
Kingston, Ontario

University of Toronto
Faculty of Law
Toronto, Ontario

University of Western Ontario
Faculty of Law
London, Ontario

University of Windsor
Faculty of Law
Windsor, Ontario

York University
Osgoode Hall Law School
Downsview, Ontario

QUEBEC
McGill University
Faculty of Law
Montreal, Quebec

SASKATCHEWAN
University of Saskatchewan
College of Law
Saskatoon, Saskatchewan

APPENDIX D
United States Institutions of Law Included in the 7th Edition

STATE AND LAW SCHOOL

ALABAMA
University of Alabama
Samford University

ARIZONA
University of Arizona
Arizona State University

ARKANSAS
University of Arkansas, Fayetteville
University of Arkansas at Little Rock

CALIFORNIA
University of California, Berkeley
University of California, Davis
University of California, Los Angeles
University of California, San Francisco
California Western School of Law
Golden Gate University
Loyola Law School
McGeorge School of Law
Pepperdine University
University of San Diego
University of San Francisco
University of Santa Clara
University of Southern California
Southwestern University
Stanford University
Whittier College

COLORADO
University of Colorado
University of Denver

CONNECTICUT
Bridgeport School of Law
    at Quinnipac College
University of Connecticut
Yale University

DELAWARE
Delaware Law School of Widener University

DISTRICT OF COLUMBIA
American University
Catholic University of America
District of Columbia School of Law
Georgetown University
George Washington University
Howard University

FLORIDA
University of Florida
Florida State University
University of Miami
Nova Southeastern University
Stetson University

GEORGIA
Emory University
Georgia State University
University of Georgia
Mercer University

HAWAII
University of Hawaii at Manoa

IDAHO
University of Idaho

ILLINOIS
University of Chicago
De Paul University
University of Illinois
Illinois Institute of Technology
John Marshall Law School
Loyola University
Northern Illinois University
Northwestern University
Southern Illinois University

INDIANA
Indiana University, Bloomington
Indiana University, Indianapolis
University of Notre Dame
Valparaiso University

IOWA
Drake University
University of Iowa

KANSAS
University of Kansas
Washburn University of Topeka

KENTUCKY
University of Kentucky
University of Louisville
Northern Kentucky University

STATE AND LAW SCHOOL

LOUISIANA
Louisiana State University
Loyola University
Southern University
Tulane University

MAINE
University of Maine

MARYLAND
University of Baltimore
University of Maryland

MASSACHUSETTS
Boston College
Boston University
Harvard University
New England School of Law
Northeastern University
Suffolk University
Western New England College

MICHIGAN
University of Detroit Mercy School of Law
Detroit College of Law
University of Michigan
Thomas M. Cooley Law School
Wayne State University

MINNESOTA
Hamline University
University of Minnesota
William Mitchell College of Law

MISSISSIPPI
University of Mississippi
Mississippi College School of Law

MISSOURI
University of Missouri, Columbia
University of Missouri, Kansas City
Saint Louis University
Washington University

MONTANA
University of Montana

NEBRASKA
Creighton University
University of Nebraska

NEW HAMPSHIRE
Franklin Pierce Law Center

NEW JERSEY
Rutgers, State University, Camden
Rutgers, State University, Newark
Seton Hall University

NEW MEXICO
University of New Mexico

NEW YORK
Albany Law School
Brooklyn Law School
Cardozo School of Law (Yeshiva University)
Columbia University
Cornell University
Fordham University
Hofstra University School of Law
City University of New York Law School
    at Queens College
State University of New York at Buffalo
New York Law School
New York University
Pace University
St. John's University
Syracuse University
Touro College

NORTH CAROLINA
Campbell University
Duke University
University of North Carolina
North Carolina Central University
Wake Forest University

NORTH DAKOTA
University of North Dakota

STATE AND LAW SCHOOL

OHIO
University of Akron
Capital University
Case Western Reserve University
University of Cincinnati
Cleveland State University
University of Dayton
Ohio Northern University
Ohio State University
University of Toledo

OKLAHOMA
University of Oklahoma
Oklahoma City University
University of Tulsa

OREGON
Lewis and Clark Law School
University of Oregon
Williamette University

PENNSYLVANIA
Dickinson School of Law
Duquesne University
University of Pennsylvania
University of Pittsburgh
Temple University
Villanova University
Widener University at Harrisburg

SOUTH CAROLINA
University of South Carolina

SOUTH DAKOTA
University of South Dakota

TENNESSEE
Memphis State University
University of Tennessee
Vanderbilt University

TEXAS
Baylor University

TEXAS (Continued)
University of Houston
St. Mary's University of San Antonio
Southern Methodist University
South Texas College of Law
University of Texas
Texas Southern University
Texas Tech University

UTAH
Brigham Young University
University of Utah

VERMONT
Vermont Law School

VIRGINIA
George Mason University
University of Richmond
University of Virginia
Washington and Lee University
College of William and Mary

WASHINGTON
Gonzaga University
University of Puget Sound
University of Washington

WEST VIRGINIA
West Virginia University

WISCONSIN
Marquette University
University of Wisconsin

WYOMING
University of Wyoming

COMMONWEALTH OF PUERTO RICO
Catholic University of Puerto Rico
Inter American University of Puerto Rico
University of Puerto Rico

APPENDIX E
Dental Schools in Canada Included in the 7th Edition

PROVINCE AND DENTISTRY SCHOOL

ALBERTA
University of Alberta
Faculty of Dentistry

BRITISH COLUMBIA
University of British Columbia
Faculty of Dentistry

MANITOBA
University of Manitoba
Faculty of Dentistry

NOVA SCOTIA
Dalhousie University
Faculty of Dentistry

ONTARIO
University of Toronto
Faculty of Dentistry
University of Western Ontario
Faculty of Dentistry

QUEBEC
Université Laval,
Ecole de Médecine Dentaire
McGill University
Faculty of Dentistry
Université de Montréal,
Faculté de Médecine Dentaire

SASKATCHEWAN
University of Saskatchewan
College of Dentistry

APPENDIX F
United States Institutions of Dentistry Included in the 7th Edition

STATE AND DENTAL SCHOOL

ALABAMA
University of Alabama
School of Dentistry

CALIFORNIA
University of California, Los Angeles
School of Dentistry
University of California, San Francisco
School of Dentistry
Loma Linda University
School of Dentistry
University of the Pacific
School of Dentistry
University of Southern California
School of Dentistry

COLORADO
University of Colorado
School of Dentistry

CONNECTICUT
University of Connecticut
School of Dental Medicine

DISTRICT OF COLUMBIA
Howard University
College of Dentistry

FLORIDA
University of Florida
College of Dentistry

GEORGIA
Medical College of Georgia
School of Dentistry

ILLINOIS
University of Illinois at the Medical Center,
Chicago College of Dentistry
Northwestern University
Dental School
Southern Illinois University at Edwardsville
School of Dental Medicine

INDIANA
Indiana University
School of Dentistry

IOWA
The University of Iowa
College of Dentistry

KENTUCKY
University of Kentucky
College of Dentistry
University of Louisville
School of Dentistry

LOUISIANA
Louisiana State University
School of Dentistry

MARYLAND
University of Maryland at Baltimore
Baltimore College of Dental Surgery
Dental School

MASSACHUSETTS
Boston University
Henry M. Goldman School of
Graduate Dentistry
Harvard School of Dental Medicine
Tufts University
School of Dental Medicine

MICHIGAN
University of Detroit Mercy
School of Dentistry
The University of Michigan
School of Dentistry

MINNESOTA
University of Minnesota
School of Dentistry

MISSISSIPPI
University of Mississippi
School of Dentistry

MISSOURI
University of Missouri
Kansas City School of Dentistry
Washington University
School of Dental Medicine

STATE AND DENTAL SCHOOL

NEBRASKA
Creighton University
    Boyne School of Dental Science
University of Nebraska Medical Center
    Lincoln College of Dentistry

NEW JERSEY
New Jersey Dental School
    University of Medicine and Dentistry
    of New Jersey

NEW YORK
Columbia University
    School of Dental and Oral Surgery
New York University
    College of Dentistry
State University of New York at Buffalo
    School of Dentistry
State University of New York at Stony Brook
    School of Dental Medicine

NORTH CAROLINA
University of North Carolina
    School of Dentistry

OHIO
Case Western Reserve University
    School of Dentistry
The Ohio State University
    College of Dentistry

OKLAHOMA
University of Oklahoma
    College of Dentistry

OREGON
University of Oregon Health Sciences Center
    School of Dentistry

PENNSYLVANIA
University of Pennsylvania
    School of Dental Medicine
University of Pittsburgh
    School of Dental Medicine
Temple University
    School of Dentistry

SOUTH CAROLINA
Medical University of South Carolina
    College of Dental Medicine

TENNESSEE
Meharry Medical College
    School of Dentistry
University of Tennessee
    College of Dentistry

TEXAS
Baylor College of Dentistry
University of Texas Health Sciences Center
    at Houston, Dental Branch
University of Texas Dental School
    at San Antonio

VIRGINIA
Virginia Commonwealth University
    Medical College of Virginia
    School of Dentistry

WASHINGTON
University of Washington
    School of Dentistry

WEST VIRGINIA
West Virginia University
    School of Dentistry

WISCONSIN
Marquette University
    School of Dentistry

PUERTO RICO
University of Puerto Rico
    School of Dentistry

PROVINCE AND MEDICAL SCHOOL

ALBERTA
University of Alberta
Faculty of Medicine
University of Calgary
Faculty of Medicine

BRITISH COLUMBIA
University of British Columbia
Faculty of Medicine

MANITOBA
University of Manitoba
Faculty of Medicine

NEWFOUNDLAND
Memorial University of Newfoundland
School of Medicine

NOVA SCOTIA
Dalhousie University
Faculty of Medicine

ONTARIO
McMaster University
School of Medicine
University of Ottawa
School of Medicine
Queen's University
Faculty of Medicine
University of Toronto
Faculty of Medicine
University of Western Ontario
Faculty of Medicine

QUEBEC
Laval University
Faculty of Medicine
McGill University
Faculty of Medicine
University of Montreal
Faculty of Medicine
University of Sherbrooke
Faculty of Medicine

SASKATCHEWAN
University of Saskatchewan
College of Medicine

APPENDIX H
International Medical Institutions Included in the 7th Edition

COUNTRY AND MEDICAL SCHOOL

AUSTRIA
University of Vienna

BELGIUM
Free University of Brussels
Catholic University of Louvain

FRANCE
University of Aix-Marseilles II
University of Picardie (Amiens)
University of Angers
University of Besancon
University of Bordeaux II
University of Caen
University of Clermont-Ferrand
University of Dijon
Scientific and Medical University
  (University of Grenoble I)
Catholic Faculties of Lille
  (Faculte Libre de Medecine)
University of Law and Health Sciences
  (Lille II)
University of Limoges
University Claude-Bernard (Lyons I)
University of Montpellier I
University of Nancy I
University of Nantes
University of Nice
Paris (University Medical and Academic
  Departments)
  U. of Paris V, VI, VII, XI, XII, XIII
University of Poitiers
University of Reims
University of Rennes I
University of Rouen
University of Saint-Etienne
Louis Pasteur University (Strasbourg I)
University Paul-Sabatier (Toulouse III)
University of Tours

FEDERAL REPUBLIC OF GERMANY
Rhemish Friedrich-Wilhelm University of
  Bonn
Friedrich Alexander University of
  Erlangen-Nuremberg
Johann Wolfgang Goethe University
  of Frankfurt
Albert Ludwig University of Freiburg
Georg August University of Göttingen
University of Hamburg

FEDERAL REPUBLIC OF GERMANY
Rupert Charles University of Heidelberg
Johannes Gutenberg University of Mainz
Philipps University of Marburg
Ludwig Maximilian University of Munich
University of Munster
Eberhard Karl University of Tubingen
University of Würzburg

IRELAND
Royal College of Surgeons in Ireland

ISRAEL
The Hebrew University of Jerusalem

ITALY
University of Rome

JAPAN
Keio University
Tokyo Medical and Dental University

NETHERLANDS
University of Amsterdam
Leiden State University

SWEDEN
University of Stockholm

SWITZERLAND
University of Geneva
University of Zurich

UNITED KINGDOM
University of Cambridge
University of Edinburgh
University of London
  Charing Cross Hospital Medical School
  Guy's Hospital Medical School
  King's College Hospital Medical School
  London Hospital Medical College
  The Middlesex Hospital Medical School
  Royal Free Hospital School of Medicine
  St. Bartholomew's Hospital Medical College
  St. George's Hospital Medical School
  St. Mary's Hospital Medical School
  St. Thomas's Hospital Medical School
  University College Hospital Medical School
  Westminster Medical School
University of Oxford

APPENDIX I
United States Institutions of Medicine Included in the 7th Edition

STATE AND MEDICAL SCHOOL

ALABAMA
University of Alabama
School of Medicine
University of South Alabama
College of Medicine

ARIZONA
The University of Arizona
College of Medicine

ARKANSAS
The University of Arkansas
School of Medicine

CALIFORNIA
Loma Linda University
School of Medicine
Stanford University
School of Medicine
University of California, Davis
School of Medicine
University of California, Irvine
California College of Medicine
University of California, Los Angeles
School of Medicine
University of California, San Diego
School of Medicine
University of California, San Francisco
School of Medicine
University of Southern California
School of Medicine

COLORADO
University of Colorado
School of Medicine

CONNECTICUT
University of Connecticut
School of Medicine
Yale University
School of Medicine

DISTRICT OF COLUMBIA
Georgetown University
School of Medicine
The George Washington University
School of Medicine and Health Sciences
Howard University
College of Medicine

FLORIDA
University of Florida
College of Medicine
University of Miami
School of Medicine
University of South Florida
College of Medicine

GEORGIA
Emory University
School of Medicine
Medical College of Georgia
School of Medicine
Mercer University
School of Medicine
Morehouse College
School of Medicine

HAWAII
University of Hawaii
School of Medicine

ILLINOIS
Loyola University of Chicago
Stritch School of Medicine
Northwestern University
Medical School
Southern Illinois University
School of Medicine
The University of Chicago
Pritzker School of Medicine
Finch University of Health Sciences/
The Chicago Medical School
University of Illinois
College of Medicine

STATE AND MEDICAL SCHOOL

INDIANA
Indiana University
School of Medicine

IOWA
The University of Iowa
College of Medicine

KANSAS
University of Kansas
Medical Center College of Health Sciences
and Hospital School of Medicine

KENTUCKY
University of Kentucky
College of Medicine
University of Louisville
School of Medicine-Health Sciences
Center

LOUISIANA
Louisiana State University
Medical Center School of Medicine
in New Orleans
Louisiana State University
Medical Center School of Medicine
in Shreveport
Tulane University
School of Medicine

MARYLAND
The Johns Hopkins University
School of Medicine
University of Maryland
School of Medicine
Uniformed Services University
of the Health Sciences

MASSACHUSETTS
Boston University
School of Medicine
Harvard Medical School
Tufts University
School of Medicine
The University of Massachusetts
Medical School

MICHIGAN
Michigan State University
College of Human Medicine
The University of Michigan
Medical School
Wayne State University
School of Medicine

MINNESOTA
Mayo Medical School
University of Minnesota
Medical School – Minneapolis

MISSISSIPPI
University of Mississippi
School of Medicine

MISSOURI
St. Louis University
School of Medicine
The University of Missouri
Columbia School of Medicine
The University of Missouri
Kansas City School of Medicine
Washington University
School of Medicine

NEBRASKA
Creighton University
School of Medicine
The University of Nebraska
College of Medicine

NEVADA
The University of Nevada
Reno School of Medical Sciences

NEW HAMPSHIRE
Dartmouth Medical School

NEW JERSEY
University of Medicine and Dentistry of
New Jersey, New Jersey Medical School
University of Medicine and Dentistry of
New Jersey, Rutgers Medical School

STATE AND MEDICAL SCHOOL

NEW MEXICO
The University of New Mexico
School of Medicine

NEW YORK
The Albany Medical College
Albert Einstein College of Medicine of
Yeshiva University
Columbia University
College of Physicians and Surgeons
Cornell University
Medical College
Mount Sinai School of Medicine of the
City University of New York
New York Medical College
New York University
School of Medicine
State University of New York
Health Science Center at Brooklyn
State University of New York at Buffalo
School of Medicine
State University of New York at Stony Brook
School of Medicine
State University of New York,
Health Science Center at Syracuse
University of Rochester
School of Medicine and Dentistry

NORTH CAROLINA
The Bowman Gray School of Medicine
of Wake Forest University
Duke University
School of Medicine
The University of North Carolina
School of Medicine
East Carolina University
School of Medicine

NORTH DAKOTA
University of North Dakota
School of Medicine

OHIO
Case Western Reserve University
School of Medicine
Medical College of Ohio at Toledo
Northeastern Ohio Universities
College of Medicine
The Ohio State University
College of Medicine
University of Cincinnati
College of Medicine
Wright State University
School of Medicine

OKLAHOMA
University of Oklahoma
College of Medicine

OREGON
University of Oregon
Medical School

PENNSYLVANIA
Jefferson Medical College
of Thomas Jefferson University
The Medical College of Pennsylvania/
Hahnemann University
School of Medicine
The Pennsylvania State University
College of Medicine
Temple University
School of Medicine
University of Pennsylvania
School of Medicine
The University of Pittsburgh
School of Medicine

PUERTO RICO
Ponce School of Medicine
Universidad Central del Caribe
Escuela de Medicina
The University of Puerto Rico
Medical Sciences Campus
School of Medicine

APPENDIX I (Continued)
United States Institutions of Medicine Included in the 7th Edition

STATE AND MEDICAL SCHOOL

RHODE ISLAND
Brown University
  Program in Medicine

SOUTH CAROLINA
Medical University of South Carolina
  College of Medicine
University of South Carolina
  School of Medicine

SOUTH DAKOTA
The University of South Dakota
  School of Medicine

TENNESSEE
East Tennessee State University
  College of Medicine
Meharry Medical College
  School of Medicine
The University of Tennessee
  Center for the Health Sciences
  College of Medicine
Vanderbilt University
  School of Medicine

TEXAS
Baylor College of Medicine
Texas Tech University
  School of Medicine
The University of Texas
  Medical Branch at Galveston
  School of Medicine
The University of Texas
  Health Science Center at San Antonio
  Medical School
The University of Texas
  Health Science Center at Dallas
  Southwestern Medical School
Texas A&M University
  College of Medicine
The University of Texas
  Medical School at Houston

UTAH
University of Utah
  College of Medicine

VERMONT
University of Vermont
  College of Medicine

VIRGINIA
Eastern Virginia Medical School
University of Virginia
  School of Medicine
Virginia Commonwealth University
  Medical College of Virginia

WASHINGTON
University of Washington
  School of Medicine

WEST VIRGINIA
West Virginia University
  School of Medicine
Marshall University
  School of Medicine

WISCONSIN
The Medical College of Wisconsin
University of Wisconsin
  Medical School

APPENDIX J
United States Institutions of Veterinary Medicine Included in the 7th Edition

STATE AND VETERINARY SCHOOL

ALABAMA
Auburn University, Auburn
School of Veterinary Medicine

Tuskegee University, Tuskegee
School of Veterinary Medicine

CALIFORNIA
University of California, Davis
School of Veterinary Medicine

COLORADO
Colorado State University, Fort Collins
College of Veterinary Medicine and
Biomedical Sciences

FLORIDA
University of Florida, Gainesville
College of Veterinary Medicine

GEORGIA
University of Georgia, Athens
College of Veterinary Medicine

ILLINOIS
University of Illinois, Urbana
College of Veterinary Medicine

INDIANA
Purdue University, Lafayette
School of Veterinary Science and Medicine

IOWA
Iowa State University of Science and
Technology, Ames
College of Veterinary Medicine

KANSAS
Kansas State University, Manhattan
College of Veterinary Medicine

LOUISIANA
Louisiana State University, Baton Rouge
College of Veterinary Medicine

MASSACHUSETTS
Tufts University, Boston
School of Veterinary Medicine

MICHIGAN
Michigan State University, East Lansing
College of Veterinary Medicine

MINNESOTA
University of Minnesota, St. Paul
College of Veterinary Medicine

MISSISSIPPI
Mississippi State University, Mississippi State
College of Veterinary Medicine

MISSOURI
University of Missouri, Columbia
College of Veterinary Medicine

NEW YORK
New York State Veterinary College
at Cornell University, Ithaca

NORTH CAROLINA
North Carolina State University, Raleigh
School of Veterinary Medicine

OKLAHOMA
Oklahoma State University, Stillwater
College of Veterinary Medicine

OHIO
The Ohio State University, Columbus
College of Veterinary Medicine

PENNSYLVANIA
University of Pennsylvania, Philadelphia
School of Veterinary Medicine

TENNESSEE
University of Tennessee, Knoxville
College of Veterinary Medicine

TEXAS
Texas A&M University, College Station
College of Veterinary Medicine

VIRGINIA
Virginia Polytechnic Institute and State U.
Blackburg Virginia-Maryland Regional
College of Veterinary Medicine

WASHINGTON
Washington State University, Pullman
College of Veterinary Medicine

WISCONSIN
University of Wisconsin, Madison
School of Veterinary Medicine

APPENDIX K
United States Institutions of Nursing Included in the 7th Edition

STATE AND NURSING SCHOOL

ALABAMA
University of Alabama in Birmingham

ARIZONA
Arizona State University
University of Arizona

ARKANSAS
University of Arkansas, Little Rock

CALIFORNIA
California State University, Fresno
California State University, Los Angeles
Loma Linda University
University of California, Los Angeles
University of California, San Francisco

COLORADO
University of Colorado, Denver

CONNECTICUT
University of Connecticut (Storrs)
Yale University

DELAWARE
University of Delaware, Newark

DISTRICT OF COLUMBIA
Catholic University of America

FLORIDA
University of Florida

GEORGIA
Emory University
Medical College of Georgia

ILLINOIS
De Paul University
Loyola University of Chicago
Northern Illinois University
Rush University
University of Illinois, Chicago

INDIANA
Indiana University, Indianapolis

IOWA
University of Iowa

KANSAS
University of Kansas, Kansas City

KENTUCKY
University of Kentucky

LOUISIANA
Louisiana State University, New Orleans

MARYLAND
University of Maryland, Baltimore

MASSACHUSETTS
Boston College

MICHIGAN
University of Michigan, Ann Arbor
Wayne State University

MINNESOTA
University of Minnesota, Minneapolis

MISSISSIPPI
University of Southern Mississippi

MISSOURI
St. Louis University
University of Missouri, Columbia

NEBRASKA
University of Nebraska, Omaha

NEW JERSEY
Rutgers University, The State University
of New Jersey

STATE AND NURSING SCHOOL

NEW YORK
Adelphi University
Columbia University
Columbia University, Teachers College
Hunter College of the City University
of New York
New York University
The Sage Colleges
State University of New York (Binghamton)
State University of New York at Buffalo
Syracuse University
University of Rochester

NORTH CAROLINA
University of North Carolina, Chapel Hill
School of Nursing
University of North Carolina, Chapel Hill
School of Public Health

OHIO
Case Western Reserve University
Ohio State University (Columbus)
University of Cincinnati

OKLAHOMA
University of Oklahoma, Oklahoma City

OREGON
The Oregon Health Sciences University
(Portland)

PENNSYLVANIA
The Pennsylvania State University
(University Park)
University of Pennsylvania
University of Pittsburgh (Pittsburgh)

PUERTO RICO
University of Puerto Rico, San Juan

SOUTH CAROLINA
University of South Carolina

TENNESSEE
University of Tennessee, Memphis
Vanderbilt University

TEXAS
Texas Woman's University
University of Texas at Austin
University of Texas Health Science Center
at Houston
University of Texas, San Antonio

UTAH
Brigham Young University
University of Utah

VIRGINIA
Virginia Commonwealth University, Richmond
University of Virginia

WASHINGTON
University of Washington

WISCONSIN
Marquette University
University of Wisconsin, Madison
University of Wisconsin, Milwaukee

APPENDIX L
United States Institutions of Optometry Included in the 7th Edition

STATE AND OPTOMETRY SCHOOL

ALABAMA
University of Alabama in Birmingham
School of Optometry/The Medical Center

CALIFORNIA
Southern California College of Optometry
University of California, Berkeley
School of Optometry

FLORIDA
Nova Southeastern University
College of Optometry

ILLINOIS
Illinois College of Optometry

INDIANA
Indiana University
School of Optometry

MASSACHUSETTS
New England College of Optometry

MICHIGAN
Ferris State College
College of Optometry

MISSOURI
University of Missouri, St. Louis
School of Optometry

NEW YORK
State University of New York State
College of Optometry

OHIO
The Ohio State University
College of Optometry

OKLAHOMA
Northeastern State University
College of Optometry

OREGON
Pacific University
College of Optometry

PENNSYLVANIA
Pennsylvania College of Optometry

PUERTO RICO
Inter American University of Puerto Rico

TENNESSEE
Southern College of Optometry

TEXAS
University of Houston
College of Optometry

APPENDIX M
Canadian Institutions of Pharmacy Included in the 7th Edition

PROVINCE AND PHARMACY SCHOOL

ALBERTA
Faculty of Pharmacy & Pharmaceutical
Sciences
University of Alberta
Edmonton, Alberta

BRITISH COLUMBIA
Faculty of Pharmaceutical Sciences
University of British Columbia
Vancouver, British Columbia

MANITOBA
Faculty of Pharmacy
University of Manitoba
Winnipeg, Manitoba

NOVA SCOTIA
College of Pharmacy
Dalhousie University
Halifax, Nova Scotia

ONTARIO
Faculty of Pharmacy
University of Toronto
Toronto, Ontario

QUEBEC
Ecole de Pharmacie
Université Laval
Quebec, Quebec
Faculte de Pharmacie
Université de Montréal
Montreal, Quebec

SASKATCHEWAN
College of Pharmacy
University of Saskatchewan
Saskatoon, Saskatchewan

APPENDIX N
United States Institutions of Pharmacy Included in the 7th Edition

ALABAMA
Auburn University
School of Pharmacy

ARIZONA
University of Arizona
School of Pharmacy

ARKANSAS
University of Arkansas for Medical Sciences
College of Pharmacy

CALIFORNIA
University of California, San Francisco
School of Pharmacy
University of the Pacific
School of Pharmacy
University of Southern California
School of Pharmacy

COLORADO
University of Colorado
School of Pharmacy

CONNECTICUT
University of Connecticut
School of Pharmacy

FLORIDA
Florida Agricultural and Mechanical University
School of Pharmacy
Nova Southeastern University
College of Pharmacy
University of Florida
College of Pharmacy
J. Hillis Miller Health Center

GEORGIA
University of Georgia
School of Pharmacy

IDAHO
Idaho State University
College of Pharmacy

ILLINOIS
University of Illinois at the Medical Center,
Chicago College of Pharmacy

INDIANA
Butler University
College of Pharmacy
Purdue University
School of Pharmacy and
Pharmacal Sciences

IOWA
The University of Iowa
College of Pharmacy

KANSAS
University of Kansas
School of Pharmacy

KENTUCKY
University of Kentucky
College of Pharmacy

MARYLAND
University of Maryland
School of Pharmacy

MASSACHUSETTS
Massachusetts College of Pharmacy

MICHIGAN
Ferris State College
School of Pharmacy
University of Michigan
College of Pharmacy
Wayne State University
College of Pharmacy and Allied Health
Professions

MINNESOTA
University of Minnesota
College of Pharmacy

MISSISSIPPI
University of Mississippi
School of Pharmacy

MISSOURI
St. Louis College of Pharmacy
University of Missouri, Kansas City
School of Pharmacy

STATE AND PHARMACY SCHOOL

NEBRASKA
Creighton University
School of Pharmacy
University of Nebraska
College of Pharmacy

NEW JERSEY
Rutgers, The State University of New Jersey
College of Pharmacy

NEW MEXICO
University of New Mexico
College of Pharmacy

NEW YORK
Long Island University
Arnold and Marie Schwartz
College of Pharmacy and Health Sciences
St. John's University
College of Pharmacy and Allied Health
Professions
State University of New York at Buffalo
School of Pharmacy
Union University
Albany College of Pharmacy

NORTH CAROLINA
The University of North Carolina at Chapel Hill
School of Pharmacy

NORTH DAKOTA
North Dakota State University
College of Pharmacy

OHIO
Ohio State University
College of Pharmacy
University of Cincinnati
College of Pharmacy
University of Toledo
College of Pharmacy

OKLAHOMA
University of Oklahoma
College of Pharmacy

OREGON
Oregon State University
School of Pharmacy

PENNSYLVANIA
Duquesne University
School of Pharmacy
Philadelphia College of Pharmacy
and Science
Temple University
School of Pharmacy
University of Pittsburgh
School of Pharmacy

PUERTO RICO
University of Puerto Rico
College of Pharmacy

RHODE ISLAND
University of Rhode Island
College of Pharmacy

SOUTH CAROLINA
Medical University of South Carolina
College of Pharmacy
University of South Carolina
College of Pharmacy

TENNESSEE
University of Tennessee
Center for the Health Sciences
College of Pharmacy

TEXAS
University of Houston
College of Pharmacy
The University of Texas at Austin
College of Pharmacy

APPENDIX N (Continued)
United States Institutions of Pharmacy Included in the 7th Edition

STATE AND PHARMACY SCHOOL

UTAH
University of Utah
College of Pharmacy

VIRGINIA
Virginia Commonwealth University
School of Pharmacy Medical College
of Virginia

WASHINGTON
University of Washington
School of Pharmacy
Washington State University
College of Pharmacy

WEST VIRGINIA
West Virginia University
School of Pharmacy Medical Center

WISCONSIN
University of Wisconsin, Madison
School of Pharmacy

APPENDIX O
United States Institutions of Public Health Included in the 7th Edition

STATE AND PUBLIC HEALTH SCHOOL

ALABAMA
University of Alabama in Birmingham

CALIFORNIA
Loma Linda University
University of California, Berkeley
University of California, Los Angeles

CONNECTICUT
Yale University

FLORIDA
University of South Florida

GEORGIA
Emory University

HAWAII
University of Hawaii

ILLINOIS
University of Illinois, Chicago

LOUISIANA
Tulane University

MARYLAND
The Johns Hopkins University

MASSACHUSETTS
Boston University
Harvard University
University of Massachusetts, Amherst

MICHIGAN
University of Michigan, Ann Arbor

MINNESOTA
University of Minnesota, Minneapolis

MISSOURI
Saint Louis University

NEW YORK
Columbia University
SUNY (Albany)

NORTH CAROLINA
University of North Carolina, Chapel Hill

OKLAHOMA
University of Oklahoma, Oklahoma City

PENNSYLVANIA
University of Pittsburgh

PUERTO RICO
University of Puerto Rico, San Juan

SOUTH CAROLINA
University of South Carolina

TEXAS
University of Texas, Houston

WASHINGTON
University of Washington